TEXAN RANCH LIFE.

A Southwest Landmark

NUMBER SEVEN

Lee Milazzo, General Editor

OUR WAGGON BEFORE ITS FINAL FITTINGS AT THE BACK. "PRAIRIE SCHOONER."

TEXAN RANCH LIFE;

WITH

Three Months through Mexico in a "Prairie Schooner."

BY

MARY J. JAQUES.

Texas A&M University Press
COLLEGE STATION
1989

Originally published by Horace Cox, Windsor House,
Bream's Buildings, E.C., London, 1894

The paper used in this book meets the minimum requirements
of the American National Standard for Permanence
of Paper for Printed Library Materials, Z39.48-1984.
Binding materials have been chosen for durability.

Library of Congress Cataloging-in-Publication Data
Jaques, Mary J.
    Texan ranch life : with three months
  through Mexico in a "Prairie Schooner" /
  by Mary J. Jaques.
        p.   cm. — (A Southwest landmark ;
  no. 7)
    Reprint. Originally published: London :
  H. Cox, 1894.
    ISBN 0-89096-394-0
    1. Ranch life—Texas—History—19th
  century.   2. Texas—Social life and customs.
  3. Mexico—Description and travel.
  4. Jaques, Mary J.—Homes and haunts—
  Texas.   I. Title.   II. Series.
  F391.J36   1989
  976.4—dc19   88-32637
                                          CIP

CONTENTS.

CHAPTER XXXIII.

CHAPTER XXXIV.

—oo⊱⊰oo—

LIST OF ILLUSTRATIONS.

TEXAN RANCH LIFE;

WITH

THREE MONTHS THROUGH MEXICO IN A "PRAIRIE SCHOONER."

———◦———

CHAPTER I.
LEAVING ENGLAND.

———

"But He that hath the steerage of my course,
Direct my sail!"

———

YES, we have actually embarked! At half-past nine o'clock on the morning of Friday, March 15th, 1889, the bell on the bridge of the S.S. *Empress* ceased to ring. The warps are cast off, the customary hoarse cries of "Forward!" "Ease her off gently there!" are heard, and the ship leaves the Alexandra Docks, and drops slowly down the Mersey. On board all is confusion. The decks are still unwashed. The *Empress* having been timed to begin her voyage the previous day, we had passed the night in our berths, lulled to sleep by the noise of the donkey-engine lowering cargo into the hold, while the operations of coaling went on without intermission, and men were busy repainting and repairing our damaged life-boats.

The *Empress* had been in dock only twelve hours and it was even considered doubtful whether she would be

B

able to fulfil her out-going engagements.   During her
former voyage from New York she had encountered
numerous gales and heavy seas, and had been so much
knocked about that the necessary repairs made her now
overdue.   Although a sailor's daughter, I am by no means
superstitious, yet I confess that I should have preferred to
sail on Thursday or any other day in the week rather than
on Friday.   And if our " tars " do not, in these enlightened
times, absolutely refuse to start on this unlucky day, I
know a great many who would assuredly not select it.
However, on Friday our start was to be, but before going
any farther, perhaps it will be well to explain why the
voyage was undertaken.

Several times my expectations of continental travel had
been disappointed in consequence of home-ties, illness, or
the whims and fancies of friends.   On one occasion the
trunks were actually packed, and our party had met at
the rendezvous in London.   But parliamentary business
detained one of its members, a fear that it would be too
late for his gout to derive benefit from the waters of
Homburg prevented another ; the expedition was given up,
and disappointment and a return home were all that
remained for poor me !

But as one approaches the third decade these little
contretemps are less keenly felt, and, in fact, I was
becoming almost a fatalist.   Looking backwards, I must
confess that on those occasions when I have persistently
fought against Destiny it has not been kind to me, and
I have now adopted as my motto : " Whatever is, is best."

" Our wills and fates do so contrary run
That our devices still are overthrown."

In the autumn of 1880, while visiting my cousins in
Buckinghamshire, a letter arrived from some old friends in

Colorado—grandchildren of the late Archbishop S. Their description of busy ranch life in that State being read aloud at the breakfast table, I became fascinated by the attractions of its wild freedom, when to my great surprise my cousin offered to write to ascertain whether I could be received at the ranch as a boarder. Another disappointment! In consequence of contemplated weddings and other domestic arrangements there was no space to spare, and, although there were no longer any home-ties to bind me, fate seemed to decide that I was not to travel.

My faithful Didymusa declared that it was "just what she had expected." Wherever I went Didymusa must surely go. Since I had been left alone we had become quite inseparable. Many years we had spent together tending our dear invalid, for Didymusa, too, had learned to love her, and shared many an anxious vigil by my beloved mother's side till the last sad scene of all.

Drawn so closely together in the first bitter days of loneliness, then, indeed, Didymusa became my great solace, and I soon grew to love her as a sister. She was ever a truly faithful and loving companion, and what are social distinctions when put on the balance against kindness of heart and sympathy?

She owed her sobriquet to her disposition to doubt. She would never bask in the sunshine of hope, and always refused to believe that "the daily round, the common task" of home-life could be relieved by a visit to North America. We had lived on quietly in our little island home, with all its tender associations, until I became haunted by visions of a trip to the Rockies, now, alas, beginning to fade. I had heard alarming reports of the expensiveness of American hotels, &c., and to think of living in them for any length of time was out of the

question.   But, taking up the *Morning Post* one day, my
eyes fell upon an advertisement for colonial ranch pupils,
application to be made to certain well-known agents.   I
immediately wrote, describing my requirements as a
" paying guest," and by return of post received an answer
to the effect that, although such an application had never
been received before, there was little doubt they could help
me to find what I wanted.   Eventually I was offered a
choice of two families—one living at Calgary, N.W. territory of Alberta, personal friends of the agents ; the other
residing in Texas, and owning a large ranch there.   And
at the present moment the head of the latter family and
his wife happened to be on a visit to England, whence they
expected to start in the course of a few weeks for the Far
West.

The agents had already cabled to their friends at Calgary, and wished me to await the answer.   But the return
cable being overdue, I, waxing impatient, determined to
wait no longer, went to London, arranged terms, and paid a
quarter's rent in advance.

I had been cautioned not to enter into a yearly agreement, and was afterwards extremely grateful for this
advice.   I was counselled, indeed, not to bind myself for
longer than a month, but the agent pressed so hard for a
quarterly agreement that at last I yielded, and arranged to
travel under the escort of my host and hostess.

When I returned home and broke the news to Didymusa there was a dismayed silence.   The same thoughts
were present with us both—of the preparations for leaving
home and all our pets.

Apart from this, I felt glad to look forward to change
of scene.   I had recently sustained another sad loss—that
of my best and dearest friend, the kind and highly

cultivated Mrs. R., who possessed all the generous and large-hearted qualities of her maternal ancestor, the great and good Lord Shaftesbury. I missed her daily in my rambles over beach and common. For ten years it had been my privilege to know her intimately, and our constant interchange of thought, and communion of soul, will ever remain fresh in my memory.

At last a caretaker was found, a man whom I had known for some time, who might be trusted to keep the garden in order, who already knew and liked my precious thoroughbred mare, and would do the best he could for the two cats.

Strange as it may appear, the parting from these was the worst. The mare would have her corn and run of the meadow as usual, with the additional advantage of no one to ride her. But with the cats the case was different. Cats—and cultivated cats—do not like to have their little habits disturbed; they become epicurean in their tastes, exacting as to the preparation of food, and, being naturally shy, timid creatures, entertain a rooted dislike to strangers and new ways. What a number of instructions Didymusa gave concerning their particular cosy corners and changes of diet!

Then, after a short round of farewell visits, we made our final arrangements, took the train to Liverpool and embarked, which brings us back to the *Empress*, as she drops slowly down the Mersey.

CHAPTER II.

VOYAGE TO NEW YORK.

THE owner of the ranch, hereafter described as the "Boss" (his invariable title on the ranch), was a retired naval officer, who had spent several years in Texas. The choice of a ship being left with him, in the first instance, he decided upon one of the White Star line, but subsequently, to my regret, changed the date of departure, and selected a vessel of the "Atlantic" line. The reputation of this line had already fallen; shortly after our voyage it ceased to carry passengers. The *Empress* was an old-fashioned vessel; her decks especially being too narrow to be fitted with modern improvements, and her engines not powerful enough for her heavy cargo.

We did not get well under way till ten o'clock, when we were all mustered on deck to undergo the usual medical inspection; a very informal proceeding as far as the saloon passengers were concerned. Then came the emigrants, about three hundred and twenty all told; sickly, puny, squalid creatures, wretched specimens of humanity both physically and mentally. All their worldly goods seemed to be contained in small bundles; some of the owners looking half-starved.

One could not help speculating whether circumstances or their own vices were to blame for their present miserable plight.

They filed before the Medical Officer of the Board of Health, and eventually all passed their examination satisfactorily. Nowhere is the contrast between poverty and wealth more striking than on board ship; the luxurious accommodation of the saloon ; the vastly different arrangements for the poor steerage passenger, who stands during his meals with a swinging table above his head; who is turned out, ill or well, at an early hour each morning for the double purpose of ventilating the bedding and airing himself — a perfectly necessary operation! His mattress consists of a bundle of rags or a few wisps of straw, which may have been dragged along with the general bundle; and men and women are huddled together almost regardless of the common decencies of life. This in my experience is the state of affairs in most vessels, American and English, though doubtless, allowances must be made, and much of the very evident misery endured by the steerage passengers may be due to the change from their customary manners and customs and mode of life on *terra firma.*

One could not but be struck by the rough good-nature and the innate politeness (with occasional exceptions) of the men towards the women; as shown by the offer of shelter or seats, and in nursing the babies, to the relief of their seasick mothers.

During the short time we were moored at Queenstown, we were amused by the persistence of the Irish hucksters, who with their sweet-sounding blarney, tried to wheedle us into the purchase of cakes, sticks, pipes, and what not. But their tones became less insinuating when they failed to do business, and, the Boss refusing to buy lemons from one old woman, she raised her voice and shouted so that all might hear : " Sure you'll know the use of lemons by-and-bye ! " A threat destined to be remembered in due course. The Boss was taking out a young pupil, Mr. Taylor, who had failed for his Army examination, the only son of his father, who had bidden him farewell from the tender, at the mouth of the Mersey. Mr. Taylor also was going to try life on the ranch, to strive for fortune like other Texan cattle kings! Our castles in the air often help to carry us through the difficulties of life, and it is an advantage to possess the power to build them, even though they presently tumble in fragments at our feet.

In the saloon, there was only one other passenger of our own sex besides the Boss's wife—Mrs. Boss, as she came to be named.

A pleasant, cheery old American, travelling with his son, Mr. D., the editor of a Chicago newspaper, was a great hand at brewing punch, and doled out the contents of the bowl so that some received an unfair proportion of the ice therein, and others too large a share of its more exhilarating constituents.

The rest of the passengers were all young men, bent upon seeking fortune in various States (ne'er-do-wells, no doubt), for the most part by manual labour. As later observation convinced me, these were likely to succeed in earning only as much—or less, when the high prices of the necessaries of life is taken into account—as many agricultural labourers at home.

They enjoyed plenty of fun amongst themselves, one of their number, as is usually the case, serving as a butt for the others. Mr. Newman hailed from a London suburb, and had been brought up in the way he should go by some maiden aunts. He was terribly distressed by the intemperate habits of Mr.

Falconer, who pretended to adopt them for Mr. New-man's especial benefit. It requires little to amuse one on board ship, and this became a very elaborate joke, lasting throughout the voyage.

The captain was let into the secret so that he should not spoil sport, when he dined with us the night before we reached Sandy Hook ; his duties during the stormy weather having hitherto prevented him from giving us much of his society even at meals. Shortly after the beginning of dinner on this occasion, Mr. Newman, who sat on my left, called attention to Mr. Falconer, who had been imbibing freely : the beverage soda water, specially coloured by the steward. Poor Mr. Newman recounted the number of brandies and soda water Mr. Falconer had consumed during the afternoon, and his own efforts to induce him to renounce the dreadful habit. At this juncture Mr. Falconer seemed to lose consciousness ; his head sank on his neighbour's shoulder and his breathing became stertorous.

" Ah," said Mr. Newman, " I was afraid he would dis-grace himself before you all. I have tried my best to keep him sober. You know he shares my cabin, and I have sat up with him two whole nights."

Of course the captain and the rest ignored Mr. Falconer's apparent condition, but as we were dispersing he suddenly roused. and rushing wildly on deck, declared his intention to jump overboard. He was closely followed by Mr. Newman, who piteously implored each and all in turn to save this victim of inebriety. A violent scene ensued between the two men on deck ; the one persisting in his attempt to jump overboard, and declaring that he was tormented by many monsters, struggling like a maniac the while ; the other upbraiding the amused spectators for their callousness in allowing a fellow creature to go to his account without lifting a finger to save him, and clinging to him in his effort to perform the act of valour himself.

The merry young Irish doctor here interposed and administered a soothing draft to the pseudo-inebriate, who recovered his senses in a marvellously short space, whereupon the Boss persuaded Mr. Newman to seek out the skipper and tell him all about it. Mr. Newman went away, to return very crestfallen at his failure to awaken the captain's interest, lamenting the necessity to sit up with his patient again that night; which he did, being well employed in restraining his constant attempts to rush upon deck, and in the delivery of temperance lectures. When Mr. Newman was undeceived just before leaving the ship, I was told that he expressed his opinion of his companions in language more forcible than polite.

Perhaps this experience served as a warning and preparation for the more serious practical jokes which generally await the young greenhorn from the hands of our American cousins.

There was a conceited commercial traveller on board much given to recitations. Upon him also the hoaxers played their pranks; performing the part of an effervescing gallery so efficiently as frequently to render his voice inaudible. Being of a fire-eating disposition, he produced his revolver to quell these turbulent spirits and compel attention—no little trouble and patience being requisite to convince him that a superabundance of animal spirits led the young men to make fun of anything and anybody as a relief to the tedium of the voyage, and above all, that their conduct must not be taken to imply a slur upon his powers of elocution.

As well as an elocutionist he was a chess-player, and according to his own account had matched himself against several famous players, and come off victorious. Strangely enough he lost all his contests on the *Empress.* I fancy he sat down prepared for an easy conquest over me, and at the critical moment, when I was on the point of check-mating him, to the accompaniment of smothered laughter from the onlookers, he suddenly placed his hands to his head, complained of intense dizziness, and, oversetting chessboard and chessmen, declared the impossibility of playing on a ship whose deck was at an angle of forty degrees. At quoits, and the various trials of strength it was always the same ; he lost on account of the angle of the deck. In the microcosm of a ship, there is the same mingling of farce and tragedy, of grave and gay, as in the world at large.

On the morning of the fifth day a shark was reported to be following the vessel, and death was soon coming to claim one of our fellow-passengers. We had observed a tall emaciated man apparently in an advanced stage of consumption, with the significant phthisic cough and hectic flush. He never appeared at table, seeking the retirement of his cabin, except on one or two occasions, when he came on deck enveloped in wraps and mufflers, for a little fresh air. Mr. J. was travelling under an assumed name, and, as the story ran, had fled from England and his wife and children, overwhelmed by debt and a complication of troubles. Whatever these may have been, " The heart knoweth its own bitterness," and he was released from every burthen at ten o'clock on Sunday morning, the tenth day of the voyage.

During the previous night we were no longer disturbed by his distressing paroxysms of coughing, but his pathetic calls for " Rose, Rose ! " as the dawn approached, were terrible to hear. The kind stewardess told me that he seemed happy at the last—when the doctor was present to administer to his wants—and that he entrusted her with many messages to the wife he had forsaken. These messages were delivered sooner than the dying man had anticipated. Having discovered her husband's destination, the poor lady had taken a berth on the *Etruria*, which passed us in fine style and reached New York some days before our arrival.

To the captain fell the melancholy duty of breaking the news to the widow, who had the poor satisfaction of hearing an account of her husband's last hours from the stewardess, who had done everything possible to alleviate the sufferings of the friendless stranger.

But I am anticipating. Mr. J.'s body was at once removed to the ship's hospital, and was committed to the deep on the following morning. Didymusa and I, with some other passengers, were present at the very impressive service, which was conducted at 8 a.m., the ship slackening speed, and the Union Jack serving as a pall.

The water was black with dolphins; it was curious to watch their gambols as they played round the vessel that morning, as if, indeed, they were rejoicing over the freed spirit! We could see them, through our binoculars, in the far distance too, shoal upon shoal, tumbling over the huge billows and forming black lines upon their white crests.

The *Empress* carried a good many intermediate passengers, from whom we were separated only by a thin wooden partition; a rowdy, disagreeable set of people, to judge by their conversation and behaviour. Amongst them were several children and eight babies. Fortunately my own cabin was some distance off, but others of the saloon passengers suffered greatly from the nocturnal choruses of the infants. It could be compared only to a number of dogs howling at the moon ; as soon as one was reduced to silence by exhaustion, another being wide awake, quite ready to continue the refrain.

Although we did not encounter one really severe storm during our fortnight's voyage, it blew a gale nearly all the time, and with a heavy cargo of crockery and the *Empress's* rather weak engines, we could not make much way through the Atlantic rollers. We were informed that she was a " good old sea boat," and her constant creaking confirmed at least one part of the statement. But she rolled, she pitched, she gave a terrible corkscrew movement ; her screw was half the time out of water, she shivered and groaned and almost came to a standstill. For two or three days we were not allowed on deck, and the port-holes were closed. But we managed to enjoy our " constitutionals " on most days, to play quoits and to watch the game of tug-of-war, &c., which the young men got up for our amusement.

In the evenings we had music, and, when the angle of the deck permitted, an occasional " hop " round the saloon. The " fiddles " were more or less in requisition, and there was a good deal of slipping and sliding about and smashing of crockery ; in one bad lurch, the steward coming to grief with the soup tureen and all the contents.

But for the unremitting kindness and attention of the stewardess, my toilette would indeed have been made under difficulties, and one morning she had to take in hand Didymusa also, who, after sliding about on the floor for some time in company with my overland trunk and after depositing two glassfuls of water in her bunk, was subsequently set upon her feet by the stewardess, who entered the cabin at an opportune moment.

But everything reaches an end at last, and on Wednesday, March 27, the stewardess came into our cabin with the good news that we were to land the same afternoon.

——oo⟨◦⟩oo——

CHAPTER III.

NEW YORK.

ALL was excitement on deck, though it soon appeared that we were not yet to set our feet upon *terra firma*. The water was crowded with small craft, and, a dense fog setting in at about 4 o'clock, there we lay, fog signals going all night. But the fog cleared early the following morning, and at about 11 o'clock we sighted Sandy Hook, and soon passed the statue of Liberty.

The docks being full, the *Empress* was compelled to steam beyond the usual landing-place, in order to reach the tug; and even then the emigrants had to remain on the ship some time longer.

The Customs' officer came on board; we described ourselves and our purpose in landing in a book kept for the purpose, and made the usual declaration that we possessed no dutiable articles. I believe that no one owned to the possession of contraband, but when the time for the search arrived, our Chicago friend was found to possess a considerable quantity of superb Lyons velvet, dozens of pairs of kid gloves, cases of eau-de-Cologne, cigars, &c. We escaped very well; in fact our trunks were scarcely opened; the Customs' officers being always more suspicious of their own countrymen. But one of our passengers, a young man, Mr. H., had undertaken to convey a box from a friend in England to her sister, having not the remotest idea of its contents. It was amusing to see his look of utter dismay and mortification when the officer opened the box, and turned out a rich and beautifully made layette! I did not hear whether the pretty things were irrevocably seized, or Mr. H. paid the duty, and the babe got its robes.

My saddle, recently new from Peat, had had its pristine freshness removed by almost indelible stains of bog while stag-hunting in the New Forest.

Didymusa's saddle, an old friend, a fine piece of pigskin from Sligo, certainly did not look like a dutiable article! The Boss had assured me that it would travel safely, packed in a sack and without a case, and promised to have it placed on the top of the hold. However, it managed to get to the bottom and sustained a broken tree and compound fracture of the left pommel—one of the old Landseer type. Let the inexperienced voyager avoid the use of leather straps on board ship. He will never see them again, as they offer too strong a temptation even to the honestest sailor. Good cording is better, and care should be taken that it is not cut by the Customs' men ; also that it is replaced after them. The best way is to replace it one's self, and in consequence of not doing this, and trusting to the promises of friends, I reached Canada with strained and broken locks, no cording, though the officials whom I met at Niagara were obliging enough to supply the deficiencies.

As we contemplated a visit of a year or more, we had brought some heavy trunks, which we left in charge of Messrs. Buckley's agent, having only those required for immediate use sent to the Metropolitan Hotel.

How we enjoyed the freedom of an uninterrupted walk to Broadway after being limited to the *Empress's* decks for a fortnight! After a visit to Messrs. Buckley's offices to change a draft and our English money, and to secure through railway tickets and sleeping berths to St. Louis, we parted company with the Boss and his wife, and, accompanied by Mr. Taylor, took a car to Central Park. It is extensive, but does not possess the natural beauties of Golden Gate, although no expense has been spared to heighten such advantages as it can lay claim to.

On alighting from the car, we were proceeding to enter the hotel with Mr. Taylor by the general entrance, when the conductor, whose nerves had evidently sustained a shock, began to shout and gesticulate as he pointed frantically to another door—the ladies' entrance. I am afraid I was taken too much by surprise to attempt an apology at this outrage on New York propriety, or even to thank the conductor for his excited energy on our behalf.

Except the remarkably large and handsome public buildings the city is not striking, while the intricacies of the elevated railway detract from the width of the streets ; although it must be confessed that it is far pleasanter to travel by this, than by the murky and sulphurous underground railway in London.

We found many novelties in the menu at dinner that night ; delicious banana and other ices being frequently served between the courses. One dish, named " Sheep's head," turned out to be a fish, so called from a fancied resemblance to the head and front teeth of a sheep. It often weighs 12lb. or more, and is common on the Atlantic coast (*Archosargus*, or *Diplodus probuto cephalous*). Dressed clams make a savoury dish, and also a kind of bivalve not unlike a cockle (*Spirula solidissima*), but not so good as a native oyster. The waiters were negroes.

The next morning we sallied forth in search of a

c

luncheon basket, for which we paid two dollars and a half at a store in Grand Street. It was a very ordinary basket, and Didymusa declared that if this was to be taken as a specimen of New York prices, the best thing we could do was to return forthwith to England. She insisted that I had been imposed upon, and nothing could prevent her from appealing to the Boss before we began to fill this expensive commissariat hold-all. Not forgetting to enter the ladies' door on this occasion, we succeeded in finding the Boss, but not in awakening his sympathy. We should soon learn what a price was charged for goods of every description throughout the States, he said. So Didymusa thought, when she subsequently paid four dollars for a pair of kid gloves !

Setting forth again, we tried to obtain biscuits at several grocery stores, but were at last directed to the baker's, where we pointed to a pile of Huntley and Palmer's tins, and, " guessing I wanted crackers," the storekeeper supplied the want forthwith. On going to purchase some white calico, several kinds of wrong material were exhibited, until we discovered that we ought to have asked for " domestic." Coloured prints, also, are so-called. If you inquire the way to the station in any city in the States, you run the risk of losing your train and your temper amid the " How's " and " Which's " with which you are sure to be greeted. What you require is the depôt (pronounced " dee-pôt "), and the " dee-pôt " you must call it if you wish to get there.

At last we laid in our little store of provisions, Mrs. Boss, who had travelled backwards and forwards between New York and St. Louis several times, advising us to make ourselves independent of dining cars and stopping places for meals, on the score both of convenience and economy. And most excellent advice this proved. The black porters would take our small tin can and get it filled with hot coffee when we did not wish to alight, and our Etna lamp was often extremely useful.

On the afternoon of Friday, March 29th, Didymusa and I separated from the rest of the party, to meet again at St. Louis, we intending to travel by the Erie and Wabash Railway, *viâ* Niagara ; they by way of Cleveland, where they wished to spend a few hours with some friends. At half-past four the conductor waved his flag, gave the signal " All aboard," and, amidst a tremendous ding-dong, our journey began.

Not knowing that all American locomotives carry a bell, for the first half-hour it seemed as if all the churches were ringing for service ; the bells following us on our way.

The bell of the locomotive is intended as a warning to pedestrians, there being no bridges over the roads, and numerous level crossings in the heart of bustling towns. Sometimes the line runs parallel with the streets, unprotected by any barrier whatever. The passengers can walk anywhere and everywhere between the metals, and a stool is placed to help one to mount the tailboard. If you hold a first-class sleeping-car ticket, you may traverse the whole length of the train, the little connecting spaces being protected by iron balustrades. From these platforms you enjoy views of the surrounding scenery and interviews with the hawkers and pedlars who come to offer eatables at the various stopping places.

A walk along the length of a train in motion is not calculated to add to one's dignity : the cars do not travel so steadily or so rapidly as the Flying Scotchman, and you require your " sea legs on " to counteract the violent oscillations. Nevertheless, when a journey lasts a week, it

c 2

is an immense comfort to be able to enjoy even this limited exercise.

The trains are sumptuously furnished with beautifully inlaid wood and heavy draperies; such lines as pass through dusty districts having their cars fitted with double windows and solid wooden partitions between the berths, the electric light being switched on and off at the will of the passenger.

Through the towns the pace is very slow, and it is pleasant at night to peep from behind your blind at the well-lighted streets, with their crowds of traffic and pedestrians. You may easily forget that you are in a train, but for the incessant clanging of the warning bell, which always peals more vigorously in such circumstances. Accidents are rare, but, of course, the trains are few, only one starting each day on these extended journeys. Generally speaking, the line is single, save at the depôts, where the trains pass each other, and there is a network of gauges for shunting purposes.

Each car is provided with hot-water pipes, a large cistern of iced water, and cups, for any passenger of any class to help himself *ad lib*.

The first night we did not feel quite sufficiently at home to go to bed properly; the ability to do this with comfort and to perform your toilette expeditiously the next morning comes only by degrees.

Being aroused by the black porter just before the train stopped at Niagara, I was surprised, on drawing my blind, to see that snow had fallen heavily during the night. Before eight o'clock we had passed the Customs on the Canadian side (a merely formal opening of hand-bags), partaken of a light breakfast, and started on a long drive to the Grand Rapids and Prospect View.

CHAPTER IV.

NIAGARA TO SAN ANTONIO.

Our hired carriage was driven by its owner, one John Ellis, a Devonshire man, quite a character in his way. Having left the old country as a young man thirty years ago, he was thoroughly Americanised. I began to regret my want of acquaintance with the West of England, until, happening to compliment him upon his team, he saw that I was a lover of horses and understood something about them, and we found a congenial and inexhaustable topic of conversation. The latest items of the English Racing Calendar were discussed, and he duly pitied my ignorance concerning "pacers" and "pacing gait" as opposed to trotting.

His remarks upon the training of the celebrated American Directum and Mascotte were wasted at the time, but I felt interested to see, on November 23rd, 1893, that the great match had come off, with the result that Mascotte holds the pacing record of the world, having paced a mile in 2 minutes 4 seconds, whereas Directum, the trotting stallion, trotted that distance in 2 minutes $5\frac{1}{2}$ seconds ; the match being for a purse of 5000 dollars.

When Didymusa was at last able to squeeze in a word, she hinted that Mr. Ellis might cease the discussion of horseflesh and expatiate on the surrounding beauties of Nature. Although the hint did not appear to move him, he ought to have credit for stopping at the specially interesting points of view, and making the most of that lovely drive.

The snow was fully five feet deep (the heaviest fall of the season), and the park, with the pretty cluster of islands, —named in honour of Lord Dufferin—the distant landscape, the steep, wooded bluff and fine belt of pines, were all enveloped in a brilliant mantle of pure white ; the sky intensely blue ; the air still ; the sun shining brightly over all.

If we lost the variety of colour, the beauty of the scene was enhanced by the solemn stillness which reigned supreme over everything ; in sharp and striking contrast to the everlasting thud of the turbulent, surging water—rolling, tossing, never ceasing to flow from that mighty reservoir of Nature.

From the Grand Rapid we enjoyed an uninterrupted view of these turbulent waters, leaping from ledge to ledge over the descent of fifty-five feet. The quantity of water passing over the falls is estimated at fifteen thousand cubic feet every minute.

The *Maid of the Mist,* the little steamer which in summer makes the trip almost under the Falls, had not yet begun to run, but failing this we did the next best thing : equipping ourselves with waterproofs and descending by the hydraulic elevator to look at the Falls from below. Perhaps it is from this point of view that one best realises the majestic splendour of the mighty cascade and the overwhelming force of its waters, the rising spray and foam ; causing the heart to quicken and the breath to tighten as one gazes.

On leaving the carriage we had previously plodded through the virgin snow along the Rainbow Ramble, where sparkling icicles hung from the banks to a length of fully nine feet, and we found huge blocks of ice below. Some-times, we were told, after a more prolonged frost, masses of ice of several tons weight were borne along the gorge and hurled over the great Fall with a thunderous crash.

Standing on the slippery rock beneath the Falls, we soon became aware that our boots, at least, were not thoroughly waterproof, and deeming it wise to keep moving, we put aside our macintoshes and set off at a trot to the " shoot," which saves the half-hour's climb of bygone days, to the Rapids, where we were tempted to sit for our photographs, just by the spot where Captain Webb lost his life.

The plucky little *Maid of the Mist* once passed these Rapids—for the first and last time. Never again will her captain attempt to shoot them. After being photographed, we walked to Clifton to buy plates for our luncheon basket, and then made an attempt to dry ourselves at the waiting-room stove, fortifying the inner woman the while, and resuming our journey *en route* to St. Louis at twenty minutes to four in the afternoon.

As the train rolled along, I could not help musing on the tragic stories (some of pathetic interest) which we had recently heard of the weary souls who had sought Niagara for the purpose of self-destruction. Year by year adds to the long list of those who, defeated in the battle of life, unhinged in mind, worn out in body, having made ship-wreck of their faith in the great over-ruling Power and Creator of these mighty waters, instead of clinging to the Rock of Ages, have cast themselves adrift.

After changing cars at Detroit, at 11 p.m., we passed through Indiana, and reached St. Louis at 6.15 on Sunday. This part of the journey was uneventful and somewhat uninteresting, with an occasional glimpse of scenery to relieve the monotony ; but, for the most part, Canada did not appear a very inviting country.   The ugly shanties of weatherboard standing bare and unsheltered by tree or shrub, compared unfavourably with our snug homesteads and picturesque cottages surrounded by productive vegetable and bright garden plots in the old country.

At St. Louis we had time for a walk and dinner before joining the rest of our party, to catch the departing train at 8.30 p.m.

St. Louis can boast of several handsome buildings, many of massive red granite, a fine old Court House, and the electric light.   Between St. Louis and San Antonio, at least within some distance of Austin, the country, for a night and a day, was all swamp.   Here the settlers were often seen with their cattle knee-deep in water, looking extremely miserable and deplorable, and reminding one of Martin Chuzzlewit's experiences at Eden.   The conductor informed us that this state of affairs endured all the year round ; it was always damp, and considerably worse during the rainy season.   Occasionally the train splashed and ploughed through the water, casting up spray on either side.

There was a great change in the temperature ; hot water pipes were no longer needed, the vegetation appeared semi-tropical in character, and we admired the Spanish moss hanging in graceful festoons from the trees (though its presence is a sure sign that a district is unhealthy) and also the Judas tree, with its pretty rose-coloured blossom in clusters along the branches.   This is a leguminous plant of the genus *cercis*, sometimes called in America " red-bud." Judas Iscariot is said to have hanged himself from a tree of this kind.

On drawing near to Texas the character of the landscape

changed, and we approached Austin through a splendid country of rolling hills, boundless prairies, with table-lands between. There was a profusion of mesquit : a tree which grows extensively throughout Texas—its name is said to be a Mexican-Indian word. The screw-pod mesquit (*Prosopis pubescos*) has spiral pods, which are used by the Indians as fodder for their horses and cattle; but the leaf resembles that of the acacia, having long sharp thorns, as those can testify who have ridden through the brush cattle hunting ! In its branches I could see little bunches, which at a distance resembled rooks' nests, but on closer acquaintance, proved to be the United States mistletoe (*Phoradendron flavescens*), which has broader leaves and more berries than the European misletoe (*Viscum album*), and is generally seen growing abundantly on the mesquit.

Austin is a fine city, situated on an eminence and appearing to advantge from the track. Crossing a bridge over the River Colorado, and leaving the valley of the same name behind us, we climbed a steep gradient, in order to cross the hills which we had seen in the distance northwards after leaving Round Rock.

Through rocky cuts, alternating with brush, we once more came upon the level plain, upon which stands San Antonio, surrounded by vast prairies. With " every turn of the wheels," as the Americans say, the weather grew warmer. We saw novel objects now—cowboys, dark-skinned Mexicans, &c. Arriving at San Antonio about 12.30, we took up our quarters at the St. Leonard's Hotel, fairly worn out, and both feeling the effects of our wetting at Niagara ; Didymusa being tormented by toothache, my own original cold greatly increased and supplemented by neuralgia and loss of taste and smell.

The chambermaid declared that I should have to become

acclimated (acclimatised—pronounced in Texas, accli-mated) to the local catarrh ; but a night's rest did wonders for us, though Didymusa must needs pay a visit to the dentist, who, as she discovered two days later, extracted the wrong tooth.

Accompanied by Mr. Taylor, we set forth in a buggy, drawn by two good horses, to visit the Missions, of which there are four, outside the city along the river, at distances of from two to nine miles below it. They are named respectively the Conception, the San Jose, the Espada, and the San Juan, all being more or less in a state of ruin, but showing traces of fine architecture, and acknowledged to be (with the exception of those in Florida) the finest in America.

San Jose, which stands on an imposing plain is the finest, the tracery of its windows being especially beautiful. All these buildings owe their existence to the zeal and energy of the Franciscans, and one cannot help regretting that so much of their ornamentation has been carried away by Vandalistic tourists.

They have suffered from storms and rains, and have been silent witnesses of many a fierce encounter with the Indians, yet much remains to convey an idea of their former grand proportions and majestic beauty.

"San Jose de Aguayo," now usually known as the Second Mission, and standing on the left bank of the river, five miles below the city of Austin, was founded in 1720, and completed in 1771. An eminent authority has pronounced it the finest piece of architecture in America. Senor Huica, one of the most celebrated artists of his day, was entrusted by the King of Spain with its decoration, and spent several years adorning it with frescoes and statues.

The Mission of "La Purissima Concepcion de Acuma"

was founded in 1716, its construction beginning in 1731. It is the best preserved of all these old monastic edifices, and having been cleaned a few years ago by the authority of the Catholic Church, is now used for services. The modern tawdry and tinsel decorations appear out of keeping with its massive walls and masterly design. Near here a handful of Americans achieved a decisive victory over more than four times their number of Mexicans.

The third Mission, or " San Juan Capistran," at present little more than a mass of ruins, also was founded in 1716, but upon a less extensive scale. For many years it was occupied by converted Christianised Indians.

Of the remaining Mission, " San Francisco de la Espada," there will, in a short time, remain only a pile of stones to mark its site. This, too, was founded in 1716.

From our driver we learnt a good deal about the horse and cattle market. In some places the road was extremely soft and after the heavy rainfall it looked as if our steeds would leave us and the buggy stuck fast in one or another of the quagmires. This is by no means an unusual occurrence even in some of the unpaved towns.

Having heard and seen enough to desire to visit the old Mission of the Alamo within the town, we turned our steps thither early the following morning. As the incidents and the heroes of this noted place were then entirely unknown to me, and others may be as little informed (I was once asked by an educated Englishwoman " whether the Texans spoke English "), it may be worth while to give a brief account of those direful times, culled from the works of Janvier, Morrison, and others, by which, subsequently, my own mind was enlightened.

CHAPTER V.

THE HISTORY OF THE ALAMO.

The Alamo was founded in 1716, and, as an inscription over the entrance testifies, was completed in 1738. It presents to-day but a shadow of its original greatness. The walls which once surrounded it are gone, only those of the Mission itself remaining. The Alamo was the chapel belonging to the first Mission established at San Antonio; in fact, its cathedral, or original parish church.

In 1835 the rebellion of Texas, which was American rather than Mexican, began, under the leadership of Houston.

A large portion of the population of Texas were emigrants from the United States, and it was this element which took the lead in the revolt against Mexican rule : a revolt precipitated by many arbitrary acts on the part of the American Government, a crisis being reached in 1835, when the Federal Government abrogated the State Constitution. The excesses of Santa Anna's army, sent to enforce obedience—notably the massacre of the Alamo and the affair of Goliad—thoroughly aroused the Anglo-Saxon fighting spirit, and made peace impossible. The Republic of Texas maintained its separate existence until 1844, and obtained recognition from the United States, France, England, and Belgium. During the administration of both Jackson and Van Buren, earnest, but ineffectual, efforts were made by the Texans to secure admission of their Republic as a State of the American Union. But President Tyler—made of baser stuff—concluded an arrangement of this character (April 12th, 1844). The treaty was ratified by Congress, in March, 1845, when General Almonte, then Mexican Minister at Washington, characterised it as an act of aggression, " the most unjust which can be found in the annals of modern history."

Bearing in mind the fact that Texas was an independent power, and was recognised as such by the Mexican Government, and consequently had a perfect right to annex itself to the United States if it so desired, this sweeping condemnation is obviously not borne out by the facts.

The war that followed was never formally declared. Each country massed troops upon the frontier, and a general conflict was precipitated (April 24th, 1846) by a Mexican ambuscade on the Texas side of the Rio Grande, which defeated a reconnoitring party of United States Dragoons, commanded by Captain Thornton. In the skirmish sixteen Americans were killed and wounded and the remainder of the force captured. After the affairs of Palo Alto (May 8th) and Resaca de la Palma (May 9th), both in Texas, and in both of which the Mexicans were defeated, General Taylor's forces entered Mexico (May 18th) and occupied Matamoras. In the meantime (May 13th, 1846) the American Congress had appropriated 10,000,000 dollars for the prosecution of the war, and 50,000 volunteers were ordered to be raised. Three facts should be here noted : (1.) The revolt of Texas probably would not have occurred had Mexico been properly governed in conformity with its constitutional law. (2.) A peaceful settlement of the Texans' difficulty unquestionably would have been arrived at had there existed in Mexico a stable

Government to treat with the Government of the United States. In point of fact, Mr. Slidell, the special envoy sent to Mexico by the United States Government, in consequence of an intimation on the part of President Herrera that a special envoy would be received, was refused an audience by General Paredes, who had usurped the Presidential office December 30th, 1845, before the envoy reached his destination. (3.) Had the Mexicans held together as a nation and opposed their united strength to the Americans, instead of weakening their force by internecine struggles ; while the result of the war must have been the same, it would not have been, as it was, almost a walk-over for the invading army. Throughout this wretched business the United States had a colourable excuse for each of its several offensive acts ; but its moral right to attack a nation infinitely weaker than itself, to conquer that nation and to strip it of more than half of its territory, never was justified and never will be.

The events of the war may be summarized in a few words : Taylor advanced from the East ; captured Monterey, September 26th, 1846, and remained victor of Buena Vista or Angostura, February 23rd, 1847, whilst Doniphan advanced through New Mexico (followed by Price, who had some sharp fighting on the way with the Pueblo Indians), and after the battle of Sacramento, February 28th, 1847, occupied Chihuahua. Early in March, 1846, Captain Frémont, acting under orders from the Secretary of War, incited a revolt in California against Mexican rule.

Commodore Stoat occupied Monterey (California), July 7th ; Commander Montgomery occupied San Francisco (July 8th); and Commodore Stockton, in a proclamation of August 17th, 1846, took formal possession of California.

The conquest was completed by Stockton and Kearney. The main invasion of Mexico was from the South, being directed against the capital. Scott landed at Vera Cruz (March 9th, 1847) ; forced the capitulation of the city after a five days' bombardment (March 27th) ; outflanked and defeated Santa Anna at Cerro Gordo (April 18th) ; occupied Puebla, without opposition (May 25th) ; entered the valley of Mexico (August 9th) ; defeated the Mexicans at Padierna (August 20th) ; and made a brilliant strategic advance across the Pedregal, thus cutting the Mexican centre and facilitating the victory, on the same day, of Churubosco. After a short truce he carried the positions of the Casa Mata and Molino del Rey (September 8th) ; stormed and carried the castle of Chapultepec (September 12th and 13th) ; took possession of the *garitas* of Belem and San Cosme, on the afternoon of September 13th ; completed the conquest and took possession of the City of Mexico, September 15th, 1847.

Peace was declared by the Treaty of Guadalupe, Hidalgo, concluded February 2nd, 1848, by which Mexico ceded to the United States all the territory held or claimed north and north-east of the present boundary, receiving in return from the United States the sum of fifteen millions of dollars. The treaty provided also for the payment by the United States of about three and a quarter millions of dollars to satisfy various claims made by American citizens against Mexico. For a treaty dictated by a conquering army in the captured capital of the defeated nation this instrument stands unparalleled in history.

The story of the Alamo, intensely dramatic and irresistibly pathetic, thrilled us as we heard it, standing on the spot where these brave men—Bowie, Crockett,

Evans, and Travis, so nobly fought and died. Stung to
the quick by the contumacy of the Texan colonists, and
their steady adhesion to the Constitution of 1824, the
usurper, Santa Anna, organised a force sufficient, as he
believed, for the subjugation of Texas, and at the head of
his well-appointed army, appeared before San Antonio,
February 22nd, 1836 ; and displaying first the red and then
the black flag from the turret of the Cathedral of San
Fernando, demanded an unconditional surrender.   The
reply of Colonel Travis was a cannon shot.

With 145 effective men, among whom were Colonel
James Bowie and David Crockett, he immediately occupied
the Alamo.

The Mission was first known as San Antonio de
Valero, but when it came to be used as a garrison for
soldiers the name was changed to Fort Alamo.

The declaration of Texan independence had not been
passed at this time, and the flag that floated from the
Alamo was the tricolour of Mexico, with the figures
" 1824 " instead of the eagle on the white stripe.

For twelve days the fire on the doomed Alamo was
incessant ; and in consequence of casualties and ceaseless
exertion, the heroic Travis and his band of devoted patriots
were well nigh exhausted.   It was determined by the
Mexican officers, after a consultation, to take the citadel
by assault on the morning of March 6th.

Notwithstanding the earnest appeal made by Colonel
Travis for reinforcements, only thirty of the determined
patriots of Gonzales, under command of Captain Martin,
reached the Alamo, and these only in time to be sacrificed
to the vengeance of the ruthless Santa Anna.   Four
thousand men under orders of Colonel Tolsa, re-inforced
the Mexican general, March 2nd.

Colonel Bonham, a gallant South Carolinian, had been sent by Colonel Travis to endeavour to hurry forward reinforcements. Failing in this mission, but true to the cause he had espoused, he returned, and, bidding his two companions adieu, rode deliberately through the Mexican lines and made his report in person to his friend and commander, Colonel Travis. Never was a more gallant spirit sacrificed on the altar of duty! On that eventful morning, March 6, 1836, at 3 a.m., the Mexicans, with their entire force, marching in three columns, equipped with scaling ladders, crowbars, &c., began the attack, with bands playing the " Hymn of the Dead." The storming of the Alamo was begun ; the walls of the outer enclosure were scaled, the defenders driven from point to point, until at last the interior of the church was reached, but not until 2000 of the enemy had been killed and wounded. Words fail to give any idea of the scene inside the sacred edifice when the grey light of morning made visible the ghastly details. No quarter was asked for or offered. The earthen floor was " shoe-mouth deep " in blood, the bodies of the defenders being surrounded by heaps of Mexican dead.

It was only when the last American had been killed that the impressive silence told that the end had come. Colonel Bowie, sick and unable to rise, was bayoneted in his bed, but not until after he had sent a score of his assailants to their long account. Colonel Crockett fell just in front of the entrance to the building, his body almost covered by the fallen Mexicans.

The story of the Alamo may be summed up in the single line : " Thermophylæ had its messenger of defeat, the Alamo had none."

The only persons who escaped this massacre were the wife and child of Lieutenant Dickenson, Mrs. Allsbury, the

niece of Governor Veramendi, Madame Candelaria, Colonel
Bowie's nurse, who was by his side when he was bayoneted,
and a negro boy, the servant of Colonel Travis. Madame
Candelaria, at the time of our first visit to the Alamo, was
still alive and residing in San Antonio.

General Santa Anna ordered the Texan corpses to be
piled together and burned, and this was accomplished by
placing a layer of wood between each two of the bodies.
The most authentic account of the final disposition of the
remains of these martyrs to liberty is that given by Colonel
Juan N. Sequin, who, in the following July gathered
together the charred bones and dust of the slaughtered
Americans, placed them in an urn and deposited them
beneath the floor in front of the altar of San Fernando
Cathedral. The names of those who perished are preserved
in the archives at Austin, but no monument other than
that of the old church commemorates the event, or marks
the ground upon which they fell. The matter is, however,
in the hands of men who never yet failed in any undertaking, and the time is near at hand when a column worthy
of the occasion will mark the spot where the heroic patriots
perished.

The declaration of Texan independence was passed four
days before the fall of the Alamo ; but the fact being
unknown in San Antonio, the battle of San Jacinto
was fought and won, and the tyrant Santa Anna made
prisoner, forty-six days after the massacre.

By the constitution of 1824 the citizens of Texas, who
had emigrated from the United States, were protected in
all their rights and privileges.

When this constitution was abrogated, and the policy
of Mexico changed towards the Americans, it was seen
that the only safety they could expect would be in the

restoration of the constitution they had abolished. Hence it was that they flew to arms and never relinquished them till the decimation of Santa Anna's army at San Jacinto made them independent of Mexican tyranny. The last of the Mexican raids on San Antonio ended in 1842, under General Velasquez and General Woll. The district court was in session at the time of the last, and judge, jury, and officers of the court were made prisoners; but after a hot contest the Mexicans withdrew.

Numerous and fierce are the conflicts that have taken place in the city and its vicinity, notably two, "the Dawson massacre" and the "Grass fight," both with the Mexicans. The latter took place near the Mission— Concepcion la Purissima de Acuma—and was so named because it occurred between a force of Mexicans, who had been sent out from San Antonio to cut grass for their horses, and a small force under Colonel Bowie. The Mexican loss was fifty men killed and many wounded, the Texans only losing two men.

Then there were the Indian raids, the period between 1730 and 1806 being one of almost continuous depredations from the powerful tribes of Apaches and Comanches, and others, who waged relentless war against the settlers.

The accounts of early travellers tell us that an Indian town existed on the present site of San Antonio. In proof of this, when any considerable excavations have been made, relics of the Indian, in the shape of arrow-heads, flint knives, and other implements of the aborigines have been found in great numbers.

The walls are in some cases over three feet in thickness, and in the building, which at present includes Messrs. Guergum's offices, an iron staple may be seen firmly embedded. To this, in the days when San Antonio was liable to frequent raids by the Red Apaches, the horses were tied, saddled in readiness for immediate pursuit.

On the old building the coat of arms of Spain and Austria still remains in a fair state of preservation. It was placed there by the Governor of Texas in 1742. Amongst other reminiscences of the Spanish domination, not yet forgotten, it may be mentioned that whilst some soldiers of the Lone Star Republic were laying a floor of this building, in 1843, they discovered a kettle containing 15,000 dollars in Spanish doubloons. Most historians agree that the Spaniards made settlements on both sides of the Rio Grande prior to 1595, and a few years later (about the time that Philadelphia was founded) they laid out a *presidio*, or military post. This was not so much in anticipation of aggression from the Indians as on account of the fact that La Salle had explored the coast region of Texas on behalf of His Majesty of France. This portion of the country, and much of the New World besides, was long a bone of contention between the Courts of Versailles, Lisbon, and Madrid. Eventually appeal was made to the Pontiff Alexander at Rome, who confirmed the title of Spain. In 1733 San Antonio was chartered by royal grant, and, as was the custom in those days, King Ferdinand III. graciously conferred upon his creation his own august name ; so that there were a parish and *pueblo* of San Fernando, embracing the white residents in the new municipality, with the present cathedral for their parish church, the Mission of San Antonio de Valero for the converted Indians, and also a Presidio of San Antonio de Bexar, named, in compliment to the Duke of Bexar, the Viceroy of all New Spain.

CHAPTER VI.

SAN ANTONIO.

———

" THE scent of the roses " still clings about the recollection of our first impressions of San Antonio : the brilliant sky, the delightful warmth of this equable climate, the rich vegetation, the pleasing novelty of everything, as from the hotel verandah we watched the busy traffic traversing the main plaza.   A few Chinese and Negroes were interspersed with the dark-skinned Aztecs, and whilst most of the colonists are Germans, many other foreign languages reached our ears.

The buggies were picturesque with their peculiar hoods and awnings, and the horses and mules, many with richly ornamented saddles, these having high cantles and horns in front, and big wooden stirrups.   The riders, wearing broad-brimmed hats or sombreros, sit easily and gracefully, never rising in their stirrups.   Most of them were mounted on pacers, of pure Spanish and Barb descent, or it may be crossed with the mustang, which ambled along swiftly with flowing manes and long full tail, well carried and showing great nerve power.

The sight of these horses, and the recollection of my " Peat " safely packed in the saddle case, having been transferred to the express with the rest of the heavy baggage, helped to drive away the neuralgia.   But Didymusa did not find similar pleasure in anticipation, having ridden only a few times previous to leaving England, as a prelude to what lay before her in the new country.

The Mexicans are being gradually driven out of the place, and, two years having elapsed between our first and last visits, we were able to appreciate the change and deplore it.

The town is being " boomed " ; the inhabitants making a great, and by no means intermittent, effort to push it steadily to the fore. The fact that so many of the largest investors are Eastern capitalists may be accepted as evidence of the confidence which the outside world reposes in the future of Mexico. Scarcely a day passes, in fact, without a record of some large transaction.

In place of the old Mexican houses and huts of *adobe* mud (pronounced a-do-bay), and of the *jacal* (pronounced hà-kal), a hut built of rough wood and roofed with dried grass and leaves, the suburbs are now thickly sprinkled with the handsome wooden residences of merchant million-aires; cattle kings who have developed into bankers, or real estate princes. And the plazas, especially the Military and the Alamo, where these people of the sunny South once held high revel with their open-air suppers and all-night gambling festivities, are now transformed into fine squares with well-macadamised roads, concreted sidewalks and pavements, and prettily-planned garden plots in the centre. All around stand blocks of business houses five storeys high, with public buildings designed by local architects, granite and stone, from quarries near the city, entering largely into their construction.

At the time of our visit the City Hall was not quite finished. It is the work of Mr. Otto Kramer, who arrived in 1888. There was a considerable stir when the official choice fell upon his plans, and a total stranger secured the appointment of Superintendent of Construction.

Built in the Renaissance style, its height is 120 feet, its width 80 feet, with three storeys above the basement, the whole being set off by a shapely clock tower 135 feet high. The material of the superstructure is dressed limestone from quarries on the Balcones, near Van Raub, Bexar County, not far from the city.

The Post Office (worthy of the city of the future) is modified Moresque in style, and notable for a frieze which represents incidents in the past history of San Antonio. There is a grand opera house, but no theatrical performance took place during our visit. However, we attended a concert given by a " Mexican typical orchestra," and heard some excellent solos by Rebagliati, a violinist of local celebrity. There were quite two dozen mandolines ; the performers making the most of their sweet-toned instruments. Some variations on the pretty air, " La Golondrina," the Mexican " Home, Sweet Home," showed more power than I had expected from the instrument. Another air, " Te volvi a ver " (I see thee again), by Estrada, so haunted me that I bought the pianoforte arrangement.

Mr. H. had joined our party at St. Louis. He was the Boss's brother-in-law, had spent many years in the United States and South America, and not only spoke Spanish fluently, but also the corrupt form of the language (mingled with numerous Indian terms) used by the Mexicans. It certainly cannot be described as pure Castilian, nor, perhaps, exactly as a patois.

On our way back to the hotel from the concert, we were asked whether we would like to partake of a Mexican *cena* (supper) and having the prospect of so excellent an escort as Mr. H., we accepted the invitation with avidity.

The lamp flickered in the evening air, illuminating the bare wooden tables and forms with their dusky company,

whose bright eyes glistened as they smiled and showed
their white teeth and gesticulated to the attendant
Señoritas. The scarlet and other brightly coloured *zerapes*
(blankets) worn by the men, lent gaiety to the scene, while
the skillets and *casuellas* (culinary vessels) in manipulation
on the ground, added a weirdness as the flames leaped into
the air or cast dark shadows around—the whole a scene
of bizarre and picturesque disorder.

Mr. H., of course, ordered the repast, the dishes being
all more or less pungent to the taste. However, we
were in for it; and perhaps it was well that the
fluctuating light hid somewhat of the preparation of the
comestibles, since later experience proved that, as far as
cleanliness is concerned, the native cookery certainly
leaves something to be desired ! So we attacked the
savouries : *Chili con carne* (meat, with red pepper), *tortillas*
(cakes), *tamales* (sausages), *tamal de casuella* (corn meal
pot pie), *chili guisado* (a kind of stew of mysterious meats,
served with green pepper sauce), &c., &c. Beans to the
Mexican are as potatoes to the Irishman, or porridge to the
Scot. Boston has a reputation for beans ; but the beans
of Mexico, if anything, would make a Bostonian deny his
birthplace,

They are generally prepared the previous day, and are
not wholesome unless thoroughly cooked, sometimes being
fried in a quantity of lard with chili thrown in. Having
tried the Boston beans on the passage out without
satisfactory results, I did not venture on these, and the
puchero and *barbacao* were also declined.

Puchero is goat flesh or mutton, stewed with various
vegetables, spices, and herbs, and *barbacao* is meat
(sometimes the whole animal with head and bones) roasted
in a hole in the ground, a fire being built underneath.

This hole is lined with stones, and covered up till it becomes thoroughly hot, when the meat is put in (the covering being replaced) and left to cook all night. The result is a deliciously crisp, well browned barbecued sheep or ox. This kind of meat is frequently bought in the market by wealthy Mexican families to avoid the tedious process of preparation.

With our *tortillas con dulce* (sweet cakes — very

PREPARING TORTILLAS.

delicious) we enjoyed some excellent chocolate. *Atole* is a kind of gruel made of Indian corn and *Atole de leche* (milk) with chocolate added is known as *champurrado.* When the bark of the cacao is mixed with this, it becomes *Atole de cascara,* or with chili, *chili atole.*

It is curious to watch the making of the tortilla either in the open square, or in the *jacal.* The corn is first soaked in water for some hours, with lime thrown in to remove the husks ; then the women go down upon their knees and beat it for hours, with any amount of tossing, patting, and flattening. The dough is next divided into small pieces of about an eighth of an inch in thickness, and then thrown on to the hot griddle (*comal*). These cakes contain no seasoning whatever, and I prefer them to the ordinary American corn-bread ; the slight flavour of lime serves to bring out the natural sweetness of the corn. The *tamales* (sausages), also, are made of ground or bruised corn, and rolled up in the husks ; one sees them often sold in the streets " piping hot." The meat is finely minced with pepper, &c., some of the dough wrapped round it ; the whole being folded in a corn husk, and fried in boiling lard.

The *metate* is a very primitive kind of mill, but none other is ever used by the poorer Mexicans. With it they grind or bruise maize, coffee, spices, vegetables, chocolate ; in some places even sun-dried salt is crushed between its stones. It consists of two pieces of rock, and is about half a yard long by a foot in width, and eight inches in thickness. The slightly-concave upper surface is roughened by indentures, and upon this the grain is placed and beaten with another stone (*marco*) resembling a rolling-pin. The stones go through a preparation of baking by fire, and are very durable ; their rough points become as hard as steel, and one *metate* will last for a generation.

With many a " Muy bonita cena " (very pretty supper) and " Adios " we left the Mexican quarters, catching a glimpse as we passed of the gambling booths, where games of hazard of every description were by this time in full swing, amidst the tinkling of guitars and little French harps, which sounded melodiously with the rich Southern voices.

The Menger and the Mahncke rank highest amongst the hotels of San Antonio, but the Boss selected the St. Leonard's Hotel on the score of economy. We found the situation pleasant and the rooms clean, whilst I received so much courtesy and attention from Mr. Lounsbery, the proprietor, and his staff, that I was induced frequently to repeat my visit, when a warm welcome always awaited me. The meals were served exactly as in the south-western part of the United States; after the soup, the whole menu (with the exception of the sweets) being served at once in numerous small circular or oval dishes, requiring some skill to arrange them round the centre plate, which is never replaced.

For the most part, the *table d'hôte* was served at small separate tables, each accommodating three or four persons, but at one larger table we counted seventy tiny dishes amongst a party of eight, or an average of about nine to each person; two kinds of fish, the inevitable beefsteak and fried potatoes, beans, a cutlet of pork and veal, liver, a sausage, two or three *réchauffés* and various kinds of stew, vegetables dressed with more or less grease, popcorn, a variety of salads, tomatoes, porridge, butter, &c. All the courses are mixed by eating a mouthful of each in turn with the rapidity peculiar to the American. The sweets, in their turn, were arranged on small dishes, and sometimes (always on Sundays) followed by a " desert " (not dessert), including ices and iced melons.

The arrangement of this menu reminded me of a story I heard on the cars, the gist of which I failed to appreciate at the time. An American from one of the South-Western States, on a visit to England, being invited to dine with an English friend, was greatly astonished to see only a tureen of soup on the table. Judging by its general appointments he had anticipated an excellent dinner. His roll and plate of soup were disposed of before the other guests had begun theirs, and he intimated a wish for more. Seeing the soup about to be removed and feeling still unsatisfied, he, nothing abashed, asked for a third portion, when, to his astonishment, was served the best dinner his eyes had ever beheld ; and he, as he expressed it, " chuck full of soup."

Owing to the heat, all the meals are early : breakfast beginning at 6 a.m., though you may procure it until 8, or 8.30, dinner at noon, supper at 6 p.m. ; but first come was first served, and we found it an advantage to be in our places at the beginning of each meal.

Iced tea and coffee were always served and frequently consumed on top of the somewhat greasy soup, but wine or beer never accompanied meals, the men frequenting the saloons between whiles, and the women taking their promiscuous " toddies " and " pick-me-ups " in their own rooms, or at the chemists' shops. If I ventured to order anything of an alcoholic nature at meal times, many scandalised glances were directed towards our table.

The St. Leonard's Hotel is much frequented by Texan ranchmen, some of whom are not very refined in their habits. On the staircase, at the time of my visit, a notice was displayed requesting " Gentlemen not to spit on the floors, walls, or ceilings " ; and the request was by no means unnecessary. We were sorry to begin our last day at this " garden City of Texas," the " Sanatorium of the West," and City of Missions. I might add this Earthly Paradise ; but no rose is without its thorn, the drawback in the present case taking the form of tiger mosquitoes. There were mosquito curtains to our beds, but this smaller striped species were on the alert all day as well as all night, and were more cunning and stealthy than their larger cousins, who are at least sufficiently honourable to give warning of their approach by singing. But the tiger mosquito seems to rest neither day nor night, and " flies round " and alights without the slightest sound. We were most cruelly bitten above our shoes, our ankles becoming so inflamed that we applied iced-water bandages when no one was looking. During our walks in the suburbs, I often could not refrain from indulging in a hop, skip, and a jump, in order to rub one foot against the other. Didymusa bore this infliction more patiently, and oddly enough, during future visits, these tiresome little creatures did not torment us. Probably they were hatched in water left for some purpose close by, the river being at a distance. There had been recent rains, and a large galvanised tank stood near at hand.

The Boss was a Job's comforter, and consoled me by a description of the venomous insects and reptiles I should encounter in the near future. He also advised me to dose myself with sulphur, in order to prevent the creatures from biting : a pet theory of his, which I never tested !

He was remarkably clever in forming theories, which seemed to have but little practical result. I found a pleasanter cooling antidote than sulphur in Harnisch and Baer's delicious ices and iced confectionery. America is acknowledged to excel in the concoction of cool beverages, and having tasted those in many cities, East and West, I unhesitatingly give the palm to San Antonio, and especially to Messrs. Harnisch and Baer ; to say nothing of the pleasant gardens behind their establishment, containing numerous shady nooks and bowers, surrounded by palms and other tropical plants growing luxuriantly, the pleasant

ripple of adjacent fountains alone disturbing the perfect
stillness. Or at night the moon, extremely bright in that
clear, lofty sky, glints between the broad graceful palmetto
leaves, with a rival in the occasional gleam of incandescent
light from the voltaic arc, fitfully leaping in the breeze
and forming miniature rainbows amidst the falling
spray.

To the left, beyond the balcony rails, the San Antonio
River flows calmly on through the entire length of
the town, with fifteen bridges, mostly of iron, on its
course.

Having bought a bridle and quirt (whip) of many
coloured horsehair (actually fashioned of the strong fibre of
Maguey) at Langholtz's, the saddler's, where Mr. Taylor
selected a complete outfit for cow-hunting, we proceeded on
the cars, drawn by sturdy little mules, which went all the
way at a hand-gallop, to Post Sam Houston. This is a
charming suburb, Government Hill being the most fashion-
able residential quarter.

About 3000 soldiers are usually garrisoned in the
military station here. We watched them drill, and the
men seemed to go through their evolutions with great
precision. After strolling round the beautiful palm
garden, we walked back, that we might admire the
suburban gardens, already ablaze with roses, verbenas,
geraniums, cacti, and many fine flowering trees and shrubs.
There were splendid specimens of the yucca, or Spanish
dagger, bearing enormous heads of pretty white snowy
blossoms. On the side-walks, the pretty china-berry tree
is planted for the sake of shade, vines and Virginia creeper
(often called ivy) affording the same protection to the
verandahs or galleries, which pertain to all houses, great
and small.

The evening was spent at the San Pedro Springs and Park, where no expense has been spared to enhance the beauties of nature by art. The band discoursed light and pleasing music : the old favourite " La Paloma " and the spirited " Himno Nacional " being greatly applauded. On our return we paid a visit to the Schultz Gardens, a favourite lounge for the German population, where they revel in iced lager and Pilsener beer, brewed in the city.

As our train did not start until the afternoon, we spent the next morning in a charming ramble to the Alamo heights, including a row on the West End Lake, everything looking marvellously clear in the bright sunshine of that perfect spring morning.

From the summits of Beacon and Prospect Hills a charming and extensive view is enjoyed. Both heights are studded with indigenous timber, and the country beyond possesses all the special sub-tropical charm presented by the ower latitudes of the Union, to say nothing of the extensive improvements in the way of parks, artificial lakes, &c., which have been made by these thrifty and wealthy Germans, whose favourite place of residence this suburb appears to be.

I often laugh when I recall our first walk in San Antonio. Having reached the side of the square opposite to the hotel, my arm was suddenly seized by Didymusa.

" Oh, look there ! " she exclaimed in horrified tones. At an open shop a man was seated, whilst another, whom Didymusa evidently took for a murderer, was holding back his head in the act of drawing a razor across his throat !

A moment later we were disillusioned. At the first glance we had failed to notice the long row of empty chairs, only one seat being occupied, but we laughed heartily on recognising that it was nothing more terrible than a barber at work in a shaving saloon, one of several in the neighbourhood, all quite open to the street, the operation being conducted in full view of the passers-by on the side walks.

———o<o>o———

CHAPTER VII.

KERVILLE AND ARRIVAL AT LECHUZA RANCH.

————

By half past four in the afternoon we were once more
"all aboard," moving from the Aransas Pass Depôt to the
ding-dong clatter of the engine bell, steaming slowly until
we left the streets and outskirts of the town behind. At
eight o'clock we arrived at Kerville, the terminus of the
line, the extension from San Antonio having been open
only about a year at the time of our visit.

The St. Charles Hotel being full, there was at first
considerable doubt whether our whole party could be
accommodated, but eventually Didymusa and I shared one
room, and the proprietor consented to give us all shelter.
This important matter being settled, we ordered a special
supper, the train always arriving later than the usual hour
of that meal. It was amusing to see the black cook with
her round beady eyes, and fuzzy hair, and gleaming white
teeth, constantly watching us from the door which
communicated between the kitchen and the dining-room.
We were informed later that the attraction was our pink
and white English complexions, and indeed these often
betray the newly-arrived Britisher in their contrast with
the sallow thicker skin of brother Jonathan.

Situated far higher than San Antonio, Kerville is
consequently more bracing, and the St. Charles Hotel is

E

usually crowded by consumptives and persons with delicate lungs, chiefly from the low-lying coast towns, where ague is prevalent. They regard Kerville as a sanatorium on account of the marvellous healing properties of its air, combined no doubt with perfect rest.

The bedroom accommodation was curious, having fixed washstands with a pipe, like those on board ship; no baths in the hotel or elsewhere, the population consisting only of about 1000 persons. We were unable to get our baggage from the depôt in time to start by the early morning train, or we should have pushed forward at once. I felt glad we were to spend only two nights here, and sincerely pitied the poor invalids, and wondered how they arranged matters during a prolonged visit; being reminded of a woman in a poor district at home who, advised to put her feet in hot water to cure a cold, exclaimed, " Lawks ! mum ; I've heard as its death to put the feet into water ! "

At six o'clock the second morning we packed ourselves into the stage drawn by four Texan horses, which were changed only once during the drive of fifty-five miles to the little town of Junction City. These animals were not much to look at, but very clever and sure-footed, being admirably driven by Louis ——, a young Frenchman, a nephew of General Boulanger.

The world is, indeed, a small place : I had been greatly amused by the career of a young lady who had spent several years in Texas, and had just returned to England. At San Antonio I was introduced to her brother, to find that his cousin was one of my intimate friends in Hants. This fair siren, his sister, had stolen or broken many hearts out here, and at the Cornfoot Depôt (between San Antonio and Kerville) one of her latest victims was pointed out to me. He was a diminutive but good-looking young Englishman, seated in a stylish buggy, and handling a pair of spirited horses to perfection; a friend of one of our professional beauties. He appeared to be thriving on his disappointment, and perhaps his great financial success in the new country proved a source of consolation. Though, as I was informed, scarcely able to write his own name, he knows a horse when he sees one, and has been a remarkably successful breeder and salesman, owning a horse-ranch and training-ground of considerable importance.

The first part of our drive was through the lovely valley of the Guadaloupe. Once the road (if it may be dignified by that name) came to a sudden termination, and we drove some distance up the river to a kind of platform consisting of one large natural block of stone, surrounded by delicious little cascades, gurgling and rippling on each side of us, whilst the pretty cardinal birds and blue-jays were to be seen in great numbers on the thickly-wooded banks.

Here we paused for a few moments to breathe our horses and give them a drink in the clear rippling water, to the accompaniment of the joyous notes of birds in their nesting season. I dipped my hand into the water, already quite tepid from the heat of the sun. This is probably the reason why horses can drink freely in passing through the creeks, even while they are hot, without suffering in consequence.

In all his ordinary work, I believe that a horse suffers far less from being allowed free access to water than from receiving it in stinted supplies at long intervals. In this regard I cannot avoid quoting the words of Mr. B. Cartledge, of the Royal College of Veterinary Surgeons, who " urges the great necessity of allowing an unlimited supply of water to horses," and alludes to the " very mistaken notion," amongst grooms and others who have control of horses, that water *ad libitum* is injurious.

While "grooms and others" drink without stinting themselves, they profess to know when a horse has drunk enough, and often take away his pail before his natural wants are half satisfied. Horses will not drink to excess if watered frequently, and in their case, at least, drinking does no harm.

I often wonder that owners, who profess to be fond of their horses, never bestow a thought on their comfort and well-being in the stable after the pleasure of the ride or drive is over, and that they do not insist on water being ready for the animals' use both night and day.

In my own stables I have constantly found the trough or pail empty the first thing in the morning, showing how much a constant supply of water is needed. My favourite thoroughbred mare has never been sick or sorry during ten years. Of course, there may be exceptions in the case of training stables ; or, at the end of a long day's hunting, properly prepared gruel may be safer and better after the fast and fatigue. Certainly hard water, just drawn from a well, almost as cold as ice, would be inadvisable, soft water, which has been exposed to the sun, being better.

But it is a difficult matter to convince ignorant grooms, and many others who have charge of horses think they know better than Sir Frederick Fitzwygram, who, also, is an advocate of frequent watering in moderate quantities.

In an able book, which should be in the possession of every owner and lover of horses, Sir Frederick Fitzwygram, in reference to the digestive methods of the horse, declares that he requires liquid before taking solid food.

This is a long digression before we pull out of the creek

and up the steep bank on the opposite side—rocky, and for some yards almost resembling a pair of steps. We had been jostled and jolted, and being unaccustomed to this kind of conveyance, the occasional lurches in bad places brought us into contact with the iron framework which supported the awning, the result being frequent blows and bruises.

But it was as well to gain some experience before crossing the Divide which separates the Guadaloupe and Llano countries. Here it was all bumping and jumping, the horses slipping and sliding, the wheels often threatening to part company from the body of the coach. This looked somewhat dilapidated, and we were informed that a breakdown was by no means an unusual occurrence.

Following, as it did, several hours of sitting in a cramped posture (although we did change places occasionally), it became quite an ordeal, and as I still suffered from neuralgia, which seems especially to resent this mode of travelling, it was a sad day for one's poor head and vertebræ.

We were all glad to stretch our legs at the small camp, where we changed horses, and, under some trees close by, discussed the luncheon which had been brought from the St. Charles Hotel.

It was half-past six when we reached the little town, and halted at the principal store, where Mr. H., the German proprietor, came forth to welcome the Boss and his wife on their return from the old country.

We were introduced both to him and his English cashier, Mr. J. R., and after a pleasant chat and a rest, Mr. H., who was at that time running the stage at this end, arranged to send us on by it to the Lechuza Ranch, about twelve miles up the river; and we were not sorry to arrive at our destination at about 8.30. The continuous drive over such country for more than twelve hours is not to be courted by the strongest.

The following morning we were awakened to actual ranch life by the Boss's reveille. This consisted of the Indian " oi-ee," a sound difficult to describe, but familiar to those who attended Buffalo Bill's entertainment at South Kensington.

As soon as we were dressed there was a regular bustle ; some being told off to attend to the cattle in confinement, some to milk the cows, others to prepare breakfast. There was the fire to light, the porridge to make, the coffee to grind, the bacon to slice, the eggs to cook, the night lines in the river to look after.

These lines are laid for catfish, a species of siluroid perhaps ; resembling a cod in the flakiness of its meat, but considerably coarser. The catfish often weighs as much as eighty pounds, the average being from fifteen to thirty pounds. Its size seemed to be its chief recommendation ; I always found it extremely indigestible, and as the menus at the ranch sometimes, after a lucky catch, consisted of catfish for breakfast, catfish for dinner, and catfish for supper on several consecutive days, it became a veritable *béte noir*.

I inwardly chuckled with delight on the happy occasions when Mr. M., a Devonshire boy, who presided over the fishing lines, returned with a long face to report that the bait was gone—devoured probably by mocassins, a poisonous species of water-snake (*Ancistrodon piscivorous*), with a dark brown body striped with black, and brownish yellow belly. These snakes are said to bite only in the water, and as I neither swam nor bathed in the river, I rejoiced to hear that they had been having a good time of it.

The Lechuza was a " mixed " ranch, running cattle,

horses, sheep, and goats, with 20,000 acres of land, fairly well-watered in most parts by the River Llano, and comprising a valuable cedar brake (plantation). The value of the land varies from 75 cents to two or three dollars an acre, depending upon the richness of the land, its proximity to the river, and upon the existence or absence of fences, several of the better portions of grazing land being protected by barbed wire enclosures, forming pastures of some thousand acres. Other portions, with good sub-soil, were under cultivation, being planted with cattle-sugar-cane, oats, maize, and millet. The garden was situated near the' river for the sake of water, the one thing needed in this fine climate (independent of rain) to produce every kind of the choicest vegetables ; tomatoes and melons grown almost wild, the former being exceedingly luscious and juicy. It was astonishing to find so few vegetables on most of the surrounding ranches, owing, as I imagined, to the deficiency of water and absence of proper irrigation, as well as, perhaps, to lack of time to attend to their cultivation, every kind of hand labour being scarce and dear. Except that of the Mexicans, who are chiefly employed to herd the sheep, and only fairly well paid, one seldom sees negroes working in this locality, and only occasionally a Chinaman or a Mexican as cook or " general help." All white " hands " demand high wages, and a " Texian," as he calls himself, must not be expected to do much out of the saddle. When his feet leave his wooden stirrups, it is generally to thread the mazy dance on the light fantastic toe, or cut capers on his high-heeled shoes—whichever you please.

Our ranch house itself quite "took the cake" in the county, both in point of size and good construction ; the extent and number of its rooms having, at the time of its building, given rise to the rumour that the Boss intended to utilise it as a private sanatorium. When it was compared with many of the surrounding shanties, this could not be wondered at. The Texan ranch, or house, is generally a rude log structure, frequently with only one compartment, to serve as kitchen, bedroom, and parlour. The rough logs of which it is built are simply nailed together, leaving numerous chinks and crevices. The floor is raised a foot or more from the ground, and rests upon four blocks of stone or timber, with a vacant space beneath, steps to reach the door, and generally a gallery on one side.

But sometimes ranches are built without this underneath space, when the ground serves as the only floor.

These mansions are anything but warm during a "norther," a snap of cold which sets in suddenly, and may continue either a few hours, two or three days, or, at the outside, a week.

On these occasions the inmates stuff up the holes in their ranches with bags and old garments, and sit crouching over the wood fire on the hearth.

The fire dogs of the Lechuza hearth; its handsome stone mantelpiece, and a bordering of the same material to form a kind of fender, were generally admired by the Texans, but the first to inspect the house after its completion informed his friends that it was "mighty bad furnished; he didn't see even a bed"—a startling deficiency to the native mind, every one of their rooms containing a bedstead, sometimes two or three, according to the size of the family.

The toilettes of these people are not very elaborate; the washing utensils consisting of a basin and towel placed in the gallery outside the ranch, where there is always a pail or bucket of drinking water and an enamelled iron or tin cup with a long handle like that of a saucepan.

On the arrival of a visitor, he is greeted with " Take seat ! " " Have off your hat ! " " Cool yourself down ! " On taking his departure the guest is bidden " Good-bye ! " and " Come again ! " To omit the latter injunction is to betray a shocking defect in manners.

In order to " cool yourself down," you take a seat on the gallery and remain inactive for a considerable time. You are invariably offered water, and expected to drink a vast quantity. I believe it is contrary to the etiquette of the country to refuse it. The men generally help them- selves ; any water which remains in the vessel being tossed far away and describing a circle of spray in mid-air. To accomplish this effort neatly requires a dexterous turn of the wrist and twist of the elbow, which can be acquired only by long and frequent practice.

To this " cooling down " process — the prolonged inactivity after exertion, and the great quantity of cold water consumed—may probably be ascribed the constant " chills " and " fever " (a kind of ague) from which so many Texans suffer. Another cause may be their custom of not wearing flannel. Very few Englishmen suffer in this way, though they are troubled with " prickly heat " or " Texan boil," due, probably, to change of diet, excess of salt meat, and deficiency of green food.

This scarcity of vegetables, however, is now almost a thing of the past, as the country is becoming settled, and the fine water utilised by irrigation. When the land is near one or other of the rivers (which never dry up in the most droughty summer) it is often irrigated by a simple system of troughs.

Everyone has a passion for chewing gum. The ostensible reason for the habit is its tendency to increase the natural flow of saliva, and thus to remedy indigestion.

The gum is aromatic and not unpleasant to chew, though the practised chewer does not care for it in its original state; not, in fact, until he has rolled it in his mouth into a large insipid ball, resembling a lump of putty.

I have constantly found one of these balls of partially-chewed gum between the joints of a rocker (chair), left there in this delectable form in readiness for future enjoyment.

Happening to pay a visit on one occasion, I received a great compliment; nothing less than the offer of a piece of gum direct from the manipulator's mouth, after she had taken all the trouble to make it " just nice " for me. I was assured that it had come all the way from Virginia, and was " real good." It was no easy task to escape the ordeal of placing it in my own mouth on the spot, and finding the most ingenious excuses unavailing to avert the immediate reception of this fine (and perfected) Virginian gum, I thought that discretion was the better part of valour, and beat a hasty retreat.

The girls are great cigarette smokers, and many of them use the " dipping stick," although they refuse to own it. The matrons, however, make no secret of this nasty and offensive habit.

For the fun of the thing, I once asked a lady what she was doing, though I confess I was perfectly well aware of her weakness. She replied without hesitation :

" Cleaning my teeth, ma'am."

It certainly looked like it, as the tobacco juice oozed from her lips, to be squirted the next moment with perfect precision into the opening of the stove; a feat requiring infinite practice ! " Dipping " is a kind of snuff-taking; the powder, which is a preparation of tobacco, being rubbed on the teeth and entirely over the gums with a piece of stick whittled at one end until it serves as a brush. The stick is almost always a root of the mesquit.

In order to make myself sociable I soon managed to take my part in the cigarette smoking, and indeed, on subsequent occasions, when camping out, or during a long day's hunting, or on encountering bad smells in Mexican towns, I found the practice very useful.

————oo;ⁿⁿoo————

CHAPTER VIII.

DOMESTIC LIFE AT LECHUZA RANCH.

NOBODY could be more active and energetic than Mrs. Boss. With the help of her husband, of some of the hands and pupils, she managed to accomplish all the cooking and household arrangements; a very praiseworthy feat, and extremely conducive to economy, since a young German girl, knowing nothing, could not be secured as a " help " under thirty dollars a month, or about £72 a year !

Lest this book should, perchance, fall into the hands of any aspiring young servant in England, let me hasten to add that this large sum does not in the end realise as much as may at first sight appear. Wearing apparel and other necessaries are so dear that a dollar does not go further there than a shilling in England; to say nothing of the rough life and the food, which would be little in accordance with notions derived from an English servant's hall. But in towns, of course, the food is better, and the life in every way more independent.

In this hot climate, butter-making is no sinecure. Taken altogether, the dairy with its churning, the bread-making and the coffee-roasting, and so forth, a considerable amount of labour was entailed to provide for the wants of our large party of from ten to twelve persons.

As is usually the case, there was only one table. At the very large ranches, to which a store is attached, there may be a separate house for the hands, but at the Lechuza Ranch we were all English or Texans. Although Americans " vaunt the equality of all men," the Texans would have declined to take their meals with the Mexicans, who camped out with their herds. Their rations of flour, beans, grocery, &c., were served out weekly, and cooked by themselves in camp.

The actual house-cleaning is much lessened by the absence of carpets and staircases, a broom sufficing instead of a scrubbing brush, though water is occasionally used with the broom, and run off through a hole made in the floor for that purpose. When there is much traffic, it may be imagined that the boards do not retain a very good colour.

The Lechuza was planned in the form of a square, with one large reception (or drawing) room in the centre, about forty feet by forty, having entrance doors opposite each other opening on to the north and south galleries. There were four bedrooms leading from the reception rooms, east and west, while the dining-room, kitchen, and other offices formed a wing on the west side, thus obtaining a desirable north-west aspect for the kitchen. The fine wide verandahs or galleries, as they are named in Texas, ran round the entire building to the beginning of the west wing (where the square became elongated), and extended in a narrow slip from the dining-room to the kitchen. The pillars which supported these galleries were covered with vines and other creepers, and some of the most luxuriant Morning-Glories (*Ipomœa purpurea*) I ever saw—red, dark and pale pink, purple, white, and variegated.

> " The lustre of the long convolvuluses
> That coiled around the stately stems."

The house and galleries were roofed with shingles, overlapping and nailed together like slates. The shingles are made of a kind of oak (*Quercus imbricaria*), and the roof looked extremely picturesque ; the interior being also very pretty, fashioned out of pine, with its fine grain visible through the varnish.

The Boss had chosen an admirable site for his dwelling. It stood upon a knoll rising abruptly from the lovely wooded banks of the river, which was within sight, and yet at a safe distance in case of one of the rapid floods which occasionally occur.

The house gained full advantage from the acceptable breezes that invariably arise in the night, baffling the attempts of the tiresome mosquitoes, which, from their extreme lightness of body, are unable to fly against the slightest wind.

I do not remember ever being bitten at the Lechuza, although we were always tormented whilst staying at places situated on the flat near the water.

All the ranches are built of a single storey, with the exception of one of very recent date, the Belvidere, which possesses a second storey. For at least three quarters of the year its galleries are used more often than its sitting-rooms, and sometimes for sleeping purposes also.

In the rear of our ranch were several buildings for housing corn, dried sugar-cane and millet, with stabling and a poultry house, of a kind of open construction, in order to allow the maximum of ventilation. There were the usual clipping-sheds, a smoke-house for curing bacon, corrals (yards) for penning cattle, and, in Texas, generally named " lots." Several of these " lots " communicated, and extended as far as the dipping vat, which was used for sheep washing.

On the first evening of our arrival, Mr. Taylor went into the " lot " with some of the hands to see the milking.

Strolling about in the dusk, he fell headlong into the vat, which is a kind of long, narrow canal, whence he found some difficulty in extricating himself.

As he was unhurt, it was impossible not to laugh at his bedraggled, bestained, woebegone appearance. It was the ruin of his pretty English grey suit, which hung outside the ranch in a shrunken form for many days to remind us of his involuntary bath.

One "hand" was told off to cut and collect wood to supply the cooking-stove; the oven being in use the greater part of the day, the demand for fuel was considerable.

Coffee can be bought only in its green condition (very cheap, costing from twenty-five to thirty cents the pound), and its roasting requires a great deal of time and attention. If it is roasted too quickly its flavour becomes disagreeable and burnt; if the oven is not opened frequently to turn the berries they "catch"; and if the vapour, which always arises as they become hot, does not escape, the delicate aroma of the coffee is entirely spoiled.

Bread was made three times a week, the sponge being set overnight with home-made yeast cakes, composed of meal, sugar, hops, and other ingredients, and dried in the sun.

This kind of bread is known in Texas as "light bread," but we dubbed it heavy "light bread" when it did not turn out quite so well as usual. No kind of cold bread is very acceptable to the Texan appetite, his table never being properly supplied without hot corn bread or hot biscuit. The latter is neither more nor less than an inferior and heavier French roll. It requires no setting, is made off-hand, raised with baking-powder, and contains about a tablespoonful of lard, or some kind of grease, to each pound of flour, with sweet milk, or soda added to sour milk.

Our ordinary meals were three a day; breakfast at 6 a.m., dinner at noon, supper varying from 6 p.m. to 8 p.m., according to the season; in fact, it was served at sundown, when it became too dark for further work out of doors.

There was not much variety in the preparation of these meals, which consisted chiefly of bacon and eggs, with beans about once a week, prepared in the orthodox manner : boiled down with bacon, until perfectly brown and the liquor quite thick.

About once a week, too, a goat was killed, and dressed in various forms : roasted, boiled, stewed. Ours not being a beef ranch, this meat was seen only on rare occasions, when a neighbour killed an ox and sent round portions for sale, or a joint was bought from the meat market of the little town.

The washing was sent to Junction City, together with soap ; the articles, great and small, being returned rough-dried and unfolded (the charge twenty-five cents a dozen), and afterwards starched or ironed, as the case might be.

Being English we indulged ourselves with table cloths, which are rarely seen, or never, in the truly typical Texan house, where the tables, supported by trestles, would be covered with American cloth, or more often its rough boards would be left bare.

Didymusa and I were supplied with sheets, and the Boss indulged in a similar luxury, but the " boys " were compelled to be contented with blankets, so that the quantity of linen was reduced to the minimum. This was also the case with our own clothing ; and the heat increasing, we shed some garments every day until underclothing became a mere trifle. Moreover, the " boys " had to shift for themselves, some washing their own clothes in wooden tubs provided for this purpose, but also utilised by us as baths ; others sending their things into the town when opportunities offered. I may mention in passing that all unmarried men are " boys," regardless of age ; but let even a youth of eighteen marry, and he is immediately designated " old man " So-and-so.

For the first fortnight after our arrival at the Lechuza, I did not become quite accustomed to these limitations.

I suffered from incessant catarrh, aggravated by the severe draughts, which our hostess declared necessary for the general health. The lamps on the supper table would flicker in an agitated manner for some time and then go out altogether, leaving us under the " Mosaic dispensation," and martyrs to excessive ventilation. Ultimately one window would be closed and the candles relighted. Finding that my complaints met with little sympathy or courtesy, after a few repetitions of this kind of thing I used to walk off, plate and cup in hand, and take my meals with greater comfort in the kitchen.

Catarrh in America is really a chronic inflammation of the mucous membrane, and although, with its subsequent lassitude, very distressing, I believe it saved me from many other complaints which are common on arriving in this hot country. From headache and prickly-heat I was quite free, but Didymusa endured a martyrdom later on.

The first time my handkerchiefs were washed (seventy or eighty having been used in three or four days), Mrs. Boss advised us to look at them after the lapse of twenty minutes. We had spread them on some wood, the average temperature being 98°, and surely enough they were as dry as buckram, some having blown away on the fresh

F

breeze, giving us a good run before they were recovered. A large shallow tub filled with cold water in the morning was quite hot enough to use for laundry purposes by noon. The ranch possessed an excellent wringing and drying machine, which economised time and labour considerably.

On Sunday we assembled in the drawing-room, where the Boss read prayers from the Episcopalian service, the nearest church being fifty-five miles away at Kerville. Sunday was a great day for salting the cattle, a most essential process, since without it they die or take themselves off to ranches where salting is a weekly practice.

The beautiful herd of a thousand mohair or Angora goats, with exquisite long silky hair, came up for this operation, many of them with sweet little kids frolicking by their sides.

Some poor mothers had lost their young ones during the night, devoured by wolves or coyotes, and their udders were in a terrible condition from want of milking, the skin in many cases being broken and bleeding. In a country like this, with such large herds, it is, of course, impossible to bestow that individual attention which we think necessary to the proper keeping of stock in England. But Nature soon healed these ruptures, when once the sufferers had been roped and the milk drawn off.

Goats had been returning an enormous profit as long as mohair materials were the vogue, but with a change of fashion trade became flat, and upon our first sight of the herd it was being kept in the hope of another change in fluctuating fashion, and for purposes of food. Mutton is never seen, the merino sheep being handled entirely for the sake of its wool. The fleeces are not nearly so bulky as those of our South Downs or Lincolns, but the wool is valuable on account of its fine, soft texture, the price of these stock sheep ranging from one and a half to two dollars.

During the whole time I was in Texas I came across only one ranch (Fort Territ, one of the largest in the country, having ninety miles of fence) where they ever killed a sheep for food. Of course, cattle always holds its own, but, from the general financial depression and other causes, of recent years the cattle man has not thriven so well as formerly. One or two bad winters may help to account for the prevailing depression, but so enormous is the recuperative power of these vast districts that cattle owners still look forward hopefully, sparing no effort to improve the native stock by the importation of beasts. The average price of an ordinary cow varies from ten to twenty-five dollars ; that of yearlings from six to eight dollars per head. Steers fetch more than heifers, a four-year-old steer in good condition commanding twenty dollars ; young calves from two to four dollars.

With regard to breeding horses, the same may be said ; several years elapse before there is any return for money expended on the ordinary Texan ponies, which seldom fetch more than twenty-five dollars, and may be often bought for from ten to twenty dollars. In exceptional cases, on the bigger ranches, where there has been a large outlay with the view of improving the straight mustang or Spanish horse, suitable for draught or saddle work, there is a good sale and ultimate profit in the stock yards of San Antonio and other large markets.

But, taking it all round, for the young capitalist of limited means there is nothing like sheep, which with proper handling yield a large, steady, and immediate profit on the wool each spring and fall, apart from the yearly increase in numbers.

The spring clipping season had now begun, the clipping being usually performed by Mexicans, who cross the borders of the Rio Grande twice a year, mounted on their " bronchos," in bands of from twenty to thirty, generally under a captain or boss. Although they bring their own cook, they are supplied with food and cooking utensils at the ranches which they visit in succession every year.

The work is done in sheds about 250 or 300 feet in length, fitted with benches four feet high by three feet in width. Two thousand sheep and lambs were brought up, although the lambs are not clipped until they are a year old.

It was a busy scene, the long sheds full of clippers, each working vigorously at a poor animal which lay on the bench in front of him. Like all artisans the clippers vary in skill and speed, some getting through as many as thirty sheep a day, whilst others could only manage ten. Some merely held the animals down on the bench, and the victims in this case were quieter and better clipped than others which were tied ; these struggling more violently, and receiving more wounds in consequence. With the greatest strength and facility, I noticed a corresponding degree of gentleness on the part of many clippers ; the slowest were generally the clumsiest, and inflicted the most severe cuts, these being instantly anointed with a black ointment to conceal the wound and keep off flies.

The incessant clattering in unknown tongues, the constant " baa-ing " of the victims, made a perfect Babel. We were gradually picking up a little of the language, and were able to understand enough to learn that the chief topic of conversation was the forthcoming evening gamble, which, to the accompaniment of music and singing, would be kept up till the small hours.

A few sheep are lost in consequence of bad cuts in clipping. Some are easier to shear than others, and it was amusing to see the shearers trying to select the animals with the fewest wrinkles.

Hard by, pens were arranged for the shorn and unshorn as they were turned out of the sheds. With each clipped fleece a check was given from the desk, to be counted and exchanged for money in the evening. Then the sport began, though occasionally, I believe, the checks changed hands before being cashed, in settlement of bets made during the day. What a nation of gamblers!

Their horses were weedy little half-starved creatures, and many of the men looked as if they, too, needed a good "feed" before beginning work. With a few exceptions, their garments were utterly dilapidated.

The next incident of the shearing was the arrival of the freighters to convey the wool to San Antonio. The fleeces were packed in large sacks. It was pretty to see the Mexicans drive through the gateway in the small fencing which surrounded the house, bringing their teams of sixteen or twenty horses to the farther gallery where the wool had been stowed.

The driver rides the near wheeler, and does much with voice and cracking of his whip towards turning the sharp corners. Sometimes the horses seemed quite mixed up, with their feet over the traces, which, with the single trees, were almost on the ground in turning the corners. The cleverness shown by the animals in righting themselves as they pulled into line, each falling into his proper place, was surprising. A freighter's horse has plenty of work and not a superabundance of corn, so that he is not inclined to jump out of his traces for the mere fun of the thing. Like his master, he takes life very practically.

The freighters live on the road, camping at noon and night, when they hobble and stake their horses.

On an average they make thirty miles a day. It is monotonous work—crawling along with a heavy load; especially during the rainy seasons, when the tracks are soft mud, like the bottom of a pond, and the waggons frequently stick in it, the poor freighter having all his work to do to keep dry his goods and the wood with which to heat his coffee.

It is astonishing, after heavy downpours of rain, which falls in perfect sheets of water, to see how quickly the clouds roll away ; the scorching sun drying the wet slush in a few hours. A day passes and you can hardly believe that rain has fallen.

BRANDING.

CHAPTER IX.

BRANDING, AND FIRST RIDE TO JUNCTION CITY.

THE " rounding up " was now in full swing. This operation, like the shearing, takes place each spring and fall, and consists in hunting and collecting together all the scattered cattle on the range (that is to say, on any ground or pasturage not under fence) for the purpose of counting the number of heads belonging to the various owners. Then the increase, foals and calves, are branded with their respective marks ; those which are not wanted are turned loose, others intended for sale being driven to the nearest stock yard at town or depôt and freighted to Chicago or some other distant market.

" Mavericks " are calves which have been allowed to run unclaimed without branding for a year, and are considered the property of whoever can rope them and affix his brand. I have been told that Maverick was a cattleman who neglected to collect his calves and yearlings and to have them branded, and so lost them.

And again, it is said that Maverick was a man who formed his original " bunch " of cattle by hunting up animals belonging to other persons—a kind of prairie highwayman. The latter is, I am inclined to believe, the most probable story.

The branding is performed with a hot iron which burns out the roots of the hair, and, effectually destroying them, prevents future growth. The animal is roped and thrown down with its fore legs tied together, as shown in the photograph. The brands are all recorded in a register which is kept at the Court House, the registration fee being 25 cents for each cow or horse. When a horse is sold, if its value permits the outlay, a bill of sale is given and rebranding becomes unnecessary ; but the record fee varies from 75 cents to a dollar and a quarter. The brands are of every imaginable device : crescents, circles, crosses, shields, trefoils, ellipsoids, angles, or combinations of these figures, often interwoven with letters or numbers, and an endless variety of forms contrived with admirable ingenuity.

When the country is more settled up in large fenced pastures, and the range system becomes extinct, I hope that this cruel custom of branding will be no longer necessary.

Horses are usually branded on the left side, cows on the right, and when they have frequently changed hands, I have seen them completely covered with various devices, a bar being always placed across the brands of former owners.

The branding takes place as far as possible at the coolest time of year, and it is the cowboy's duty to dress the wounds and keep flies away until they are cicatrized.

When not engaged in " rounding up," about which I shall have something to say farther on, the cowboy takes his turn at " line riding " to repair defects in fences. For this purpose he carries the necessary tools, and also blankets for the night, the fences varying in extent from twenty to seventy or ninety miles, so that he cannot always return to sleep. A certain distance is supposed to be allotted to each cowboy in order that they meet one another on the line.

BRANDING.

Fencing is an expensive item in buying a ranch, mortgages often being raised, and paying 12 per cent. To stretch the wire, of which the tension varies with the temperature of the day, requires considerable experience. But on ranches not under fence the cowboy has more trouble, as, while allowing the cattle to graze in all directions, it is his duty to keep them as far as possible within certain limits. Of course some must stray, even with the closest vigilance ; hence the need of branding and also of the " rounding up " each spring and fall.

If the cowboys neglect to tend the cattle after branding, they fall into a terrible condition or occasionally die. Then the turkey-buzzard (*Cathartes aura*) arrives, does his work upon the carcase, and soon leaves only a skeleton on the prairie to tell the tale. I have seen flocks of these birds watching an animal till the breath leaves its body, when they will cover it so completely that the carcase looks quite black.

The turkey-buzzard is regarded as a useful scavenger, and to kill one entails a fine of twenty-five dollars. In high flight they appear graceful, anything but that when devouring their prey, with their naked warty necks like vultures !

Apropos of scavengers, the Tumble bug (one of the species *Scarabeus*) is a wonderful provision of nature in default of sanitation. Thousands of these creatures may be seen working in the most assiduous manner, the female laying her eggs in a globular mass of manure, and using her hind legs in regular treadmill fashion to roll it to some chosen spot, where she buries it in a hole in the ground which she has excavated for the purpose.

These beetles swarm wherever there is any attraction, but they are very inoffensive and do not bite. One cannot give the same good character to the ticks, fleas, and chintz-bugs. To a person with an abnormally sensitive skin, ticks are indeed a pest ; a sad drawback to picnics and camping-out expeditions in summer.

Whether they were in the grass or fell from the live oak trees, I never quite discovered, but my sufferings from them were very real.

They are parasites ; a kind of magnified mites, attaching themselves to the skin, and sucking the blood until they swell to such an extent that they resemble miniature birds' eggs, though naturally they are flat, having innumerable legs but no wings. They will adhere in this way for a fortnight, until they drop off, when they are supposed to die. Once having fixed the mandible or proboscis in the unfortunate victim's skin, their tenacity is so great that no amount of mere force will remove them. If you dislocate the neck, thus breaking off the body, you only increase the discomfort, as the decapitated head apparently still continues to suck, and causes as much inflammation and irritation as before ; as they possess no lungs, the only method of killing or removing them is to cover them with oil or grease, which prevents respiration. I have been told that the common kind of this horrible insect is the *Iodes albipictus,* but Dr. Curtice, of the United States, has investigated the life history of the various species of ticks, and recently written a very clever paper on the subject. He speaks of that usually called the " lone star " as *Amblyomma unipuncta,* and, though this is not so numerous as the common variety, its habits are quite similar.

The investigations of the United States Department of Agriculture, concerning the relation of ticks to Texas cattle fever, have produced such astonishing results that any information regarding these creatures at once commands attention.

The question that occurs to one's mind on reading the reports is : Are there other species of ticks capable of transmitting the disease ?

This question has not yet been answered, though the first steps have been taken to decide the matter.

On July 3rd, 1893, Dr. Curtice made experiments on ten adult females of the *Amblyomma unipuncta* (commonly called the "lone star tick"), which were collected from cattle. These had an average weight of forty-four drachms. They were confined in the laboratory under ordinary conditions, and began depositing eggs July 7th. This continued about ten days, they by that time having deposited forty-eight per cent. of their original weight as eggs. They were alive July 25th—that is, six days after having ceased to lay eggs—though apparently dry and lifeless. The larvæ appeared August 8th, which, on comparison, will be found very similar as to length of time required for the common variety.

The result of these experiments on the larvæ of cattle-parasites will be published as soon as they are concluded ; but, up to the present, nothing further on the subject has reached me.

My first acquaintance with a tick was one night a few weeks after our arrival, when I became afraid I was going to be troubled with Texan boil.

At breakfast the following morning, when Didymusa described the supposed abscess, with its loose "head," or scab, she was greeted with roars of laughter, and, grease being applied, the disgusting, bloated creature tumbled off, although its mark remained for nearly a year.

I thought that this tick had been picked up from the

sheep.   The Mexicans not staying to shear the bucks
(about ten or twelve in number), as these had wandered off
and had not been brought up in time, and this part of the
clipping falling upon the home hands, Didymusa and I
accompanied Mrs. Boss to the sheds.   There was a good
deal of fun in capturing these consequential, butting
gentlemen, and between us we managed almost to shear
one of them, holding him down and wielding the shears in
turns.   The task occupied about an hour, and left my hand
and fingers very stiff.   After this trial, I felt more than ever
surprised at the rapid manipulation of the Mexicans.

" Chintz " bugs were very prevalent, perhaps on
account of the pine-built houses and wooden bedsteads.
During the Boss's two years' absence, the ranch had been
left in charge of a young English visitor and his father,
with the Devonshire boy, who, as well as being the fisher-
man, was a capital cook and general all-round hand.   They
had for the most part slept on the gallery, and the
" chintzes " (neither more nor less than the common bug
of London lodging-houses) had it all their own way.

These pests were waiting for us, but the first night we
were too tired, after our long drive from Kerville, to notice
anything.   Like all Americans, however, they did nothing
by halves, and the second night we were quite able to
appreciate the vigour of their attack.   The following day
the bedstead was taken to pieces, but the slats could not
have been put together again properly ; and that night,
after falling through several times, I followed the example
of my host and hostess, who always moved their mattress
to one side of the gallery, the boys occupying another side.
We could not very well divide our mattress, and Didymusa
would not be induced to sleep anywhere but within four
walls ; so that I betook myself to my own particular

portion of the gallery and there lay down on the floor. I never mind where I sleep; the harder the bed the better the night. In fact, the simplicity of one's habits stands one in good stead in this kind of life, and even the ability to eat a few slices of mild onions proved desirable when one could not easily obtain other vegetable diet—a plebeian taste in the opinion of many persons, but these onions, less pungent than the small spring onions which decorate our salad bowls at home, act as a useful stimulant to the appetite.

Their odour conjured up the familiar picture of an English ploughman sitting beneath a quickset hedge with a crust, a piece of cheese, and a raw onion in one hand, a pinch of salt in the hollow of it, a knife in the other, enjoying his hard-earned "bait," whilst his horses stand discussing theirs close by, the regular crunch of their grinders his sweetest music. But this old-fashioned type of English ploughman with his respectful salutation is fast dying out, alas!

During my first week at the Lechuza I had nothing to ride, and the Boss was too busy, after his long absence, to find me a mount; so that I was pleased when, after looking through his stock of horses, he assigned "Maize" for my use, a sprightly little bright bay with flowing mane and tail. He stood about fourteen hands, and I soon became very fond of him; but he had one drawback, not being quite able to carry my full-sized and rather long saddle. The girths always slipped under the arm of the shoulder and rubbed him. A crupper might have kept it in position; but not being intended for pony use, the saddle had no T-iron to attach one to.

However, Maize and I became great friends, and he carried me pleasantly for some weeks. Having been out on him a few times, and feeling anxious for news from home, as the Boss and all the boys were too busy to go, on the following Saturday, April 20, I suggested riding to Junction City to fetch the mail, &c.

During the past few days the thermometer had been from 80° to 95° in the shade and over 130° in the sun, while the intense stillness of the atmosphere seemed to forbode a storm. The Boss regarded the suggestion rather dubiously, and insisted that I should carry a " slicker " in case of a sudden downpour. A " slicker " is the kind of waterproof used by the cowboys ; and I was provided with one of Mr. Taylor's ; a frightful, gaudy, new mackintosh, bright yellow and red, in all its pristine freshness.

This was attached to the saddle together with various bags (for the mails and other articles), suspended by strips of leather to the studs, some of which were used in the ordinary way for the breastplate and others for the small sandwich case. Altogether a truly ludicrous spectacle to my unaccustomed eyes ! Round Maize's neck a rope was fastened, the end being coiled and secured to the saddle. This appearing a quite unnecessary encumbrance, I took it off and threw it behind me in spite of combined shouts and entreaties from the cowboys and the Boss. But after further experience, a few weeks hence, I was careful never to stir far without this appendage ; extremely useful in so rough a country.

About seven miles down the river I fell in with Mr. H., senior, father of the young Englishman who had been left in charge of the Lechuza during the Boss's absence. Mr. H. was now staying at Ranch Viejo, which he had bought for his son.

He emerged from behind a large chaparral thicket

where the road from Bear Creek united with that which I was following to Junction City, and feeling somewhat diffident to enter the strange town alone, I was pleased with his company. We seemed to resemble the golden goose as we went on our way, being joined by quite a little crowd of cowboys one after another. I afterwards learned that Saturday is a favourite day for marketing and inquiring after mails.

There was a blacksmith at Junction City, and as Maize required shoeing, I left him at the forge, and walked on to Mr. H.'s store to do my own shopping and execute one or two commissions for the others.

I was so warmly received at the store by its agreeable German owner, and by Mr. J. R., his English cashier, that it seemed more like paying a pleasant visit to old friends than shopping. They sent for my mails, and, one of the letters requiring an answer, kindly offered pens, ink, and paper, and the use of their snug office " back of " the store—always a pleasant spot in my memory, on account of the hospitality shown on this and subsequent visits by Mr. J. R., whose offers of biscuits, ginger ale, &c., were extremely welcome after the long dusty rides from the ranch.

Just after Maize's return from the forge the wind suddenly " lifted " with a curious hissing, rushing sound, and some black clouds, which had been gathering for some time on the horizon, drove up with it. After a vivid flash of lightning and a tremendous crash of thunder the clouds burst over us.

There happened to be a waggon-yard or feed-yard connected with the store ; a square plot of ground enclosed by a very high fence, with sheds arranged on two of its sides for horses, these being secured by a bar-chain fixed across the ends, or sometimes simply tied to the fence. If they are lucky enough to get a feed of corn, they eat it from an old box on the ground, the stage horses generally occupying the sheds.

This place was frequented by freighters, cattle owners, and cowboys, who convert it into a cheap hotel and livery yard combined. A couple of horses at a livery stable in Texas would cost about two dollars (or between eight and nine shillings) a day; whereas at the feed-yard they can be provided for at from 10 to 25 cents.

Dried sugar-cane, millet, and corn are purchased from the owner of the yard, and if the nights are cold, the freighters take refuge in their waggons, which are always provided with blankets and camping utensils. Otherwise they sleep in the sheds or any warm corner that happens to be available.

Occasionally some lively cowboys will disturb the slumbers of their quieter neighbours; when a free fight is the result.

As I was not ready to start, Maize was taken to the yard, and now I wanted the rejected rope, to tie him to one of its feeding troughs. But my new friends supplied the deficiency, and the rain still falling, and the bells of the two little hotels ringing for dinner at noon, Mr. J. R. invited me to accompany him to one of them.

A funny meal! with fourteen Texan ranchmen, cowboys, and others waiting outside for admission; two little boys waving mesquit branches over our heads to ward off the flies; the table, as Mrs. Naudain, the proprietress, expressed it, spread with " all the seasonable dainties which Junction City could afford."

The grease on the handles of the knives and forks made one shudder, to say nothing of the fumes of the black over-roasted coffee, loved by the Texan as fondly as his molasses, which imparted an unpleasant stickiness to everything. The Texan never suffers from gout. I remember seeing one mix oysters and molasses together, with hot corn bread sopped in it. The oysters were given to him as a great treat, sent already opened in a can with ice from San Antonio. The oyster beds are at Galveston, Rockfort, and Corpus Christi. We had a plentiful supply of " biscuits," with poached eggs, bacon, fried steak, some uninviting boiled bones with a little meat attached, gristly, freshly-killed, and tough ; custard also, and pudding, peaches, and dried apples cooked up in pastry ; on the whole, a feeble imitation of the more elaborate menus of St. Leonard's, with its multitude of small plates. Although Irish potatoes are sometimes served and specified as such, as a general rule, when you hear of potatoes in Texas you must expect the sweet potato, which tastes not unlike a parsnip, and is extensively grown in this country. Not a *pomme-de-terre* by any means, its tubers growing upon a climbing plant akin to Morning Glory (*Ipomœa batatus*), supposed to be a native of Brazil, and the original potato of the southern part of the United States.

The storm passed off about four o'clock, when the sun began to shine brightly. On leaving the store it seemed like entering a stove-house, the ground hot and steaming—and such mud ! I felt as if I were carrying tons on my feet, and with my well-filled mail and shopping bags, poor Maize had a pretty good load. I left the town with Mr. H., who also had been detained by the storm, but on account of the mud, the ride home was not accomplished very quickly, although the absence of dust was delightful.

G

CHAPTER X.

ROUNDING UP CATTLE, AND COW OUTFITS.

On reaching the ranch, about seven o'clock, everyone looked out eagerly for letters. One boy was sent to deliver the mail which I brought for two little ranches higher up the river.

There was great excitement at the Lechuza, a large herd of cattle, over a thousand head, having just been driven into the pens for the night on their way to some distant place. The company's "outfit" were camping out about a mile off at the first creek. I had observed their waggon (similar to that shown in the photograph) on my ride home, but supposed it belonged to squatters on the move.

These rounding-up "outfits" vary very much in size and formation. Large owners or companies send from ten to twenty-five of their own hands, supplied with a properly-fitted camping waggon and provisions, a boss, a cook, and a horse herder, there being from six to twelve horses for each cowboy. The cowboy finds his own blankets and saddles, and receives from twenty-five to thirty dollars a month.

> I am a Texan cowboy,
>   Light-hearted, gay, and free,
> To roam the wide, wide prairie
>   Is always joy to me.

COW OUTFIT CAMPING.

My trusty little pony
  Is my companion true ;
O'er plain, through woods and river
  He's sure to " pull me through."

I am a jolly cowboy,
  From Texas now I hail ;
Give me my " quirt " and pony,
  I'm ready for the trail.
I love the rolling prairie—
  We're free from care and strife—
Behind a herd of " long-horns "
  I'll journey all my life.

The early dawn is breaking,
  Up, up ! we must away,
We vault into our saddles,
  And " round up " then all day ;
We " rope " and " brand " and " ear mark "—
  I tell you we are " smart " ;
We get the herd all ready,
  For Kansas then we start.

When low'ring clouds do gather,
  And lurid lightnings flash,
The crushing thunders rattle,
  And heavy rain-drops splash,
What keeps the herd from running,
  And " stampede " far and wide ?
The cowboy's long, low whistle,
  And singing by their side.

And when in Kansas City,
  The " Boss " he pays us up,
We loaf around a few days,
  Then have a parting cup ;
We bid farewell to city,
  From noisy marts we come
Right back to dear old Texas,
  The cowboy's native home.

[These lines have been set to music by Mrs. Robert Thomson.]

If the country to be " rounded " is very extensive, or if
the cattle have to be taken up trail any distance before

G 2

being sold, the expedition may last three or even six months. Branding takes place every day when necessary, the cattle which are not required being turned loose again. A certain number of cowboys drive the selected herd, riding at stated intervals on each side. Sometimes there is a break out, followed by a stampede and much hard " running " to cut off the escaped animals and drive them back into a compact mass before continuing the journey. Other cowboys are told off in turn to drive the unridden horses or hunt for more cattle. Hobbling the horses at night and taking them up in the morning, with other duties for securing the herd, also are undertaken in regular turns.

The camping ground is always chosen by the cook, the boss giving him some idea of the desired locality. The cook generally drives the waggon also.

Smaller ranches combine in getting up such outfits, settlers joining independently to hunt up their own little bunch (pronounced boonch), clubbing together to pay the cook and commissariat expenses.

They generally manage to choose a spot near a good sized ranch with available corrals to pen the cattle. Roping is very skilful, and in the hands of an expert the rope is a dangerous weapon. In Mexico it is called the lasso, the lariat, or la reata, and it is difficult to say whether the Texan cowboy or the Mexican vaquero uses it the more expertly. In the art of riding, too, the one and the other are perfect.

The cowboy would no more speak of his rope as a lasso than describe the evolution of his pony as bucking ; this is always " pitching." The country is always called Téxas, never Texass. The rope measures forty feet in length, and varies in price from 45 cents to a dollar, according to its quality and the finish of its noose, either with leather or an iron ring, or more often with nothing but a simple knot at the end for the length to pass through. This running noose is swung horizontally over the head, with the elbow at the height of the crown. By this circular motion sufficient force is acquired to project the whole length of the line, the remainder of the coil being held in the left hand until the noose falls upon the object to be roped. A well-trained pony will stop dead on feeling the strain, and the rope is wound round the horn of the saddle. There is a tremendous strain from a full-grown steer; but these small ponies are strong in the shoulder, and show wonderful intelligence, throwing themselves back on their haunches to resist the pull the moment the rope tightens.

If the rider fouls (misses), the pony gallops on and trots up again, until the animal is captured and ready to be branded.

The rope ought to fall, and when thrown by a skilful hand, generally does fall, upon the horns or feet, and I have been told that some of these ponies will even pass on if it catches the neck; but this example of their intelligence I have never witnessed.

Mexican and Texan saddles are both extremely heavy and cumbersome, high in the cantle, with a long horn or peak in front—to which the rope is secured—sometimes being adorned with goat-skin pockets. I tried to lift one of these saddles from the ground quite in vain. Those of the Mexican ranchers are really costly, often being trimmed with gold or silver to match the rider's own highly ornamental suit of clothes. He has three rows of buttons down his legs, and his handsomely braided jacket is stitched with gold and silver thread, the whole being surmounted

by the expensive sombrero, costing from thirty to three
hundred dollars. The cowboys also wear a similar broad-
brimmed hat, but made of plain straw with a leather band
round its high crown, and occasionally with another band
of gold and silver twisted over that. A leather strap passes
under the chin to prevent the hat from falling off when the
pony pitches, or in riding through thick brush.

Ordinary saddles are made of hard wood, covered with
leather or parchment tightly stretched; from the peak to
the cantle an open space runs down the middle, which I
concluded was for ventilation in this hot climate. They
are not in any way stuffed or padded, but a thick blanket,
folded square, is placed beneath to protect the horse's back
from the frame. They do not often gall, except after some
hours' "cutting out," when very sudden swerves and
stoppages at full speed become necessary to turn the cattle,
causing an unavoidable wring of the saddle and consequently
sore shoulders.

The Texan spurs are heavy and large, but not so enormous as those used by the Mexicans, which weigh several
pounds; and whilst the rowels are two or three inches in
diameter, they are not nearly so sharp or cruel as the
smaller English kind. The bits are very severe, but the
cowboy never rides on his reins, these generally hanging
slack on the horse's neck, except in rounding and cutting
out, when the poor pony is most unmercifully jerked.

In Texas the bridles are managed in a manner quite
different from our own, the object being, I imagine, to
leave the right hand free to throw the rope. Instead of
bearing on the right or left rein, according to the desired
direction, the hand, with both reins, is drawn outwards and
across. When you wish to go to the right, for instance,
the hand is drawn out on that side, the left rein pressing

against the horse's neck. In driving, you take the right side instead of the left ; and it is contrary to etiquette to overtake and keep just in front of another carriage. Unless your team be sufficiently superior to show it a clean pair of heels, you must stay behind.

MEXICAN BIT.

A snaffle is never used, the curb being about an inch high in the crossbar or port, but short in the cheekbits or branches. The bit shown in the accompanying photograph is Mexican, and of chased silver. It is now in my possession, having been bestowed upon me as a mark of high esteem ; but it is nothing less than an instrument of torture, a type of many (perhaps not quite so cruel) in general use in Mexico ; for the Mexican, like the Oriental, prides himself upon riding with a finger, although the uneasy curvettings and fretting and frothing of his steed, with his trick of throwing his nose in the air, betrays the cost at which this apparent ease is attained. Both Texans and Mexicans ride with extremely long stirrup leathers.

CHAPTER XI.

" ROPING "—HAILSTORM—COYOTES, SKUNKS, AND FLOWERS.

THE rope, on the frontier, is frequently employed as an instrument of vengeance. Not so often as the six-shooter or the bowie knife, though many a score has been wiped out on the prairie by the fall of the fatal noose upon the surprised enemy ; when his neck is broken, hurled from his saddle, the lifeless body is dragged along the ground for some distance, exactly as if the man were one of the deer which are occasionally treated in the same fashion.

An instance occurred at the Spring rounding-up at some pens not far from the Lechuza. It was said to be a pure accident—greatly to be wondered at on the part of so expert a roper ! But a deadly feud was known to exist between the two men, although the affair was hushed up, and the assassin would have fared worse if he had stolen a horse.

I waxed indignant on one occasion, when some mixed cattle (that is to say, cattle owned by various persons) were being roped, and a cow's leg being broken, the poor animal on account of the calf by her side, was turned loose to shift as best she might, instead of receiving the more merciful *coup de grâce*. Didymusa's wrath burst forth in spite of the Boss's warning that it was often as much as one's life is worth to give free expression to opinion in such a country. But a woman escapes scot free, when a man would have had bullets through his head again and again. Certainly, the young fellow who owned the cow, must have been any-thing but gratified by Didymusa's frankness. She reminded him that one day his own turn might come and, singularly enough, before the end of the year, he suffered a painful death from a kind of typhoid fever. He died in his bed, however—a rare occurrence for a Texan, who generally " dies in his boots."

There is a story told of William ——, one of seven brothers. The other six had all been shot. William took to his bed, turned his face to the wall, lay for some days, and died apparently a natural death. His mystified relatives examined the body thoroughly, but could find no wound of any kind ; nothing to account for his strange end.

At the large Exhibition about a year later at San Antonio, we enjoyed the roping contest and tournaments, and the cowboys' favourite game of " lifting the ring " quite as much as the military display at the Agricultural Hall at home.

The rain, which had detained me at Junction City on Saturday, was very local, and after passing the last creek before reaching the ranch, all traces of a storm were lost. The Sunday following was very sultry, without any corresponding rise in the thermometer, the heat being the more oppressive in the absence of the delightful day breeze which nearly always prevails at this altitude. The Sunday's rest was appreciated, and those hands who did not go out for the day indulged in longer siestas than usual. About two o'clock in the afternoon, the hottest part of the day, when the wind is inclined to drop, there is mostly a little relaxation, at least, during the summer.

We had just prepared supper when we heard an unusual noise, something like a very rough sea beating on the shore, from the direction of Bear Creek. On going outside we saw a dense cloud rising above the mountain, and the Boss ran swiftly towards the house calling upon the boys to help him to close the shutters. Every ranch of any pretensions is provided with shutters to protect the glass during hailstorms. But before they could be closed, the hailstones began to rattle down, breaking some of the windows and injuring the shingle roof.

We could not hear ourselves speak, or perfectly understand one another even when shouting at the top of our voices, so deafening was the noise upon the roof. For half an hour the storm lasted, and we wished to weigh some of the stones. At first the Boss refused to allow anyone to leave the house, but a little dog having been left tied up outside, he pressed a hard hat down tightly on his head and presently ventured out for a few seconds to bring the poor brute under cover.

He was bruised even in that short time, but managed to secure some trophies, the hailstones being as large as a fair sized hen's egg, and weighing just under two ounces.

The storm was followed by a beautiful evening ; half a mile distant nothing had been seen of it. While we were enjoying the Sabbath quiet of the evening on the gallery after supper, we heard a great disturbance amongst the goats a little way off. The Boss and one or two of the boys proceeding to the scene of action, found some coyotes (pronounced kiotee) worrying the herd, a kid having already been killed.

The coyote is a wild dog or prairie-wolf (*Canis latrans*) and the cause of much trouble amongst the sheep and goats. Into the breast of the uninitiated camper, also, it strikes terror, as it invariably approaches near to see what it can find. The querulous, snapping bark of a single coyote, ending in a shrill prolonged howl, conjures fears of a hundred, in the stillness of the night.

They are cowardly, sneaking animals, and never attack man ; rarely tackling even a kid or a lamb single-handed, but working together in small numbers, not as a rule in large packs like wolves. Two or three coyotes will attack and kill a good-sized calf. They are extremely crafty, and the Boss failed on this particular occasion to get one within range of his gun.

Soon after his return, our olfactory nerves being very painfully offended, he explained that a skunk had been killed at a ranch distant half a mile as the crow flies, on the further side of the river. The Boss's explanation was confirmed on the arrival soon afterwards of one of the boys who had been taking part in the chase. Even at this distance the odour was excessively pungent and unpleasant, and it seemed that the highly electrified air carried sound as far as scent, for we could hear the hunters' voices and almost distinguish their words.

Skunks (*Mephitis mephitica*) have white bodies and tails, with black backs. The Texans name them polecats, but they are larger than the European carnivora of the weasel family.

We were not greatly annoyed by wolves at the Lechuza, but the Paint Rock and Bear Creek districts were dreadfully troubled with them, their cattle sustaining considerable damage during the winter. On one occasion when we were returning home from a dance, at Bear Creek, we were pursued by wolves.

Many suggestions have been made for some organised effort to exterminate these creatures, but nothing had come of them at the time of my departure, though they were hunted by any enterprising individuals who kept a few hounds.

I was invited to a wolf hunt at South Llano. We staked our horses and proceeded, principally on foot, amongst the cañons and hollows which form their lurking places, and Mr. P. managed to work some mischief amongst the quarry.

Since my arrival at the Lechuza, I had ridden all over the country, besides going out several times after cattle and horses with the boys; but Didymusa could not join in these mountain climbs, not being a very good horsewoman. Roche, her little pony, had thrown her once, and made her nervous; in fact none of the horses are to be trusted by riders not possessing a firm seat.

Rain lilies, lovely white flowers, are so named because they spring up in one night after rain. Texan " violets " are scentless purple flowers, more like the iris; and linums, quite scentless also, of a bright crimson hue. Many a time I wished I was a botanist! As I desired Didymusa to see them, we arranged to set forth early one morning, in order to avoid the heat of the day. The Boss did his best to frighten her by declaring that anyone we met would be sure to take a shot at us, persons travelling on foot being always regarded with suspicion. However, we decided to take the risk, and started at 5 a.m., although the threat was not without its grain of truth, a pedestrian being never seen outside a town.

It was a delightfully fresh morning, and, having climbed the mountain, of which the Lechuza commanded a view from the North, we sauntered along the table land between it and the next range, and enjoyed a fine view of the surrounding country. Didymusa was in raptures with the flowers, but as she stooped to pluck some, suddenly I saw a large snake rear its head and strike almost over her shady sun-bonnet. Its ominous rattle told only too distinctly what it was, and we regarded one another in terror at the narrowness of our escape; but as it withdrew, still hissing and rattling, followed by the dogs, we began to breathe more freely.

Didymusa suggested that we should return to the ranch, and we began to pick our way amongst the rough stones and thick vegetation with the most extreme caution. We had not advanced many yards, however, before we saw another snake curled up asleep on a large rock. I was preparing to collect some stones to take vengeance upon this one for the fright inspired by his mate, but Didymusa clung to me tenaciously, and, her one idea being to reach home in safety, the snake escaped, and we got well laughed at for our pains. But it was our first encounter, though not our last, and subsequently Didymusa went so far as to skin the dead snakes very successfully, and we brought home many a fine skin and rattle as trophies; though, for my own part, I shrank from touching the creatures. They make a rattle every year, so that you can tell their age by the number possessed, the button at the end counting as one.

I believe this variety is the diamond rattlesnake (*Crotalus adamanteus*), inoffensive, inasmuch as it always tries to escape and never attacks unless disturbed or hurt. It cannot strike at a greater distance than three feet. One of the cowboys gave me a piece of a root, which they generally carry in their pockets; when scraped and eaten it is an antidote to snake poisoning, but otherwise a poison in itself.

CHAPTER XII.

TEXAN DANCING, RIDING, AND DRIVING.

———

A FEW days after the adventure with the snakes, we received an invitation from Mr. J. R., the cashier of the stores at Junction City, to a lecture on the Holy Land, to be given by Brother Coleman, a Freemason, at the Union Church. The invitation arrived whilst I was out riding in the morning, and included ourselves, Mr. Taylor, the Boss, and his wife, and I found Didymusa in a great state of alarm on my return.

"A queer place, this Junction City," the Boss had told her; "I expect we shall all have to sleep in one room."

As the "Buckboard" accommodated only two persons, we were to set forth in the springless waggon. Each took a vacant seat beside the Boss in turn, the remaining three occupying two chairs and a reversed box; but as the road was rough, and tree stumps were frequent, we bobbed about and were jostled and jolted in so extraordinary a fashion, that we finished our journey on the floor of the waggon.

These waggons contain a seat or two, fixed on an iron frame and movable, to allow the sides to be heightened when the five bows, or wooden arches which support the canvas tilt, are attached. When the sides are heightened, the seat is fixed on top of the extra frame and becomes quite lofty, whilst the waggon is better suited to the conveyance of freight.

The lecture, which might have been more interesting, was varied by the singing of hymns, suggesting the rise and fall of a wailing wind. The company, to several members of which we were introduced, proved rather amusing; the ladies dressed in very bright colours—in light washing dresses for the most part, the scene being graced by the presence of a bride of fifteen.

When Mr. J. R., all politeness, showed Didymusa and me to our room at the hotel before supper, the rest of the party entered and stayed a few minutes, the Boss exclaiming,

" I told you what to expect ; " and his wife confirming Didymusa's fears, with—

" This is very nice ; just sufficient accommodation ! "

Poor Didymusa was greatly concerned all the evening, and not entirely without excuse. As I have already mentioned, a Texan generally has three or four beds in his principal sitting room. It would not be properly furnished without them, and this particular apartment was used partly as a general reception and ladies' room, partly by the " drummers " (commercial travellers) for the display of their goods, as also by the Judges during the Court week.

Subsequently Mr. Taylor declared that he had been similarly hoaxed, no room having been taken for him at the hotel, as he was to occupy Mr. J. R.'s own sanctum adjoining the store.

This invitation presently brought another to a dance in the town, and as Didymusa could not ride, the Boss kindly offered his buckboard and a team ; one, a white horse, named Spider, which scared (shied) badly, and had a tendency to bolt ; the other, Jim, a bad baulker (jibber), a somewhat ill assorted pair. Directly I gathered the reins Jim threw himself upon the ground and declined to budge, Spider resenting his conduct by plunging violently, snapping one of his traces, and rearing over Jim's back. Didymusa sprang down with the agility of a lamplighter, and the Boss jumped into the vehicle. The harness was patched up, and, with his shouting and whipping, whilst several of the hands pushed the horse, and others turned the wheels, we at last made a start, driving round and round in a circle, and slackening the pace sufficiently to permit the Boss to alight, and Didymusa to be helped back to her seat amidst many remonstrances.

However, we had made a start somehow, if with an unsatisfactory pair of horses, and drove down the hill and through the first enclosure at something like a runaway pace. But I was determined to let them go, rather than risk another standstill, and the Boss had cautioned me not to stop at the first creek. So we rattled along, by degrees they settled into a steadier pace, and Jim did not favour us with any more of the baulking pranks at which he was an adept.

We were to sleep at the new hotel, where we also made our toilettes and supped. The landlady wished to know " whether we were going on the floor "; and, making a guess at her meaning, I said, " Yes, if I am acquainted with the dances," having been previously informed that the squares were very intricate.

" Then you don't belong to the church ! " she exclaimed. " Yes, we both belonged to the Church of England," I assured her; but she remained sceptical, as no one who belonged to the " church " was in the habit of dancing. By " church," I think she understood one of the several bodies of dissenters, many of their members being forbidden to dance.

H

"You've a fine suit of hair, and mighty long, too," she said, and went on to inquire whether I was "full-blooded English," and where I was "raised." "Wale, I'll declare!" she cried, when I had satisfied her desire for information.

The dance was quite a smart affair, supper being provided at 10 o'clock, and dancing kept up vigorously until 2 a.m. Of course, the men considerably outnumbered the ladies, and many were compelled to wait for partners till the night was far advanced. A number is given to each man, who dances when it is called out by the musicians. At a public dance each number costs from fifty cents to a dollar, the money going to pay the fiddlers. During the pauses in the intricacies of the mazy square, there are exchanges of candies, chewing-gum, and *billets doux*, which may be compared to the flowery mottoes in an ordinary bonbon, with an advertisement thrown in. The style of chewing-gum correspondence may be judged by the following lines:

"ADORABLE ONE!—Where is the light of my eyes this dreary night? Darning papa's socks? Ah, me! the weary, weary injustice of cruel fate! Tell me, dearest, tell me that as soon as your tiresome task is finished you will hasten to me. Remember the old meeting place. * * * I shall be there, with my heart beating in a wild double-shuffle. * * * I will bring whatever change I can raise *to buy more of Heisel's delicious love-letter juice.*

"Yours till we meet,   "EVER THINE."

There is a kind of master of the ceremonies in the person of the prompter, who sometimes dances, or sits beside the fiddlers to direct operations. "Now, then, gentlemen, get your partners on the floor"; naming the dance. "Quord-reele," a "shorteesche," a "glide polka," or a "set." He also directs the figures of the "sets," ordering a *chassez*, *dos-a-dos*, *reversé*, *galopade*, or ladies' chain, at his own sweet will, throwing a good deal of life into the affair with his—

" Balance all—swing your partners, now the ladies to the left, back again, swing your hands round, right hands across and how do you do, left hands back and how are you. Swing or cheat or swing somewhere and don't forget the broncho-rider, join hands round and promenade home," and so forth, making an endless variety of figures.

The Texans cannot be described as graceful dancers, although they have some power of expressing the poetry of motion ; their figures are supple, and they swing and sway a great deal, with much facial by-play.

Cowboys are not exactly light-footed, but they are very springy, and make fun with their high action, while they pirouette on their high-heeled shoes. They are extremely particular about their shoes, which are always of the best make and fitting to perfection, whilst most of them possess the distinguishing mark of small, shapely feet. A cowboy's garments may be sometimes rather dilapidated, but he would go without a coat or deny himself luxuries rather than wear a boot that had not a fine upper to its sole, or that did not fit like a glove. The boot is to the cowboy what the sombrero is to the Mexican ; its extra-ordinary high heels being partly to prevent the foot from slipping through the large wooden stirrup. Their boots are certainly not made to walk in. Spurs are now dispensed with at dances, except in the case of " rangers " or under-sheriffs in uniform. These men display their six-shooters, and are occasionally required to keep the peace. Sometimes the exuberant cowboy becomes uproarious, when he begins to shoot at the lamps and windows—a signal for the company to make a general stampede.

After one of these gatherings at a small and rather rough ranch, a perfect specimen of its kind, where spring water is as cold as ice, and straight coffee (that is to say, without milk or sugar) with cakes, and slices of goat's meat and biscuit, only, were handed round, I met my friend Mr. W., the lively and polished Bostonian, who smilingly remarked that " if some of my friends in old England were called upon to dance a quadrille after the manner of these backwood people, it would be a revelation to them ! "

The next morning I had some trouble to start the team, but thanks to the help of several friends and possibly to the baulker's conviction that he was about to return home, we improved upon our setting forth from the ranch,

Mr. H., knowing that Didymusa could not ride very far, and thinking that she must be considerably handi-capped in consequence, insisted on lending me his light, two-wheeled, trotting buggy without a head, together with his bay-horse Button, standing fifteen hands.

The pilotage of the buggy was undertaken by Didymusa in fear and trembling. She was told to follow close on the heels of the buckboard, but when we came within four miles of the Lechuza, we overtook one of the trainers and another English friend who was staying there, Mr. A.

Whether the sight of his companions inspired Spider I know not, but at this juncture he " scared " in the most remarkable manner and bolted. The ridden horses joining in the sport, poor Didymusa was left to her own devices. Her story was that as my buckboard disappeared in the distance Button refused to move, jerking his head, backing, and switching his long tail until at last he managed to get the reins under it. Whilst Didymusa was leaning forward over the dashboard to release them, with her heart in her mouth, he took advantage of the opportunity to turn his head towards his home, and she found considerable difficulty in getting it round again. She was thinking it would be necessary to alight and lead the horse, when somehow she succeeded in starting him in the desired direction, though as this implied driving down the steep pitch to the last creek, her satisfaction was only partial. However, M. happened to be there fishing, and was only too glad of a lift.

In the meantime I was careering along at full speed, and as we flew down a steep pitch which ended in a sharp curve, the wheels swirled, and I began to think my chariot would really come to grief, for it had seen service and the wheels looked as if they might easily part company from the axle. However, the opposite rise told upon the horses, which were nearly pumped out ; and so was I, for having no purchase for my feet, and no companion to wedge me in my place, I had been bounding about like an india-rubber ball during the violent oscillations of the buckboard. It was no easy matter to steer clear of the worst stumps and other obstacles, collision with any of which at this breakneck pace meant instant destruction.

Mr. M., now acting as Didymusa's knight-errant, was a good whip, and overtaking me before I reached home, we enjoyed a fine race to the ranch.

A Texan road or track, it must be remembered, is not level, like an English highway, although no stumps higher than four inches are supposed to be left in the middle of the track, and all able-bodied men are called out once or twice a year to take their share in repairing and clearing the roads. This duty can be avoided by payment of from one to one and a half dollars or by sending a substitute.

Nevertheless there are always a good many stumps

left in the middle of the track which makes it extremely
awkward to drive a single horse or spike team (two
wheelers and one leader). But the single horse buggy is
seldom used for these long rough country journeys, and
with the double or four-in-hand team one can generally
manage to avoid the stumps between the horses. Indeed
the horses will take care of themselves on rough ground,
and for this reason their drivers are much too wise to use
tight bearing reins. Nor could the distances be accomplished, to say nothing of the pace, in such an unnatural
position. Few of the horses bore, and they carry their
heads remarkably well. In New York, San Francisco, and
other large towns I was sorry to notice that very tight
bearing reins were in general use. Not to prevent the
horses from "falling down," as an obstinate old coachman
in England once suggested! Oh, no, the American is
honest enough to admit that he does not use the bearing
rein for that purpose. "Appearance, ma'am," he says,
" is why I use it."

All honour to Her Majesty, our beloved and respected
Queen, for setting so excellent an example in forbidding
the use of bearing reins on her own horses!

Frequently, in joining a *posse* of cowboys on my rides,
or helping them to drive when I came across a herd " Up
trail," I listened curiously to their numerous tales of
adventure on " rounding up," " roping," or running helter-
skelter down steep mountain sides. Their ponies' legs
were sometimes broken, or perhaps a back; they might be
strained or cut, but I never heard a fear expressed of their
" falling down," or a hint of the necessity to hold them up.
It is perilous riding at times, and occasionally fatal
accidents have occurred, riders turning head over heels
during these rapid descents. But there is no jumping, a

cow-pony generally swerving at a cactus bush, although I have seen a few of the more eager take them in their stride.

I once witnessed a somersault of the kind just referred to. The "bunch" of horses which was being hunted had reached the level, and when once this happens you have to make time, or you soon lose sight of them in a wooded country. We were about half-way down the steep side of a range, and begun to put on speed, when T. E.'s horse suddenly heeled over. A moment of awful suspense ensued. T. E. lay on his back, apparently sobbing his life out, but, the shock once over, he soon recovered, shook himself, remounted, and both rider and horse escaped without apparent injury, those ahead knowing nothing of the accident.

A little while before, a similar slip had occurred down a cañon between Junction City and Kerville, when the rider broke his neck and the pony his back.

In hunting in some sections where the rocky nature of the ground makes the horses very liable to slip, the shoes are "caulked"—a sharp-pointed piece of iron projected downwards from the shoe ; very similar to our roughing nails. But in many instances, where the riding is principally confined to the prairie, shoes are dispensed with altogether.

The cow-pony, of mustang origin, in some cases crossed with the Spanish breed or other imported stock (in the case of Canadian horses, generally French), is a weedy-looking little animal, but plucky, and possessing great endurance, frequently doing a hard day's work on nothing but his native grass, and keeping himself in fair condition in a territory where grazing is good and the mesquit grass (*Bouteloua oligostachya*), a rich native grass, is abundant.

I have been surprised to see how gamely these ponies

between thirteen and fourteen hands will carry twelve, fourteen, or even over sixteen stone, to say nothing of the heavy saddle. They have no knee action—a great advantage when riding in military fashion—but their lope or canter is very easy, and they gallop evenly with a long stride, on account of their length of leg to the hough, and move with their hind legs well bent and under them. Their staying power is not great, and I found later on with my larger horses that I won any race longer than half-a-mile. For the quarter or half-a-mile they are extremely swift.

"Pacing," "fox-trotting," or "single-foot" gaits are not desirable in the true type of cow-pony, and are unsuited for travelling over rough ground; nor does the cowboy require high knee action. He often rides twelve or fourteen hours a day, week after week, "shucking" along and never rising in his saddle, the exertion of which the livelong day, with the thermometer at ninety-eight degrees in the shade, is not to be dreamed of. The pony, knowing his duty, jogs along with the reins hanging on his neck, whilst the cowboy twists his little cigarette between his deft fingers, or chews his tobacco, or the gum which his "best girl" has given to him at the last dance.

Very often the particular cow or pony or bunch of either is not found for weeks, perhaps never, when there is no "running." I used to think that in some cases this existed only in the imagination.

Although in running it is desirable to keep pretty near, if you "crowd" or run the animals too close, they are liable to break up and scatter, which is fatal to a good capture. Range after range is climbed to survey the surrounding country, without the use of glasses, and at first I was astonished to hear Charlie C., the Lechuza trainer, say, " No ; that ain't our boonch," whilst the only visible cattle were a mile distant on the opposite mountain or intervening table-land.

But with experience I found that he judged by the general appearance of the bunch, it being manifestly impossible to distinguish the brand. The movements of heads and tails would show him whether they were cows or horses, and he was familiar with all the bunches on the range, whoever their owners. He possessed a pretty little bunch of his own, although he owned no land. I soon grew familiar with his bunch, on account of its predominating dun colour. It comprised a few skewbald ponies, too, these and the piebald being named paint, and chestnuts sorrel. Some of the bunches contained curious mixtures : flea bitten brown and flea bitten grey being prevalent in one, with some sorrels. This was a bunch of superior cow ponies, crossed with foreign bloods, and standing from fifteen to sixteen hands. Mares are never used in Texas for the saddle, and very seldom in harness, unless for slow draught, or agricultural work.

CHAPTER XIII.

SHEEP DIPPING, BREAKING IN BRONCHOS, VISIT TO TEXAN SQUATTER.

———

THE evening after my return from the dance, the sheep were brought up and driven into the corrals in readiness for dipping on the morrow. Very young lambs were not put through the vat, and those old enough to undergo the process were divided from the sheep, as they did not require so strong a solution. The Boss this year was buying a new preparation for the dipping, which seemed poisonous and unusually strong.

The object is to destroy the scab, which is contagious and so general that all the sheep suffer from it more or less. Through some misunderstanding of the orders, the herders brought up their flocks a day too soon. Some people from a small neighbouring ranch had been using the dipping vat, and it was not yet prepared for the reception of our own sheep. There was a consultation to decide whether the flocks needed water before the operation. Sheep are not very thirsty animals, the dew and the succulent roots (when these form their food) supplying all the moisture they required. Finally the Boss settled that they should have their bath before going down to the river to drink.

But the night was very hot, the fretfulness caused by their separation from the lambs doubtless accelerated their thirst, and the result was disastrous.

A certain number of sheep are caught and thrown into the vat at the end by the pens, whilst the Mexican herders and other hands stand by with forked poles to dip the frightened animals as they swim past. Then the sluice gate is opened at the further end to release them, a sloping board being fixed for the water to run back into the vat. There was a fearful crowding at the place of exit, and the sheep seemed very glad to be free again.

We had seen many of them drinking as they swam the length of the long vat, and during the night 150 died in consequence of swallowing the new dipping preparation. The following day fifty more succumbed.

The carcasses were carted away some distance, but the wind happening to change, the stench became awful the next day. It was then decided to try cremation, and after supper the Boss, who was terribly cut up at his loss, went with some of the boys to see how the bodies could best be burned. As we watched the flames rising in the darkness we all felt exceedingly depressed and somewhat unwell. On the Boss's return a bowl of punch was brewed, and, Didymusa and I having returned to our room to write home letters, Mrs. Boss brought some of it there.

After this there was not much annoyance to the household, but for weeks subsequently, on passing North Creek, I fancied there was an unpleasant odour, and the ashes smouldered for a long time. Of course, the Turkey-buzzards collected, thirty or forty of these useful scavengers doing their best to help us; but there was really so ample a feast, and decomposition takes place so quickly, that on this occasion the result of their efforts was incomplete.

A team of young colts were waiting to be put for the first time into harness; and being glad to find something to divert his mind, the Boss set to work on them. He did not know the meaning of fear, and it was impossible not to admire his courage. He was always ready to ride or drive any of the young bronchos, and indeed, like most naval men, to go anywhere and do anything.

He had not been a successful man; a perfect gentleman, honest and straightforward, he was easily imposed upon, and had been completely duped by the worthless person he took into partnership on his first advent in Texas. The marvellous gift which some seem to possess, the ability to turn all they touch into gold, was not his. More sinned against than sinning, he may have lacked that power of dogged perseverance, which, allied with a thick-skinned unsusceptibility, appears to help people along in the world better than more brilliant endowments. He would soon flag and grow tired of manual labour; and was always prepared with a convenient excuse; how could he keep on, when he had already sprained his back once when roping a steer?

Well, the bunches of colts in the corral were roped and thrown by the trainer, thus to expend some of their strength in pitching. This was their first handling, then, the waggon having been brought up, they were at last harnessed. Despite the united efforts of the hands, they broke away from the pole time after time, damaging the harness, which had to be " hitched up " again and again. Presently there appeared a chance of success; the Boss was in his seat with the " lines " in his hands, Mr. A. H. and Charlie H. climbed up stealthily by his side, each holding a rope tied to the fore-leg of one of the bronchos, so as to throw them to the ground if they really got beyond control.

Then came the word of command, " Loose their heads." What a rush, what a clattering, as they plunged on their mad career, with loud snortings and wild screams, such as

I never heard from any other horse but a broncho. The Texans call it "bawling."

The Boss succeeded in steering clear of the posts and rails round the first corral, but they actually charged a large heap of firewood, and in their pitchings managed to leave it behind, the waggon wheels of course being much entangled. It was indeed a "prairie-schooner," opposing great waves, we all following in its wake, either to lend assistance or to pick up the pieces, as the case might be. The waggon was soon free of the firewood, but its rattle and jarring whilst surmounting these obstacles increased the terror of the young and previously unhandled team; in fact, it was enough to frighten the oldest "screw." Off they dashed at a greater pace than ever, leaving the track and making for the mesquit, until lost to sight. The course of the waggon as viewed from the rear, with its swaying tail, was indescribable; we could trace it for some distance by the broken mesquit, and see that it had had a narrow escape from a spill against a larger tree, from whose trunk a piece had been torn clean away.

However, after some hours, the chariot returned in triumph, all unhurt except Mr. A. H., who had received a slight kick; for, on nearing an almost impenetrable thicket of chaparral, the Boss could not turn the horses' heads, and was compelled to have recourse to the ropes to throw them down. In getting away again, one of the team kicked Mr A. H. on the ankle. Poor little beasts! they returned greatly subdued, covered with foam, and completely worn out.

The breaking to saddle is a process of still greater severity, so sudden and rough that it may almost be described as brutal, and the better and the more courageous the pony, the worse its treatment. Considering the high price of all manual labour, and the comparatively small value of animals, it would not pay to spend much time over their training, which is usually accomplished in one day.

The ponies having been "rounded up" and driven into the corral, and those not required "cut out," they are "roped" (lassoed), and thrown again and again, until the trainer and his assistants can work their hands along the rope to get sufficiently near to bridle and bit the young colt, the bit being invariably a very severe one. All this time the pitching and bawling are something terrible to hear. In the same manner, when the colt is on the ground again, an attempt is made to put a saddle on his back. This will be thrown off a dozen times or more; but having eventually succeeded in fastening the girths, the stirrups always being tied down, the trainer vaults into the saddle. During the saddling the pony is generally blindfolded; but, the bandages now removed, the assistants throw the end of the rope to the trainer and lose no time in jumping aside, this being the moment for renewed and violent pitching.

Even if the pony were of so tractable a disposition as to start without this usual gymnastic display, he would be spurred till he began it. Occasionally the trainer is thrown, when roping, throwing, and blindfolding begin all over again. But these men are wonderful riders; they could sit a flea, or an animal with the extraordinary jumping powers of that insect. Their agility and suppleness are marvellous, but they all relinquish the training business at twenty-five; often before attaining this age.

The breaking-in of the bronchos in this sudden manner by mere brute force was, like the branding, no pleasure to witness, and only a desire for information induced me to visit the corrals while it was going on, and this but seldom. Didymusa and I always endeavoured to induce these people to be kinder to their animals, and in some instances I hope we succeeded. But I must confess that, taking into account the large number of ponies to be broken in and the short allowance of time to do the work in, it is difficult to discover a remedy for the sudden terror awakened in the poor bronchos, though in a few cases this might easily have been mitigated.

I remember one broncho—a black—of great courage and determination, which would have turned out a better horse with more gradual and gentle treatment. In pitching, it is, perhaps, needless to say the horse lifts his four feet simultaneously from the ground, his head and tail almost meeting, his back arched like a bow ; in fact he nearly doubles himself in halves. The only way to keep your seat is by perfect balance, suppleness of the loins, and the use of the stirrups, for which reason they are always tied.

This black broncho possessed extraordinary pitching powers ; threw his trainer several times, and was unusually difficult to bridle and saddle. He was so severely jerked with the cruel bit, besides being thrashed with the end of the rope, that blood poured freely from his mouth, and he was tied up all night, saddled and bridled, to a corral post. This was done to tire him out, and though the blood still continued to flow, the poor beast refused water. The following morning he was again blindfolded, when he began to pitch once more, but his strength failing, the trainer was able to keep his seat, and the horse was ridden almost to death. He became a confirmed pitcher, and little wonder, after the treatment he had received. But almost all these horses are prone to pitch under the influence of fright or excitement, or during a snap of cold, if the saddle be put on their backs without first having the chill taken off; even the coldness of the bit has the same effect.

When the trainer, especially if he is a Mexican, starts off victoriously the first time on a broncho, he waves his large sombrero and shouts frantically; his wild cries mingling strangely with the bawling of his terrified steed.

These wild horses naturally dread the near approach of a human being; since if they retain any recollection of the incident, their last encounter was for the painful purpose of branding. Having been once ridden in this fashion, they are sent to market and described as " broken in ! "

Unless the burden of grief is very heavy, one's troubles in this climate, with its busy, active life, and invigorating air, and constant sunshine, soon pass off. It is impossible to nurse depression for any length of time, and so the Boss's disappointments in connection with the sheep dipping were quickly forgotten.

During my wanderings on Maize I never missed an opportunity of becoming acquainted with the small squatters, who were remarkably friendly and hospitable— always ready to place all they possessed at one's disposal.

Thinking a little change desirable for Didymusa, I persuaded her to saddle Roche and accompany me to call upon my new acquaintance Mrs. B., who intended shortly to migrate with her husband farther west, " this country being no good to them now—quite used up." Which meant that, as so much of the land was being brought under fence, and they had no money to buy, their cattle were pretty well starved out.

Captain B., who had held a commission during the Civil War, was a tall, thin, gaunt man, with a typical American head. He used to talk a good deal of his position " 'fare the ware," when he owned slaves, and was not obliged to wait upon himself, his son " Buster " (I never heard him called by any other name) listening the while with evident admiration.

Their abode was of the log hut description, its crevices stopped up with odd garments, and so forth. Two large bedsteads, and one small one in a corner for their little girl Mattie, occupied the best part of the reception room. Near the hearth stood the large spinning wheel, with which Mrs. B. industriously spun the yarn, and made by hand the "domestic" (calico) for her household. The great wheel flew rapidly round and round, while she manipulated the threads, which soon got mixed up when I tried my prentice hand. Mattie, a little girl of ten, with luxuriant red hair, and large freckles on her face and hands, trotted about, with naked legs and feet covered with dust and dirt. Boots were quite a punishment; but, on special occasions, when these were thought necessary, she always wore bright red hose. She could milk the cows and help her mother in the house—a perfect child of the back- woods. Buster promised to be the counterpart of his father.

There was a small, narrow addition to the building, where the meals were cooked and eaten, a rude trestle table standing at the farther end barely leaving space for the broken chairs and stools.

A small gallery was attached to the front of the shanty, with steps, by which one entered. Not having forgotten the inevitable ropes, we fastened Maize and Roche to some posts fixed for the purpose in front of the house, and then went through the usual preliminaries of "taking off hats," "cooling down," &c. Didymusa's face was a study at this first introduction to a Texan at home !

But she became very deeply interested in the spinning, and the time slipped on, Mattie showing us her pretty pet deer, and creating a diversion by her constant efforts to thwart the hens, who were desirous to lay or sit under the beds. Noon and the dinner hour were fast approaching, and the report of Captain B.'s gun could be heard in the distance.

We had received a pressing invitation to stay, and Mrs. B. would take no refusal, so that we were interested to see her husband enter with a squirrel, which he immediately began to skin. This was a new dish to us, and the inevitable fried eggs and bacon also were preparing, with some kind of stew, which did not smell very appetising.

During the affair of the sheep I had not felt very well, and any disagreeable odour brought on a relapse. Didymusa and I happened to be left for a few minutes to ourselves, rather dreading the approaching meal, when— " Oh ! there must be something wrong, decidedly wrong, with that stew ! "

When Mattie opened the door it smelled worse than the dead sheep, and I bolted outside the house, intending to mount and fly, followed by Didymusa, entreating me not to leave her alone. I never knew whether Captain B. overheard our discussion, but there had been another report from his gun, and now he emerged from the rear of his house carrying a dead skunk ; this fully accounted for the stench, which we had unjustly attributed to the stew.

" Hold hard, Miss Jaques," he cried, " you're sure not going to leave us yet. Mees B. will have the squirrel fried directly ; she's a right smart cook ! "

I must have looked sceptical regarding the squirrel, as I

informed him that I had not much appetite just then; but he assured me he was not " shenan-neganning " me, and that the dish would prove a delicacy. He was " mighty sorry I didn't feel good " (always used instead of well), and finally I consented to remain.

After all the meal was not very bad, the squirrel tasting very much like a young rabbit; there also we first tasted Algerita jelly.

Directly after dinner Captain B. perceived signs of a Norther, and as we did not wish to stay all night, it seemed expedient to be making tracks. We had only two or three miles to ride, but the wind " lifted " ominously, driving through the mesquit trees accompanied by a sharp shower of sleet and a sudden fall in the temperature.

On reaching the Lechuza we were glad to draw near the cedar-log fire in the drawing-room where the Boss was seated having a " trade " with a Texan. Such persons were, as a rule, not invited further than the gallery, which allowed freer play for their chewing and spitting operations. Very often the trading took place outside, where the Texans invariably alighted, and assumed a squatting posture on the ground.

When this man took his departure we all gathered round the bright fire, work being suspended for a time on account of the sudden cold, taking care to avoid that part of the room recently occupied by the trader.

Both by man and beast a wet norther is more dreaded than a dry one, and its effects are more serious. A Texan will crouch over his fire, or, if overtaken while camping, he lights a bonfire, sleeping or sitting close beside it until the cold passes off.

It is impossible to maintain circulation even by the most

violent exercise, and as there is no trotting or rising in the saddle, an equestrian would be frozen.

This particular norther came late in the season, but it was over before dark, to be followed by a lovely evening, when the boys, being less tired than usual in consequence of their rest, indulged in boxing and various games.

———○◦⁄◦○———

CHAPTER XIV.

MILKING COWS, BIRDS, AMBULANCE CASES, TWO BENIGHTED TRAVELLERS.

ALTHOUGH the Boss had lived in Texas seven or eight years, he was still an Englishman to the backbone. To have taken out letters of naturalisation as an American citizen would have entailed the loss of his pension from the English Navy. As he not only retained this, but had lately paid a visit to his native land, he was greatly respected as one who had not been forced to leave the old country in consequence of any shady transaction.

This is not quite so obviously the case with all the Englishmen one meets in Texas, though Brother Jonathan never makes any painful allusions, welcoming every Englishman—especially if he happens to have money in his purse.

It was evident that the stains on the nicely-kept floor were an eyesore to the Boss, who would have had it as clean as a ship's deck. In the morning one of the boys was told off to wash the drawing-room floor with water and a broom, Didymusa coming to his aid. It was a regular turn out, all the ornaments being moved and dusted, and the goat and panther skins beaten. From my bedroom I could overhear F. H. and Didymusa arguing the point, he being a little too much inclined to scamp his work in order to get outside again, whereas Didymusa was nothing if not thorough. When he began to beat the mats against the meat-safe she protested forcibly, even though he informed her that the dust would keep the flies away. In the end, I believe she took the broom to him, as I heard a good deal of scampering about, and "You really do hurt, Miss Hartley!" With her handsome face and fine dark eyes she looked quite a little queen, when she managed the house department, and for the most part the boys proved very amenable to her rule. She soon succeeded in curing some of their slovenly habits, to be accounted for by the fact of their having formerly kept a bachelor ranch.

M. was invaluable—clever both inside the house and out; helping to kill the goats, a good milker, a skilful rider and roper, able to handle the "sulky" (plough) and the cultivator in a workmanlike manner, to say nothing of his dexterity in catching and preparing my friend the catfish. He could make capital bread, was really an excellent cook, though not so handy with his needle as F. H.—a very useful accomplishment for the young ranchman. F. H. used to make famous darns on his socks and patch his clothes, which often got sadly torn riding through the thick bush. He re-covered the deck-chairs with fresh sail cloth, repaired sacks, &c., &c.

"Duck and pants" were the usual wear, with the addition of leather leggings for riding through very thick brush. But these are cumbersome appendages, and many good riders dispensed with them, taking their chance of slits and scratches.

Mrs. Boss left the clearing away and washing of the supper things to me and Didymusa; this was always a merry time, and we never lacked willing helpers. In many ranches, with the object of lessening labour, plated knives are used, which merely require washing and do not stain. These are not very suitable for cutting meat, however, as they have a very blunt edge. At the Lechuza we had English steel knives, but it cannot be said that they were not the cause of much additional labour, whereas Didymusa objected to uncleaned knives. Not many days after our arrival she hunted up the knife-board and some earth which served for bathbrick. The hint was taken, with the result that the knives were cleaned once a day in the evening.

The lowing of the Texan cows is not very musical, and they had a habit of returning to their calves in the corral at awkward times and in detachments. Sometimes when we needed the milk badly before supper we saddled up and rounded them in ; at other times they came in bellowing after we had retired for the night, when the Boss would call some of the boys to attend to them. But for the most part they turned up before eight o'clock, and we used to go to the corral for the milking, at which Didymusa was becoming quite expert.

The Texan cow does not stand patiently to be milked like the more gentle shorthorn or Jersey. If her calf is not allowed to suck first, she utterly refuses to have her milk drawn, or may take it into her head to upset both milker and pail. When the calf has sucked for a few minutes, you get it away as gently as circumstances permit with a rope round its neck, and the milker attempts to take the vacant place. The cows vary in disposition ; some are fairly quiet, but young ones cause a lot of trouble, and the calf gives you a lively time, frisking and jumping in its efforts to return to its " mar," as American girls call their mothers. These calves are very strong, and I have been pulled to the ground on battling with one three weeks or a month old, very nearly receiving a kick in the face into the bargain. They are never brought up by hand, or the cows would soon be lost sight of. Not being heavy milkers and having no artificial food or succulent grass, they never yield more than half a gallon each night and morning. Then the calves were allowed to finish, thus getting the richest part of the milk, the "drippings," in which the greater portion of the cream remains, and also relieving the bad milker from the odium of not having "milked out" and "dried off" the cow.

It is very usual, on coming across a newly-calved cow, to drive her up for milking, even if she bears another brand, and neighbours never object, as you are supposed to give the calf sugar-cane or something to eat when it is able, by way of recompense.

Indian corn was now standing between six and seven feet high; the cultivator, with one horse, being used between the drills instead of hand-hoeing.

Birds were very numerous in the trees by the river and about the buildings; flocks of black birds with golden breasts, which were occasionally shot, and made excellent pies. Night and day the air seemed full of song and joyous twitterings. The eaves of the gallery were lined with martens' nests, or more correctly, this bird is the American barn-swallow (*Hirundo horreorum*); the twitterings could be heard all over the house, the doors and windows being always open to admit air and sunshine. And from the distance the red cardinal birds could be heard, their note being rather loud and shrill at times; not equal to that of the mocking bird (*Mimus polyglottos*), who, when his red brother went to roost, would take up his position in a belt of trees to our right, as we sat in the south part of the house during the evenings, and warble throughout the night. I prefer the nightingale, although the mocking bird is a sweet singer. Nor did he have the night all to himself ; the air always thrilled and vibrated with insect life, and at supper, or whenever a light was visible, legions of small creatures would come in and swarm over the table, falling half burnt into the milk jug and cups, and sticking in the butter, molasses, and jams. Mosquito blinds to the windows would have been an immense comfort, and I often wondered that when building so good a house the Boss neglected to add them.

Fireflies darted about, lighting up the thick growth on the river banks at a discreet distance, but moths, mantis (a long-legged insect, of slender form and grotesque appearance), devil's darning-needles, and others, intruded upon our privacy.

I grew rather fond of the katydid, which seldom entered the house, and was very cheerful with his long, shrill chirrup. Although it belongs to the locust family, I never heard of its committing any ravages ; a green insect (*Cyrtophyllus concavus*), and arboreal.

There were numbers of "blue" jays (*Cyanocitta cristala*) ; and the green jay (*Xanthoura luxuora*) is a very handsome bird, large and crested, having also a pretty note. The dear little humming-birds, too, were very fond of the belt of trees where the mocking-bird lived. When the boys found one of their tiny nests they would break off the bough on which it was built, and bring it to us as a souvenir. I have one that is ridiculously small, appearing incapable of holding even the minutest egg. Other birds were the Texan swallow (*Embernagra rufivirgata*) and the chaparral cock, which was always in evidence wherever you travelled, with his head stuck out and his legs moving at a great pace. I believe he is a member of the cuckoo family. Whilst deer-hunting, some of these birds fell to our guns, their brown and white wings making trimmings

for our hats.   They are so plentiful that I felt little com-
punction, though I confess to a pang of regret when the
humming-birds were robbed of their nests.   One thing
that struck me was the absence of large and rare butterflies ;
very remarkable, with such swarms of birds and insects
around us !

One morning a mare was brought up, her colt having
broken one of its hind legs.   Mrs. Boss, who had attended
some ambulance lectures in London, was often very successful in bandaging wounds.   In the case of a Mexican
herder we had almost feared lock-jaw, but the disaster was
averted by her skilful treatment.   Poor fellow ! he was
very grateful when she had dressed his thumb, and retired
with many smiles and bows : " Muchas gracias, adios,
señorita."

Both Didymusa and I, also, wore Ambulance medals,
but we were nothing loth to remain in the background when
there was anyone else to render the necessary aid.

On this occasion Mrs. Boss did not seem disposed to
leave her kneading to turn " vet.," and, as she truly said,
her efforts would probably prove useless, since we
possessed no means to make a sling to keep the animal
quiet.   But the Boss having got some splints ready,
Didymusa and I went to the corral and finally it was
decided that I should be the bone-setter.   The poor little
colt was lying on the ground, held down by four of the
boys, whilst the trainer supported the injured leg.   It was
a simple fracture, and, as he held it, no one would have
supposed it was broken ; but directly the colt was allowed
to struggle, the increased mobility became apparent, and,
in moving the cannon or shank bone, the seat of the
fracture, we could all hear *crepitas.*

The colt, being six weeks old, was big enough to prove

a troublesome patient, but the limb was held very steadily, the splints could not have been better, and Didymusa kept them in position, while I padded and bandaged it to the fetlock. The bandage was so firm that we hoped it might not slip off for some time; but before many days the leg was dangling free, though I believe the bone united after a fashion, or else the lower end withered, as it was still able to limp after its mother.

After the domestic work was finished, we seldom went to bed without a game of whist or chess or " reversi." By placing the table inside the drawing room window and the lamp outside on the gallery, we succeeded in obtaining sufficient light, and yet in baffling the moths, though occasionally they tumbled down the chimney of the lamp and extinguished it.

One evening, having sat up later than usual to finish a rubber, we had just turned in and began to doze, when there was a tremendous commotion amongst the dogs; and we distinctly heard a voice attempting to silence them, together with sounds of a horse's hoofs. This was followed by a consultation amongst the boys, and presently by the Boss's going to learn the cause of the disturbance.

Mr. H., senior, having been to Junction City, and thinking he would return in the cool of the evening by moonlight, had lost his way, it appeared. He threw the reins on Tommy's neck, trusting that the horse would take him safely home; with the result that he found himself at Lechuza, where Tommy had been "raised," Mr. H. having bought the animal from the Boss.

There was not much ceremony; an unexpected guest could generally be supplied with a blanket, and find a place on the floor to lie down. The night being warm, Mr H. elected to sleep on the gallery, which was occupied by the

boys.   He carried his own and other persons' mails, a piece
of beef from the town for Sunday's dinner (he was a great
hand at beef steak puddings), and some delicious little
spring onions grown on irrigated ground near the city.

Very kindly, he gave me a bunch of these, at the same
time reminding me that I had not yet paid my promised
visit with Didymusa, to him and F.   I explained as the
reason, that Didymusa did not think our slight one-horse
conveyance particularly safe ; and indeed, as its narrow seat
possessed neither back nor sides, there was really nothing
to hinder us from falling out in case of a collision with a
tree stump.   The road, too, was a bad one, and I had
never travelled over it before.   Mr. H. suggested that I
should ride over alone, and that if I cared to stay the night
Mrs. M. would put me up, or I could sleep in the corn
crib.

Accordingly I started on this expedition, Didymusa
asking rather wistfully when she might expect to see me
again.   She was always anxious about me, wherever I went,
either alone or with others, and I felt a little guilty afterwards because I told her carelessly, that I should return
some time during the evening, unless I slept in the corn
crib.

I declined to take the shorter and rougher track through
the cedar brake, as I had not yet explored it ; the alternative
route followed the road to Junction City for about eight
miles, when it was necessary to cross the river and ride
through some mesquit, in order to reach the parallel track
to Bear Creek.

All this I accomplished without trouble, but experienced considerable difficulty in finding Mr. H.'s ranch.

As I went to several wrong ones first, I did not reach
my destination very early in the day.   One ranch that I

"struck" in my wanderings was interesting, being nearly, if not quite, the oldest in this part of Texas ; built with a quadrangle, in order that it might be better fortified against attacks of the Comanches. The country was wilder than the Lechuza district, the track leading for several miles over a table land, which skirted an extensive cañon formed by Bear Creek, a tributary of the North Llano, on my left, whilst to the right, beyond, lay a fine stretch of grazing land, bounded by a range with numerous grand bluffs.

I spent a pleasant afternoon rambling along the course of this pretty winding creek with my friends ; sometimes immediately under the bold bluffs which I had seen in the distance. Although I was sorely tempted to stay the night with Mrs. M., and to go on to Roca Springs the next morning, the recollection of Didymusa's anxiety led me to decline, but I consented to remain for an early supper and ride home in the cool of the evening, by the light of the full moon.

There is no twilight in this country, and the darkness sets in even more suddenly than usual when a high range of mountains shuts off the setting sun.

I found this particularly the case on reaching the spot where it became necessary to strike off through the mesquit again, in order to cross the river and gain the other road. The sun was just disappearing, and the moon had not yet risen over the mountains to supply its place. The trail I followed in the morning was narrow and indistinct even by daylight, being, in fact, merely a sheep-walk winding in and out the mesquit. By the dim light of evening I could not distinguish it at all, nor the landmark, consisting of a dead stump and a big stone, which I had observed in the morning on emerging from the brush.

However, an opening presenting itself, and, Maize being inclined to take it, I hoped it was the right one, and rode on without taking much heed, and feeling sure that the horse would follow the shortest cut home.   Suddenly it occurred to me that he was taking anything but a short cut ; we ought to have been through the mesquit and over the river long ago.   This was perplexing, and to retrace my steps would be more so.   It had now become quite dark, fireflies darted through the bushes, the air rang with the noisy chirrup of the katydids ; while the moon was behind me and had not yet risen sufficiently to be of any service.

I came to the conclusion that it was best to trust to Maize, although he was now taking me through some thick chaparral.   Little did I imagine that he had come into the Boss's possession by way of a " trade," and was calmly making for the ranch of his original owner on the other side of the cedar brake, where he had been raised ; serving me, in fact, exactly as Mr. H.'s horse had treated *his* rider.

It was the roughest ride I ever had ; sometimes Maize nearly slipped on his haunches as we went down a draw— a kind of pass by which you can descend a cañon ; or, as we rose again, scrambling with his nose between his knees and his body on the ground.   I began to wonder how long this kind of thing was going to last, when we came across a bunch of horses, probably his own original bunch, since it was his evident intention to " run " them.   There appeared to be no alternative, I had entirely lost my bearings, and could only hope that Maize would round the horses up to the ranch.

This became even more exciting than climbing up and down cañons in the nasty light, and, the moon being still behind me, I had quite enough to do, at the smart pace

Maize was travelling, to dodge the trees and bushes. A good cow-pony always looks out for himself during a "run," taking the shortest angles, and making the sharpest swerves round trees, and you have to dodge right and left, to lean upon his neck, and lift your feet in order to avoid the higher bushes. In spite of the utmost alertness, I managed to get my elbow pierced by one large mesquit thorn, which broke off in the flesh, and, while I protected my face with the hunting crop, there was a constant sound of slits as others rent my skirt. But I did not care much about my old habit, as I had another at the ranch, provided that my boots (which Crichel, of Chichester, had taken so much pains to fit) were preserved in a wearable condition. I was in an agony on account of these, as I had no second pair, and my heart sank when I heard the thorns and bushes dragging against the uppers as we tore through the thickets.

At last we drew near a more open space and Maize began to slacken his pace, but to my dismay the bunch were disappearing without bringing us nearer the Lechuza or any other habitation. As Maize gradually dropped into a walk, I found time to think seriously of my position.

I felt exceedingly hot after the brisk run—so did Maize, who soon stopped entirely, and with his muzzle in the air, blew sharply through his nostrils, emitting a sound between a deep sigh of relief and a snort of triumph at having gained the upper hand and gained his own way.

Then he calmly began to browse !

Beyond a doubt I had lost my way, and, as Maize apparently did not intend to take me home again, I should probably be compelled to stay out all night.

My present posture—leaning over the saddle to facilitate his feeding—was conducive to back-ache, and, seeing a large, tempting-looking rock, I dismounted and sat down upon it. How I appreciated the inevitable Texan rope, now uncoiled, with one end in my hand, giving Maize its length to feed.

The night was warm, the temperature never rising after sundown in this healthy region ; indeed a blanket is often acceptable, as a sharp breeze generally rises about two a.m. The benighted cowboy stakes his pony, makes a pillow of his saddle, and rolls himself in his blanket or slicker. Should the night be chilly, he makes a fire and sings himself to sleep with his favourite song.

> " Then bury me not on the lone prairie.
> With the turkey buzzard and coyoté
> In a narrow grave, six foot by three," &c.

But I did not feel sufficiently at home to stretch myself at full length on the " lone prairie." No music, as far as I know, has ever been written to these words, but I had heard them sung once or twice, and as I tried now to recall the air, I must have dozed. I was startled by a tremendous crash and crackling in an old dead tree a few yards behind me, and some wild animal bounded like a cat to the ground and pounced upon some prey in the bush. The animal must have been a panther ; its victim uttered a piercing shriek, and I became wide awake on the instant. Without losing a minute, I clutched my rope, drew Maize to the stone, and felt better when I was once more in the saddle.

For a few seconds I had been possessed by fear ; every story I had heard of Indians, panthers, wild boars, coyotes, wolves, and rattlesnakes, flashed upon my mind. Feeling angry with myself for leaving the saddle, and still more with Maize as the indirect cause of my fright, I determined that instead of browsing to his heart's content, he should carry me steadily on throughout the night.

The moon was now at its zenith, shedding a flood of silvery light all around me. Remembering the direction in which I had come, and not wishing to explore the difficult paths of the cañon again, I turned the pony's head in the contrary direction, and, perceiving a large belt of trees, rode nearer and discovered that these were cedar. I now felt no doubt that I had arrived at the farther side of the Lechuza brake; and, in any case, decided to risk it and ride through. Once more, with the trees and the dark shadows, the riding became difficult, but after taking a circuituous route to avoid the denser places, I perceived a long streak of light, and to my intense delight, realised that I was out of the wood.

Profiting by my hunting experiences, I climbed a peak not far distant from the cedar brake, and surveyed the surrounding country. My best hopes were confirmed— there lay the Lechuza below, looking beautifully serene with the moonlight shining on its shingle roof. The air feeling rather chilly and damp, I loped along with renewed spirits, away from any track, straight across country. I knew it must be considerably past midnight, and wanted, if possible, to get in and steal a march on my friends. The dogs, who had become very fond of me, helped my plans; instead of rushing out and barking furiously as they did when Mr. H. arrived the previous night, they must have recognised the horse; for they came bounding towards me, whining and fawning, and jumping to lick my hands.

I quickly off-saddled, and having turned Maize into his lot, carried my saddle and bridle to my bedroom, where I always kept them for safety. Didymusa was lying awake speculating as to the comfort of the corn crib in which she believed I was sleeping. My appearance at the breakfast table created great astonishment the following morning,

K

but when the Boss and the rest heard of my adventure, instead of laughing at me, they agreed that I had shown a great deal of pluck and grit. So far my escapade ended very agreeably; it is pleasant to win the good opinion of others and to be on easy terms with yourself.

—◦○◦◦○◦—

CHAPTER XV.

DUTIES OF YOUNG RANCHMEN—RESOURCES OF KIMBLE COUNTY, TEXAS.

THE following night I was slumbering peacefully on the gallery, when I was awakened by a great commotion amongst the swallows. It must have been between two and three o'clock, and the light of the moon, now on the wane, flooded the gallery floor. The birds would not begin their busy day so early, in the natural order of things, and their screaming and sudden flight to and from the nests under the eaves, was quite different from their usual manner of heralding the morn with sweet, liquid, gurgling notes and twitters of love and happiness as they fed their young.

My attention was attracted by something bright, sliding down one of the pillars, to the accompaniment of sounds of slipping and scraping, and the next moment I saw a large snake, four or five feet in length, glide rapidly along the outer ledge of the gallery in a line parallel with that in which I was lying. There were not two yards between us; the moonlight gleamed on its writhing body, and brightened the sheen of its silvery scales; then, to my intense relief, it disappeared over the opposite end of the gallery.

Although this was a far more " creepy " experience than that I had acquired on the " lone prairie " the previous night, pride prevented me from taking up my blankets (it could not be called a bed, since the only mattress was a travelling rug) and joining Didymusa within the room.

It was a perfectly harmless snake, although scarcely less loathsome to me on that account, being one of the fangless variety known amongst the Texans as the mouse or chicken snake, and often encouraged at the ranches to destroy the mice, which are very troublesome. In the present case it was seeking martens' eggs, but the hatching season being over, I hope it was disappointed.

Mrs. Boss's antipathy was as intense as my own, and she told me that though at one time there were a good many about the house, she had hoped and believed they were all killed. I have never seen a specimen of this snake at the Zoological Gardens.

Our party at the ranch had recently received an addition. Two new pupils, Mr. Field and Mr. Steelson, had arrived, one having failed to pass his examination for the army, the other to qualify as a doctor. They were not in the least fitted for a colonist's life, nor did they frame well as incipient ranchmen. The premium for a pupil was five hundred dollars (£100) for the year, out of which the English agent received fifty dollars commission. In the present cases the money was quite thrown away.

The careers of all these young men formed interesting studies. However well lined their pockets had been on leaving home, they generally arrived without a cent, often finding it necessary to draw on the Boss to pay the stage fare from Kerville. They were usually supplied with an elaborate outfit, utterly unsuited to the life on which they were entering, their dressing-gowns and such luxuries being only in the way. Unless they were destined to become the prey of the mice and weevils (which, unless one is extremely vigilant, destroy everything), these superfluous raiments passed into the hands of the Texans; traded away for ponies, cows, or some kind of animals, the English boy, you may be sure, not getting the best of the bargain.

Mr. Field very soon parted with some of his gorgeous apparel in exchange for "hogs."

A few hogmen in this country seemed to monopolise the business in swine, keeping hounds to hunt up these half-domesticated wild boars, who made terrible ravages in the Lechuza garden occasionally, this not being provided with hog fences.

So Mr. Field made a "trade," and, bartering some of his best suits, became the proud possessor of hogs. But from that day until he quitted the country two years later, he never succeeded in recognising his own property. Hogs which run on the range are generally ear-marked, and I may say that the disputed ownership of these animals is the cause of more "six-shooting" than any other kind of pilfering.

The people thereabouts, as an old Scotch surveyor explained to me, "don't understand the difference between meum and towem." About this time a noted hog-stealer had been hunted down, and Mr. C., the under-sheriff, was compelled in self-defence to use his revolver with fatal effect. Cavillings arising out of the similarity of brands often end by a bullet being put through the head of one of the claimants.

Mr. Field's hogs became a household word at the ranch, and if ever we happened to catch sight of any swine during our rides, the other boys began to "chaff" him.

"Look, Field, there go your hogs!"

Off he would ride in the expectation of getting near enough to gain some idea what his recently acquired property was like, but with squeaks and grunts the animals were soon out of sight, leaving him disconsolate and none the wiser for his chase.

Later on in San Francisco I was informed that an Englishman might always be known by his heavy boots and ponderous footsteps ; and new hands are nearly always laughed out of wearing their good English boots, with their "ugly square toes, thick soles, and low heels." Then they try to squeeze their feet into the dandified, lightly made, high heeled boots, such as the genuine cowboy are so proud of.

The Training College in England which prepares young men for a Colonial life is a very necessary and useful institution. For, as a rule, they come out entirely un- prepared for the life in store for them, and the sudden change to hard manual labour and plain fare often proves a severe trial to the stoutest heart, even when there is a sincere desire to overcome difficulties and fight a way strenuously to success. To those who have left home merely to escape reproaches for wasted time and opportunity, the life must be really insufferable ; being brought into contact, as they are, with matter of fact, determined bread winners, and finding "loafing round" a game which scarcely meets with success.

Money is always wasted upon such as these ; gambled away in some town before their arrival at the ranch, or otherwise drawn into the pockets of sharper-witted Brother Jonathan. Probably it will change hands even during the voyage across the Atlantic, and in this case some attempt to gain a livelihood on landing will become absolutely necessary.

Of course, I am now referring to the more pronounced type of ne'er-do-well, but it is to be feared that many such abound in every town in the Union.

But a steady man, who is master of any particular profession or trade, is seldom or never at a loss ; while, in default of this, a brave, stout heart, a good pair of honest working hands, with a modicum of common sense, will generally ensure a good beginning, and command a satisfactory result.

Even with this desirable outfit, it is well for a young man first to gain experience of the country and its resources, and the ways of its people ; to find out whether he is likely to suit them and they him ; whether he has any bent and capacity for stock-raising. When he has learnt his own mind, and gained sufficient experience to judge of an opening, then is the time to help him with money to good advantage.

The duties required of a ranchman are numerous and varied. No knowledge comes amiss. He should be a Jack-of-all trades. That he must be a first-class rider goes without saying ; a good horseman will soon adapt himself to the different saddle, seat, &c. He needs to be a cattleman and agriculturalist combined ; and, although he will not be called upon to follow the plough, the " sulky " being invariably used, a knowledge of all machines and implements of husbandry, and of gardening tools, will be found useful, and, unless he possesses a natural aptitude for handling them, as occasionally seems to be the case, save him from many awkward mistakes.

The ideal ranchman must be butcher, baker, carpenter, wheelwright, blacksmith, plain cook, milker—a formidable list truly ; but it is a fact that each of these trades will have to be practised to some extent sooner or later.

It is desirable, also, that he should know how to render first aid to the injured ; that he should, indeed, have attended the first five-course ambulance lectures in England.

Accidents often happen when one is many miles from surgical help, just as a horse may require shoeing at a long distance from a forge.

Large ranches have their own forges, and make the necessary shoes. To travel thirty miles to the nearest blacksmith's on every occasion would be out of the question.

A man who can do the plainest cooking commands from twenty to thirty dollars a month, with board and lodging. A young ranchman starting with limited capital will not be likely to keep such a one, and should accordingly know how to make and bake bread, in case he runs short, as also the hot biscuit; to prepare his porridge, fry his eggs and bacon, and perhaps to turn out a good plain pudding. When a man is quite single-handed, as often happens to begin with, the pressure on his time prevents the fulfilment of some amongst his multifarious duties. He invariably neglects, at first, either the domestic arrangements or the outside calls upon him. But, by-and-bye, he is able to adapt himself to circumstances and effect a compromise—distributing his labour as far as it will go, doing a little of this and a little of that, and so attaining a happy medium.

The interiors of some bachelor ranches would startle many affectionate relatives in well-appointed English homes. But often enough an untidy, not over clean shanty, with its unwashed crockery and general disorder, is indicative of a thriving cattle-man and agriculturist, too intent upon success, and too active in securing it, to bestow attention upon the minor details of housekeeping and personal comfort.

If two or three young men club together, forming a partnership or a well-agreed little colony, there is division of labour and less weary up-hill work. Of course, it is a mistake to think of farming-out in Texas as in the old country, but a knowledge of husbandry is extremely helpful, though the differences of soil and climate need to be allowed for.

The land having been selected, a portion will have to be stubbed (cleared of mesquit and other trees with their roots), and holes dug for the cedar posts to support the wire fence, which will border the ground set apart for Indian corn, cattle-sugar-cane (sorghum), maize, oats, &c. Then there will be the sowing, harrowing, and "hoeing" or cultivation; and later on reaping and stocking. "Cutting machines" are difficult to hire and reaping must, for the most part, be done by hand. The cows have to be milked, the oxen, goats, or pigs as the case may be, to be killed, and the latter to be cured for bacon or hams; a "smoke-house" being attached to most ranches for this purpose. In addition to all this, the young ranchman will require to hunt up the cattle, break in horses (if he can), to superintend the sheep herding, if he does not actually take part in it, and to camp out during the lambing season.

And even if he should be fortunate enough to employ hands for all these operations, he will be better able to direct them and judge of their capabilities, if he is competent to perform the duties for himself. In such a country, with such a climate, with steadiness and perseverance, the young ranchman has before him a magnificent prospect; and to lend force to my own opinion I quote the following :

" No doubt with the extension of the line from Kerville to Spofford Junction the land will become very valuable, and those who invested early will then congratulate themselves. A great deal is already under fence, and becoming so rapidly settled up that all the smaller squatters are fast disappearing from the scene, and are one by one driven on further West to a country, as they term it, less " used up." Of course, the fencing system is starvation to the impecunious squatter ; occasionally he actually gets enclosed and has to take up his camp and start whether he will or not."

The following description of Kimble country is taken from the last report of the Commissioner of Agriculture. It contains some interesting statistics, showing the progress and development of the country :—

" Kimble County was formed in 1858 from Bexar County. It was named in honour of George Kimble, who fell at the Alamo. It is situated in the South-Western portion of the State and has Menard County for its northern, Mason and Gillespie for its eastern, Edwards and Kerr for its southern, and unorganised county of Sutton for its western boundaries. Llano River runs through the centre of the county, which, with its tributaries, Bear, Copperas, Johnson, James, Saline, and Paint Creeks, furnish an ample supply of water for all purposes. There is sufficient timber for domestic purposes. The county is distinctly a stock-raising county, though the soil, which is a rich loam on the streams and in the valleys, is highly productive, and farming is carried on successfully on a small scale. The general surface is broken, in some places mountainous. The county was organised in 1876 and contains an area of 1302 square miles. The Methodist, Baptist, and other Christian Churches are represented by church organisation. Junction City is the county seat, population 700. Improved lands sell from two to six dollars per acre, unimproved for from one to four dollars. The average taxable value of land in the county is one dollar twenty-three cents per acre.

"It has a total school population of 570, with twelve school houses, and gives employment to eighteen teachers ; average wages paid teachers forty to fifty dollars per month. Kimble County lies between thirtieth and thirty-first degrees of latitude and just east of the 100th meridian. The rainfall is an average of thirty-six and a-half inches per annum ; the altitude about 2310 feet above sea level. The census of 1890 gives a population of 2243 souls, independent, intelligent, quiet, Christian people, contented at home and satisfied that they occupy one of the most favoured sections of this great State.

"As a stock country it is unexcelled, and its valley lands are of the richest description and especially adapted for cultivation. The surface of the country is greatly diversified. The high mountain divides back from the rough breaks, and cañons bordering the water courses are generally flat table lands ; while the valley lands lying along the water courses are smooth, level, well-drained, rich, agricultural lands. All the elements seem to conspire to give us an incomparable climate, unsurpassed on any part of the globe.

"Gentle Gulf breezes temper the sunny days of summer and make a blanket a comfort at night. Sunstroke is a thing unknown ; nor do we have any close, hot, sultry days. The winter months are as pleasant as the summer ; a moderate, steady cold, just right to enable the farmers to save and cure their meat. Snow seldom falls, and is a rarity. We seem to be out of the range of cyclones, hurricanes, and blizzards, as we never have any. Out door avocations can be followed throughout the year. With regard to health, it seems superfluous to say anything under this head, except for the benefit of strangers. There being no swamps nor stagnant waters, with the whole

surface of the country well drained, with an elevation of
2100 feet above the sea level, we are high above the
malarial districts, an altitude that yellow fever and cholera
cannot climb. We might justly claim that we are exempt
from most of the ills that affect the rest of mankind. Our
dry and bracing atmosphere, in connection with our mild
and pleasant climate, presents a natural sanitorium to all
sufferers from weak lungs, bronchial troubles, or consumption in its first stages, their maladies passing off so quietly
and surely without physic, that, before they are aware of the
fact, they are surprised to find themselves sound and well.

" This high, dry atmosphere creates an appetite to eat
and sleep, which are Nature's great renovators of the
broken down human system. By breathing this bracing
atmosphere, drinking these pure sparkling waters, away
from all malarial tendencies, a person will greatly add to
his natural life.

" Bountifully supplied with a great abundance of pure,
running water, there being about twenty-five large flowing
creeks, Kimble is probably the best watered county in
Western Texas. The streams are all bordered with heavy
growths of pecan, oaks, elm, blackberry, live oak and
mesquit. In the Eastern part of the county, large bodies
of post oak and black jack. On the mountains, scattered
in different parts of the country are large bodies of fine
cedar, suitable for pickets, posts, rails and telegraph poles.
The Llano valley seems to be the natural home of the
pecan, the tree growing to enormous proportions, some of
them measuring six to seven feet in diameter at the butt,
and attaining a height of eighty to ninety feet, and often
throwing out limbs fifty to sixty feet long. The majestic
trees border every stream in the county, and are a source of
considerable revenue.

" Taking one year with another, the yearly sales of this nut amount to about 50,000 pounds, the price received ranging from five to nine cents per pound.

" This is an exceedingly profitable crop from the fact that it requires no labour but to gather and market it.

" Many distinct and different characters of soil are found, embracing black land, red and black sandy, alluvial, mulatto, and chocolate ; all very productive of crops best suited to its character. Corn and cotton crops on the black bottom lands ; wheat, oats, and all small grains do better on the mulatto or chocolate, as they grow too rank, get top-heavy, and fall before ripe, on the rich black bottom lands ; vegetables, root, and all vine crops, do their best on sandy soils, although they produce remarkably well on all the different soils of the country.

" Stock-raising has been the chief avocation of our people, and no section is superior to this.

" Horses, mules, cattle, sheep, goats, and hogs, all do equally well. Feeding range stock is never resorted to. Hogs run loose and fatten on the mast, of which there is a great abundance and variety. Kimble County offers, to those seeking homes, great inducements. Good rich land, wood and water all combined on the same tract, can be bought for from two to five dollars per acre, and they will soon command a much higher price.

" For the capitalist the field is broad and open, offering unequalled and safe investments in needed enterprises that always return a profitable dividend. Cotton, corn, wheat, oats, rye, barley, potatoes, pumpkins, melons, millet, and sorghum are all grown with satisfactory results, averaging with the favourable sections of the State. All kinds of garden produce do well and yield abundantly. It is however, in the raising of small grain that this county excels, wheat especially doing remarkably well. Tobacco has been grown experimentally with success, but no attempt has been made to cultivate it as a field crop.   Stock-farming, as it is usually called, is the ideal of the farmers profession. It is also the most profitable, since it affords a happy combination of what has hitherto been considered two distinct avocations in Texas, to the mutual advantage of both It is conceded by all acquainted with the country that the hill lands are without a peer for pasturages.   Horses are hardier and better developed if raised in such a pasture, they have better wind, better feet, greater strength of limb and endurance.   It is a well-known fact that sheep do not thrive well on low flat lands, and anyone who has watched the habits of cattle will bear testimony to the fact that they exhibit the same predilection in this matter as do the sheep. It will be readily seen that when one can combine the advantages of such pasture lands with the fading facilities of a farm, it presents an opportunity for the production of stock in the highest stages of development and perfection.

"Kimble County has two towns, Junction City and London.   Junction City is the county seat, and is situated on the confluence of North and South Llanos.   It is beautifully located and is almost the exact geographic centre of the country.   It does a large trade with the stockmen and farmers of an enormous territory.   London is situated in the north-east part of the county, nineteen miles distant from Junction City.   It is most favourably located in the post oak belt, surrounded by a very rich agricultural country.   It has a mill and gin, which put up over two hundred bales of cotton in 1891.   It has a population of three hundred people.   In addition to these there is the nucleus of a town at Noxville, with post office and store.   Noxville is surrounded by numerous irrigated farms and gardens, and has a bright future."

CHAPTER XVI.

PICNIC, TEXAN DANCE, FIRST VISIT TO THE "FIELD."

————

DURING the last days of May, Mrs. Boss planned a long day's outing to gather Algerita berries ; we were to picnic for dinner and return in the evening, the Boss "running the sheebang" (keeping house), so that the whole party might go.

There were quantities of Algerita bushes, with extremely prickly leaves, and little red berries about the size of a currant. They seemed to be a species of barberry—of an acid flavour, and making a very nice preserve.

We mustered twelve or fourteen saddle horses, whilst the waggon, with a two horse team, driven by the boys in turn, carried Mrs Boss, Didymusa, the provisions, and a large empty barrel, which danced about from one end of the vehicle to the other, to receive the berries.

We were to go steadily, out of consideration for the new pupil. He said that he had not ridden much at any time, and it was almost his first experience in a Texan saddle ; a fact easy to believe when one saw the daylight between it and himself.

The boys soon began to indulge in "running" and other pranks, with the consequence that Spider, an excellent cow pony, and therefore a bad swerver, who carried poor Mr. Field, soon left his rider helpless on the ground, There he lay for some minutes insensible, having, no doubt, been badly stunned, as his head lay near a large rock. After a plentiful application of cold water he returned to consciousness, however, though he complained of a bruise over his temple.

This was a sad beginning of our day's jaunt; the boys put him in the waggon, but he became unconscious several times during the day, and anxiety on his account damped our ardour. The bushes being excessively sharp, it was impossible to gather the Algerita berries quickly in any quantity, so we tied pieces of sail-cloth and slickers round the bushes, which were then belaboured with heavy sticks until the fruit tumbled off, bringing with it numerous bits of leaves and wood. The sail-cloth was next spread out on the ground, and with large fans we winnowed the chaff from the grain.

The berries are full of seeds, and rough in flavour like the barberry, but they make an excellent jelly somewhat similar to red currant. We came across some prickly pears of the cactaceous genus (*Opuntia tuna*), the first ripe ones I had seen. Mr. A. H. having prepared some of them with his penknife, I put two in my habit pocket.

Our party scattered in all directions in groups of two or three, and on returning to camp, I put my hand in my pocket, intending to offer the fruit to Didymusa, but the sateen lining was full of the sharpest little thorns imaginable, and I took care never to repeat the process; these thorns being so fine that it is impossible to extract them from the skin, whilst yet extremely irritating.

The Texans caution one not to eat many prickly pears, having an idea that they are conducive to what they call " cholera morbus." Before dinner most of the boys indulged in a bath in the creek, where one of them found, as he thought, a great prize—a turtle, which was subsequently conveyed to the ranch with the pleasant prospect of soup and cutlets. It proved a most unamiable animal, snapping at everything within reach, right and left, and, worse than this, to the general disappointment, the Boss declared it to be inedible—an alligator turtle or snapper, (*Machochelys lacertina*). It was not a large specimen, weighing in fact under 20lb., but there was something very uninviting about the appearance of its scaly head.

We saw plenty of rabbits (called by the Texans cotton-tails), but these are never eaten, as they have the reputation of being full of worms. The dogs put up a "Jack rabbit," and created a little excitement by chasing it for a consider-able distance. But the rabbit was one too many for them; a great deal too swift to be caught by one of these Texan mongrels—a good kind of dog in his way, faithful, affectionate, an excellent guard; originally bred from collies, but crossed in some instances, I am told, with the lobo (wolf), or even the coyote, which makes him savage.

I never saw one swift enough to catch a "Jack rabbit," which is a species of the large American hare, with very big ears and long legs (the Texan *Lepus callotis*). They have black marks on the tail and eartips, and, their flesh not being sufficiently esteemed to be hunted as game, run perfectly wild in immense numbers.

Well-bred English dogs cannot stand the heat, and some which were imported soon fell victims to the rattle-snake.

F. H. was an authority on snakes; it was he who taught Didymusa to draw the fangs before skinning the odious creatures, the fangs being poisonous after death. He would let the harmless snakes wind themselves about his body at their own sweet will. On one occasion, having caught and stunned a rattlesnake, supposing it to be dead, he slung it across his saddle.   He had not ridden far before it revived and fastened its fangs in the upper of one of his boots, but though they penetrated the leather, fortunately, they did not touch his foot.

Most cowboys carry a small piece of the rattlesnake root in their pocket, and one of them presented me with some, which still lies amongst my other little souvenirs of the country.   It is a species of the *Prenanthes*, and scraped and swallowed after a bite is considered an antidote, otherwise it is a virulent poison.   I was fortunate enough not to require to test its efficacy.

A rattlesnake brought about my first experience of a " pitch."   I was returning from Junction City after dark, taking a short cut through some undergrowth, when Maize placed his foot on a snake.   I heard its rattle immediately, and the horse got a sudden " scare."   The bite I believe is not fatal to horses, although an indelible scar is sometimes left by the fangs.

The day after the picnic we were all busy getting the berries boiled down; the result being ten gallons of preserve.

Mr. Field did not entirely recover from the effects of his fall for two or three days, and then the boys organised a " coon hunt " for his edification.   Between nine and ten o'clock in the evening when M. generally started to the river to look at his night lines, they all sallied forth.

The sport began by placing Mr. Field close to a hole in the steep bank, holding a sack with its mouth open while they ostensibly went in search of the raccoon (the *Procyon lotor*, somewhat resembling a large rat) which was to be driven up to the burrow, when he was to intercept the animal, and catch it in his sack.   The boys appeared to be hunting industriously for their quarry, beating and shouting as they proceeded, but gradually going farther and farther from the river side and making a detour by way of the small pasture to the ranch, when they turned in, leaving Mr. Field patiently watching by the hole for the appearance of the raccoon.

About three o'clock we heard them hilariously finishing the " hunt," driving the long-looked-for and still imaginary raccoon before them and showering upbraidings upon the defenceless head of the victim of the hoax, who, they declared, had fallen asleep, and thus allowed the quarry to gain its hole, instead of being cut off, and captured in the sack.

One night Mr. Steel was taken out to shoot deer, to a cedar brake named Up-Indian, some miles from the ranch and quite away from all tracks. Having carefully staked his horse, he was sent up a tree ; and there the boys found him the next morning, Winchester rifle in hand, stoutly declaring that no deer had passed near ; he was quite sure that he had not fallen asleep, his position (as his companions had taken care) being scarcely comfortable enough to induce slumber, or at least he had only dropped off for a few minutes now and then—but of course it was those few minutes, the boys told him, which had proved fatal and lost him the deer.

About this time Charlie H. very kindly gave a dance in our honour. His ranch was within a few miles of the Lechuza, and, except the Boss, we all went in the best waggon ; the old waggon was used for breaking in colts, because it got accustomed to being smashed up. It was a glorious night ; a fortunate circumstance, the company being numerous, a good deal larger, in fact, than the shanty, which could not accommodate half the guests.

The various waggons and buggies, with their teams and several hacks, were tied outside, where we also sat on all kinds of improvised seats, chatting agreeably until we were called to dance. One room had been entirely cleared of furniture, but its dimensions were small, and some of the boys remained patiently outside until the small hours before their numbers came round, and some went away disconsolate, having waited in vain. The other room was a kind of crêche, crowded with the displaced furniture, which included a bedstead, this and every available space being covered with sprawling babies, some slumbering peacefully in the prettiest infantile abandon, some crowing, laughing, rolling over and over, and playing with each other, others fretful and tearful at the sight of so many unfamiliar faces.

Charlie H. had married a girl of thirteen, who, although only nineteen at this time, looked more like an English-woman of forty. They had three children ; one sweet little fair-haired girl of three soon recognised me, and held out her plump little hands to be taken, possibly with visions of candy.

To these country dances, families from surrounding ranches will travel long distances, if the host and hostess are popular. The young mothers love a dance, and, having no nursemaids, are compelled either to bring their babies or stay at home themselves; a room being nearly always provided for the little ones' reception. If such a room is not set apart, they are left in the waggons.

On one occasion the Boss heard frantic cries, and going to see whence they came, found that a baby had fallen half through a hole in the broken floor of a waggon, where it hung suspended head downwards. For a long time I declined to believe the story, until subsequent observation convinced me that such an occurrence was quite probable.

We had a stand-up supper arranged on a little table in the narrow cooking-room, it consisted of black coffee without sugar, hot biscuits, and all kinds of cakes. On the centre of the table stood an erection which was intended to represent a cake, but composed of clay or stone, frosted with white of egg, and looking like a bride-cake. Being deceived by its realistic appearance, Didymusa asked for a piece—to the amusement of the company, who quite understood that it was only intended as an ornament. We saw several similar table decorations at one time and another later on.

Though we had come provided with wraps, these, not being needed, were left with our hats in the babies' room. When the time came to depart we went to recover our properties, but the lamp had gone out, and the rays of early dawn being as yet too feeble to enable us to distinguish one object from another, we groped about amongst babies' heads and hands and toes, till at last Didymusa lighted upon what she thought was my blue llama shawl.

" Oh, you have got my baby ! " a young mother exclaimed, and the slight mistake being rectified our hostess brought a lamp, and with the usual compliments and *adieux* and " come agains," we set forth, having thoroughly enjoyed the party.

If there had been the remotest chance of the daily routine of ranch-life becoming wearisome, the monotony would have been entirely relieved during these few weeks by my efforts to make the most of my remaining time, and to become acquainted with the country and people.

Didymusa had been informed at the dance that I was

" a lively box " and " peart " (pronounced peert), also that I had " caught on mighty quick." I had certainly tried to do my best, and now began to feel considerable regret at the prospect of leaving this sunny land and all my friends. For, a few weeks earlier, I had arranged to depart from the Lechuza about the middle of June, my intention being to set forth to the ranch at Calgary, in the North-West territory, taking San Francisco *en route.* It may be remembered that on applying to the agent in England in the first place, I was offered a choice between two ranches : one being the Lechuza, the other situated at Calgary, to which I now thought of removing.

However, the hand of Fate again interposed. The day after the dance, Didymusa and I drove the light buggy into Junction City, in order to try to procure some lighter and simpler loose-fitting gowns, as we found those we had brought from England, with their heavy drapery according to the prevailing fashion, too heavy and quite unsuited to our present mode of life. Full blouses, which can be easily washed, are the best for bodices, with perfectly plain skirts.

At the store Mr. J. R. asked us to carry back a basket of delicious mulberries (Russian, and on the average an inch long, and large in proportion) as a present to Mrs. Boss. In answer to my inquiries, he said they grew at " The Field," just beyond the town, and, as it was only a few minutes walk, he offered to take me to see the trees.

The farm had been thoroughly stubbed, and ten acres planted with fruit trees—peaches, plums, a few apples and pears, besides a hundred or more of these Russian mulberries, which had been put in about three years ago.

The greater portion of the orchard and garden ground was irrigated by means of ditches, the water being conveyed from a dam constructed a few miles higher up the South Llano River. The estate formed one block, including six lots as shown in the plans of the town, and the streets were cut in straight lines from the squares intersected. Two sides of this property faced the street ; one the main, the other a continuation of the road up to South Llano, the remaining two sides adjoining some other town property.

There was a dear little one-roomed cottage, with a tiny gallery and trellis work porch running round it, covered with creepers and surrounded by ornamental shrubs. The place was for sale ; I was " stuck " on it, and determined to become its owner.

No sooner said than done. Instead of returning immediately to the ranch, I went to the snug little office and wrote home several business letters in order to have the necessary sum at my disposal that the title deeds might be signed and transferred on my return from California. I intended to " run " " The Field " myself for a year or so, to build a shanty, and thus become landowner householder in America at óne and the same time.

Mr. J. R. undertook to write to Mr. Schmelter, the owner of the property, brother-in-law of my kind German friend, the merchant prince and principal store-keeper of Junction City. Mr. Schmelter had been very prosperous as a cattleman, &c., in Kimble Co. and its neighbourhood, and, desiring a wider scope, opened extensive stores at San and Antonio, where he was equally successful.

This delay made us rather late in leaving the town, and the shadows of night began to fall upon us before the first creek was reached. As we walked up the last hill, what with the late hours of the previous night's dance, and the excitement of the day, I felt rather drowsy, but there was little chance of composing one's self to slumber with Didymusa as a companion !

She quite failed to appreciate the charms of this lonely drive, with only the fireflies to brighten the dark chaparral thickets. Numerous stars studded the lofty sky, the milky way appearing very clearly defined, whilst the cry of the katydid was incessant. But it was all wasted on Didymusa, and, as she hinted, on me also. Between her efforts to watch lest my eyelids should droop, and her sharp look out for tree-stumps ahead (I confess we made one or two rather close shaves), her anticipation of objects at which Button might conceivably shy, and the frequent application of her elbow to keep me on the *qui vive*, she certainly found ample employment. It seemed so ludicrous that my drowsiness was soon overcome, and I could not resist the temptation to " play possum," that is, to sham.

It had been later than we imagined on leaving the city, or else we failed to make time on the road, which was really too dark for fast driving, and by the time we reached the Lechuza all the good folks were sound asleep. But we unharnessed and attended to Button ourselves, finally entering the bedroom as the drawing room clock struck midnight. Mr. J. R. had thoughtfully put some crackers in our small conveyance, with a bottle of gingerade upon a lump of ice, all of which we thoroughly appreciated before we retired to rest.

CHAPTER XVII.

SITE AND PLANS FOR OUR NEW HOUSE—BUYING A WAGGON AND TEAM.

THERE was so much to do and arrange in consequence of this new turn of events that it appeared doubtful whether we should be in a position to fulfil our engagements for starting to San Francisco. I abandoned the idea of going to Calgary, and arranged to have telegrams forwarded from San Antonio. "The Field" was already needing attention, delicious ripe peaches lying on the ground, and some acres of oats being ready for cutting.

I had been advised to secure the services of a young German whom Mr. Schmelter had employed to plant the trees, and who also understood irrigation and pruning as practised in this country. In the morning, therefore, I saddled up and went in search of this young man, Anthony M—— (afterwards called Tony), and having come to terms, arranged that he should occupy the cottage with his mother.

Although I undertook to make a small addition to accommodate their cooking-stove, &c., he was to enter upon possession in a few days. Then there was our own house, with its site, to be considered, the Boss, who had been the architect of his own, very kindly drawing out numerous plans. Having eventually decided upon one of these, I took counsel with the builder and the mason, for it was to be a superior kind of shanty, with a stone foundation, a chimney in the centre, with a good hearth for the drawing-room, and two fire-places arranged diagonally all in one block for the bedrooms.

I looked forward to the winter and the possibility of a severe norther with considerable apprehension, and intended that the dining-room, &c., should be well heated by stoves. The large block of masonry which formed the chimneys was well executed by Mr. Archer, an Englishman, a relative of the late famous jockey, the stones being drawn from the bed of the river. I also directed that the floor should be boarded over the stone foundation, and that there should be no open space under the galleries, such generally becoming a receptacle for fowls, dogs, and all kinds of rubbish.

The Boss planned my " lot " also, with a stable—a kind of open stall building, a coach-house, harness room, and a rat-proof granary (lined with tin), and over the whole a capital loft for sugar cane and millet.

Having received estimates for the building, I selected that of Mr. Lightfoot, who forthwith ordered the lumber, expecting that all would be ready for occupation about two months hence.

Although houses are run up so quickly, in this climate there is no fear of damp from new bricks and mortar. But the solid stonework of this house consumed more than the usual time. Most of the lumber comes from the neigh-bourhood of Trinity River, and from the extensive pine forests of Eastern Texas, but these woods are supposed to furnish timber of inferior quality.

It was estimated in 1880 that of long leaf pine alone the Eastern Texan forests had twenty billion feet standing, and that there were other pinewoods besides, making the timbered area of Texas twice as large as that of Alabama and the Mississippi combined. Hard wood also abounds in many parts of the state; the latest accounts of its "timbered acreage stood thus: 46,302,000 acres; and the timber standing, of all kinds, 67,508,500,000 feet."

All the cedar required for my "lot," posts, stables, &c., was drawn from the Lechuza brake. In the evening the Boss gave me quite a lecture on irrigation, but although he also lent me several valuable books; I fear I did not sufficiently master the subject to profit by his advice.

I made another journey to Junction City, where I hired a cutting machine at a dollar the acre; and with this, and a loan of horses supplied by Mr. H., we begun to reap the oats. Instead of partaking of the hotel delicacies on this occasion, we bought some provisions and crackers and enjoyed an al-fresco repast with some of "The Field" peaches, in the pretty porch of our new home. The cutting machine proved to be an antiquated arrangement, and did its work in a very untidy fashion.

The Boss advised me to purchase mules for the farm work; but good mules fetch a higher price than horses in Texas, and apart from the question of cost, I wished to combine business with pleasure. The small acreage under cultivation would not employ a team more than six months out of the year, and for the rest I intended to drive it myself; so that mules were out of the question, as, though I had never driven any, I had heard a good deal that was scarcely in their favour. Their hardiness and endurance are undoubted, being surpassed, indeed, only by their stubbornness. On arduous journeys they will exist longer than horses, and forage better for themselves; but when really overdone, a mule will not move another inch, he will lie down rather and be killed. As an old Texan told me, a mule can "rustle"—this word meaning, in the Lone

Star State, to stir about energetically ; but I believe that
in Nebraska and other places it implies stealing, and a
hapless person got into pretty hot water by the innocent
but erroneous use of the word during his travels.

Later in the day, the team which I had hired for the
cutting machine was offered for sale, but it had been
worked almost to death on the stage, and showed more bone
than flesh, with not a few galls when the harness was
removed.

Many of the stage horses were covered with galls at
times, and I often thought what a field there was here and
elsewhere for the Society for the Prevention of Cruelty to
Animals. Neither Didymusa nor I ever lost an opportunity of trying to arouse sympathy for the dumb creatures
we loved so well, but our efforts were generally in vain,
though I flattered myself bye-and-bye, that the fine
condition of my team, the marked improvement in their
general appearance, to say nothing of their gentleness and
increased intelligence, was not entirely without influence.

Whilst declining to become the owner of the cutting-
machine, I made an offer for Button, for whom I had taken
a liking—an excellent saddle horse, as well as all one could
desire in harness. His price was seventy dollars, but in
England he would certainly have been worth forty pounds
or more.

Mr. H. possessed a young horse of the same height
(fifteen and a quarter hands) and rather a brighter
bay. He had been in harness and saddle only a few times,
was full of courage, fast, a pacer, and of a very kind
disposition, provided you were gentle with him ; "but,"
Mr. H. added, " sakes alive, just upset him and he can
pitch ! " We went to the feed yard to inspect the said
" Dandy," who, when loose, was not amenable to anybody

but his owner, who had intended him for his own use in saddle. But, as usual, the almighty dollar proved a temptation, even to a merchant prince. The figure was 120 dollars—a big sum for a horse at Junction City.

At first Dandy could not be seen, so we made a tour of the yard, and presently his head appeared from the corner where the big "stage," which was used only on special occasions, stood. Such a bonny crest and eyes! Mr. H. called him, but quite unavailingly, for Dandy put back his ears, and, with a merry twinkle in his eyes, bounded off in an opposite direction, and seizing a pony by the tail, bossed him round and round the yard. Dandy was exactly what I wanted, and I suppose Didymusa perceived the admiration and pleasure in my face.

"Oh, Mr. H.," she cried, "don't persuade Miss Jaques to buy that horse. I shall never sit behind him. Look at him, he is like the very devil himself."

I often asked Didymusa where she gained her experience of his Satanic majesty. Mr. H. assured her that Dandy was "a very nice horse when you are used to him," and I felt convinced that he would prove interesting. He showed great nerve power by the way he carried his tail, though this was not quite so full as with most of these horses, having, probably, been slightly docked and pulled to give him a stylish appearance.

Dandy's poverty of tail, as compared with other horses in Texas, became a standing joke against me, and the boys used to offer additional switches from their own ponies' appendages to tie on—of course, demanding fabulous prices for the concession! However, Dandy's tail improved in course of time, if it never rivalled the sweeping proportions of some.

After a considerable amount of "trading," Dandy was

transferred to me, together with Button, for 160 dollars the pair.

Mr. H. was agent for the Studebaker waggons, one of which I bought for sixty-eight dollars, also a set of double harness for eighteen dollars and a half, a sack for ten cents, and two bushels of corn for a little less than three dollars. This being put inside the waggon, Didymusa and I climbed to our perches, and presently, in all the glory of new red and green paint, with everything spick and span, and the harness glittering, drove back to the Lechuza.

And we did spin along! Dandy was a trifle too fast and eager for Button, and when descending the abrupt pitches, left all the holding back from the pole to his yoke fellow, but on the whole they were a good pair, Button, with his year of seniority serving to steady the more volatile Dandy.

These waggons being fitted with "grasshopper" brakes, which constantly get out of order, it is desirable to have a more serviceable one made and adjusted by the blacksmith —this costs five dollars. The poles of all waggons, backboards, and buggies, are not fixed like those of our waggonettes, &c. When not in use, they rest on the ground, and at other times swing free between the horses, the weight depending from their collars. This is supposed to be an advantage when travelling over very uneven or broken ground, such as we frequently met with. Sometimes one horse will be on a level two feet higher than the other, when the roads are full of ruts or small watercourses, or, on entering a creek, and a pole fixed in the ordinary English manner would be utterly impracticable.

The following morning I tried Dandy in the saddle, the Boss and Mr. Taylor holding well on to his head whilst

Didymusa lifted me into the saddle as usual with the greatest precision and nicety. We had a good deal of wild careering, but I kept his head up and there was no pitching. As he gradually ceased to gallop, I gained my first experience of pacing. It reminded me of a horse going dead lame, but in time I grew to like it, and in such a hot climate it is the pace *par excellence* for a lady, or indeed for any hack-work. It may well increase the price of a horse, as it always does. As my new steed sobered down and gave me an opportunity to think, he reminded me of Sir Walter Scott's description of the "Ambling Palfrey." Dandy's pace was inherited ; he was supposed to be nearly pure Spanish or Barb breed, although I suspect that his pitching accomplishments betrayed a strain of mustang blood. He had several "gaits," and for a long time I could not distinguish one from another. I liked the "fox-trot" least ; trotting with his fore, and indulging in a rapid shuffling walk with his hind legs. As Dandy in harness had a high rolling trot up to 14 or 15 miles an hour, his knee action was too high to be quite pleasant in a "fox-trot."

Mr. Stillman, in "The Horse in Motion," accurately describes this "gait" under the name of "single foot."

"An irregular pace, rather rare, distinguished by the posterior extremities moving in the order of a fast walk, and the anterior extremities in that of a slow trot ;" again, Mr. W. S. Clarke describes "single foot as an irregular gait which many very fleet horses when overdriven adopt, a disagreeable gait which seems to be a cross between a pace and a trot, in which the two legs of one side are raised almost, but not quite simultaneously."

When the legs are perfectly simultaneous this becomes

"pacing," and of Dandy's three "gaits" it was the one I preferred. I have seen Mrs. V. in the Row riding a handsome skewbald, a remarkably fast and good pacer. This was before I went to America, and on asking for information, heard it described as "racking." By this name I believe it is known in Syria where the friend of whom I inquired had met with it. It is eminently essential in a hot country since you have merely to sit still and enjoy the breeze as your horse ambles along; for cold winter days a brisk trot is preferable.

Artificial pacing, as I have been informed, is taught by logging, and also by removing some of the shoes, and riding the horse lame. Doubtless it is a form of lameness in the first instance.

I set forth before 6 o'clock the next morning to see about stacking my oats, making good time on Dandy. Mr. H., who was already at "The Field," thought that they were quite fit to cart; he was deceived, however, for later on, finding they were heating, Tony was compelled to open them again. There being no threshing machine at hand, we used them just as they were; the straw and chaff with the grain was thought better for the horses, but for corn, maize is usually given.

Mr. H. had heard from his brother-in-law, Mr. Schmelter, who had arranged to meet me on my return from California, when he would be prepared with the transfer deeds, and I on my part with the purchase money. The price named was about twenty-five dollars an acre, with no valuation, and I was to take immediate possession, and the standing crops.

We entered into a long consultation before finally deciding upon the site for the house: its aspect and position towards the street, and in case the property should ever be divided. The lot with the stable, granary, &c., was to be built near the cottage.

Tony introduced his mother, who had left the banks of the Rhine while still a girl in her teens, when her parents made a long voyage of three months, as colonists, leaving their Fatherland and "Groszmütter." By which name she, also, became familiarly known, for we grew much attached to her.

Nearly fifty years ago she had seen troublous times on her parents' settlement, with the "Injuns" as she named them. She was a first-rate milker, clever with the cattle and poultry, besides being quite an herbalist: concocting innumerable nauseous draughts, remedies for all ailments under the sun, and with which she was only too delighted to dose us on the slightest excuse.

As in the case of the "prepared" chewing gum, we were driven to many small subterfuges to avoid these unpleasant panaceas.

————oo⊱⊰oo————

M

CHAPTER XVIII.

BY "SUNSET" ROUTE FROM SAN ANTONIO TO SAN FRANCISCO.

ALL was at last in train for departing from the ranch, except the re-packing of our trunks, most of which were to be warehoused at the store in Junction City. Our kind friends in England had advised us what to take and what to leave behind, one lady, who had great experience of travelling in Europe, urging me strongly to take a few boxes of night-lights. But she had not considered the heat of the climate, and when we subsequently dived into a box containing reserved linen and other articles, we found the whole contents in a peculiar condition, the effect upon one's olfactory nerves being decidedly disagreeable.

It recalled one memorable afternoon I spent, a child of five, with a large family of other little ones, when a wax doll was roasted before the dining-room fire. I don't know which made me laugh more, the recollection of the long-past scene with the entrance of the head nurse, or Didymusa's face when she handed me the empty boxes which had contained the night-lights, now all melted.

Before our departure, we were to take part in a dance which was given at the Lechuza, and which proved to be much like the other dances we had seen, except that the company was more numerous, every ranch, little or big, within a considerable distance, sending representatives. A few had come so far that they were compelled to stay all night, one gentleman, dressed *de rigueur*, looking very conspicuous in his swallow-tail coat—even more so at breakfast the next morning, with a portion of the previous night's coffee spilled over his elaborately frilled, cambric shirt-front. The cakes were stupendous! " Cookies " of every description, chocolate and coffee, cakes, lemon snaps, apple turnovers, open tartlets, with Algerita and wild-grape jelly. The coffee was made outside in two large cauldrons, holding about five gallons each. There the supper, also, was laid on a large trestle-table forty feet in length. It was fortunate that the night was fine, the moon shining brilliantly, we having looked forward with some dismay on account of yesterday's rain, which had fallen in " buckets-full," as it can fall only in a semi-tropical climate. But by this evening all the mud was baked hard again.

Although a babies' room had been provided, no babies arrived, owing to the fact that some wag had placed a notice on the door of the small school-house by the creek, to the effect that " babies were not wanted at the forth-coming dance." In default, however, the room was extensively patronised for " dipping sticks," powdering and hairdressing, the young ladies laying on the powder in perfect " chunks," and retiring several times to arrange their hair in different styles.

In the Far West, convention dispenses with chaperons, and it is quite the correct thing for a gentleman to bring a lady with him in his buggy. If he is not the happy possessor of such a vehicle, and his means permit, he hires for the occasion ; otherwise he escorts the lady on horse-back.

A United States lawyer once expressed his astonish-ment very openly at our English customs regarding chaperons.

" Why," he asked, " do you send inferior, or what you call common men, such as coachmen or footmen, to take charge of ladies in preference to gentlemen ? " He seemed to think our system a reflection upon the gentlemen in particular and our nation in general.

I confess I found not a little difficulty in answering him. Doubtless the moral tone of the United States is in this regard extremely lofty, and woe betide the man who departs from this code of honour ! He is quickly confronted with a six-shooter or tried according to the methods of Judge Lynch, the slightest disparagement of wife or sister, by word of mouth or otherwise, being speedily and effectually avenged.

A marked instance came under our notice at a neighbouring ranch. The owners being absent, some of the hands were entertaining a few cowboy friends, and cards and " red-eye " whiskey were the order of the day. An Englishman happened to make some light and inconsiderate remarks concerning the sisters of one of the boys, whereat the Texan immediately turned upon him, and battered his head with the butt end of a Winchester. He became unconscious, and the others went to seek assistance ; but, during their absence, the Texan returned and inflicted a terrible gash with his knife across the prostrate Englishman's throat. On their return, his companions found him lying in a pool of blood, and for several weeks he hung between life and death. Although he eventually recovered, he will carry the marks of that night's adventure to his grave.

The perpetrator of the deed, who, although " raised " in Texas, was, as his mother termed it, " full-blooded Irish," escaped over the Mexican border, but before I left Texas he reappeared on the scene. By that time the excitement had cooled down, the witnesses would have been difficult to collect, and no steps were taken to prosecute or arrest him. The theft of a horse would have been considered far more serious ! The people are quiet and gentle in the ordinary way, but if the old frontier spirit be roused, their bold, lawless character crops out, and so it will for many years to come, in spite of all the effects of modern civilization.

My friend the lawyer, without exactly advocating lynching or, in our own case, a return to the duel, seemed to insinuate that the "good old days" possessed certain advantages over the present ; with their alternative appeals to the Law and Divorce Courts, and the lamentable and inevitable perjury.

On the 16th June our "tricks" were packed and placed in the waggon, and all the little party at the ranch assembled to witness our departure. C. H., who was out horse hunting, had charged one of the others to "tell" us good-bye—the Texans never "say" goodbye. Dandy and Button had wandered off to some remote corner of the big pasture, and our start was delayed while they were hunted up, but, making good time when once we got away, Junction City was reached just as the supper bells began to ring—at least the City Hotel could boast only of one bell, but Mrs. Naudin was in the habit of announcing that "the best luxuries the city afforded" were ready for consumption, by vigorously beating a tray with a large iron spoon.

We intended to pass the night here, to be in readiness for the six o'clock stage the following morning, and, Didymusa having alighted at the store to expedite matters, I thought I might as well drive down to the feed yard to show a group of admiring friends how beautifully I could turn in.

But just at the critical moment, the wheels seemed to become locked, there was a grating sound as of a skid on a steep hill, and Dandy began to plunge. With a warning cry " hold hard, or you'll be over," Mr. Van Buren ran to the horses' heads and turned them in the opposite direction. Until that time I failed to realize that my new American carriage required a turning circle of about a quarter of a mile for perfect safety—the bed of the waggon being perfectly straight, with no space for the wheels to turn under it. The construction of the buggies, the front wheel being the same size as those behind, made them very awkward in turning and dangerous with a shying horse.

Now that we had become seasoned to the rough mode of travelling, the return over the Divide to Kerville seemed far less of an ordeal than the outward drive had been. We passed one night at the St. Charles's Hotel, another at the St. Leonard's Hotel at San Antonio, where the return to civilization and to Harneck and Baer's excellent ices, was fully appreciated, then, having secured tickets for San Francisco with " stop overs " at a few places on the way, we set forth at 12.40 the following day by the " Sunset route." Before nightfall we began to leave the prairie and that characteristic feature of Texan scenery, the mesquit tree, behind us, crossing the Rio Grande or Rio Bravo del Norte, and, passing through the fine scenery of the Apache Mountains and Sierra Blanca, arriving the next day at El Paso del Norte, now known as Ciudad de Juarez, in honour of the Mexican statesman of that name.

Five lines of railway meeting here, the little town has attained considerable importance, and is thoroughly Mexican-American in character. It is well situated in a fertile valley fifty miles long, and stands about 3500 feet above the sea-level, its climate resembling that of the table lands of Mexico. Passing over the long footbridge, which spans more sand than river, we enjoyed a peep at the old adobe houses and fine cathedral. Although this edifice still bears traces of exquisite workmanship in its nave, chancel, and ceilings, it has been robbed of the greater portion of its interior decorations ; its grandeur has faded. The town itself was founded in 1680, and there is an interesting old church of about the same date.

Our walk was marred by clouds of dust, which seemed to penetrate everything ; but the mountains to the north-east of the town shelter the city from the keen winter winds that sweep from the plains of Kansas. Wheat and corn crops were abundant ; the irrigating trenches, with stately cotton-wood trees on each side, still serving the purpose for which they were dug by the Jesuit missionaries 300 years ago. Delicious grapes grow plentifully, and are shipped to all parts of the country.

We grumbled at the dust in the streets of Ciudad de Juarez, little imagining what we were to encounter the next day when we crossed the great Colorado desert before reaching Yuma. The sand fell like heavy rain all around us, and we could scarcely see across the cars from the tail-board. The temperature was 120° in the shade (Didymusa, indeed, declared that the conductor once read 130°), and we could not bear to touch the woodwork of the cars, whilst the air was so scorching that it was impossible to have the windows open. Our luncheon basket not being lined, its contents were completely spoiled, except in the case of hermetically sealed tins ; but this fact caused slight inconvenience, since we felt little inclination to eat, though it was hardly possible to have too much to drink.

What a number of journeys we made along the cars to fetch iced water! Didymusa, in fact, drinking so freely that she brought on internal cramp, to be followed later on by " prickly-heat."

I sat, as it were, in a Turkish bath, but, the cars being fortunately not full, managed to keep at a distance from Didymusa, who was hot as a furnace. For companion I had an English lady, the wife of an American, who lived and throve near El Paso, and the pair of us presented a queer spectacle, our thin dust cloaks having a dark wet line all down the back !

Near the track was a salt, alkali lake ; a marvellous mirage creating the illusion of a boundless, distant ocean.

It was a treat to stretch one's legs during the half hour's halt at Yuma, and, with the absence of motion to breathe air freer from the dust, which had been dense enough to hide the mountains of San Bernardino in the distance, and resembled a blizzard of hot, stinging, suffocating particles. Whilst we walked back and forth near the station, the cars were swept out and sprinkled with water. We bought two melons from some Apache Indians, whose hair, short and ragged over the forehead, grew to a considerable length behind. For the melons we paid a dime (ten cents) each ; they were very delicious and proved extremely refreshing when we resumed our journey. On leaving Yuma we passed extensive salt-works, mud-volcanoes and boiling springs. This group of mud-volcanoes in the desert is a remarkable curiosity of San Diego county. They are sometimes known as *fumaroles* or *salses*, being vents by which the steam and gas make their escape from what appears to be a pond of thick hot mud.

A vent having been formed, the mud gradually rises till it becomes a cone about eight feet in height and the same in diameter at the base, though the shapes and sizes vary considerably. After a time, the supply of gas being exhausted, activity ceases, the mud sinks down to its former level, and becomes covered with a hard level crust resembling solid earth.

These mud volcanoes extend over a surface of several square miles, continually changing as fresh vents are formed and new cones arise. It is dangerous to venture too close, as the crust is liable to yield, precipitating one into the mud beneath, which has a temperature higher than that of boiling water. Some of the cones are curiously fringed with little crystals of sulphur, &c., deposited by the out-rushing vapours. The " Death Valley," or the " American Avernus," as it is sometimes named, owes its title to the circumstance that an entire party of Californian emigrants, having strayed from the overland trail in search of a short cut to the gold diggings, died there from thirst in 1850. As a matter of fact, the title of the valley is well deserved, if only because of its inhospitable sterility. It is situated on the most eastern part of California, near the Nevada line, and is probably the hottest place on earth.

In the central Sahara Desert, a mean temperature of 94° has been attained in July ; and South California and Arabia are as hot. But each of these places is cool in comparison with the Death Valley, where the lowest temperature in the shade during July is 99°, the highest 120° ; the mean being above 108°. The total rainfall during the hot months is less than an inch and a half, but strong winds prevail, those blowing from the south having a velocity of from thirty to forty-five miles an hour.

As we left the desert on our right, and drew near to the coast with its tempering breeze, the air became gradually cooler.

The beautiful city of San Angelo was planned by the Spaniards in 1781, and well might they name it El Pueblo de la Reina de los Angelos (the town of the Queen of the Angels). It is only fourteen miles east from the Pacific Ocean. The Los Angelos river rises at the mouth of a gorge in low hills, and flows past a wide plain near the western end of the San Gabriel or Sierra Madre, a spur of the Coast Range. The average height of this mountain is about 7000 feet, rising towards the San Antonio peak to over 10,000 feet.

The snow had disappeared from the summits before our arrival, but in the early spring the mountains are snow-capped, although luxuriant orange orchards flourish within ten miles of their base. Whilst the climate is well-nigh perfect, it is not exempt from frost. The mountains to the east, within thirty miles of San Angelo, are thickly clad with snow in winter, and this fact helps to lower the temperature sometimes even to 24°, causing serious damage to the orange and lemon nurseries, but not to the older trees or fruit, which is mature before the frost sets in. On the other hand, there are hot north winds and summer sand-storms occasionally.

At Santa Barbara, on June 17, 1859, the temperature rose to 133°, trees being blasted, fruit blistered, and calves destroyed, rabbits and birds killed from exposure to the hot wind; but during the last thirty-two years nothing approaching the intense heat of that summer has been experienced in any part of the State. The inhabitants assert that the dryness of the atmosphere protects the orange and other fruit trees from destructive insects. Time would not permit us to visit the San Gabriel Mission, which is considered the best in California. It was founded in 1771, and sometimes known as the Mission of the

Temblores (earthquakes). This building did not suffer to the extent of those at San Juan Capistrano and Santa Inez, in 1812, or that of Santa Clara, where the church was thrown down in 1815, and rendered unfit for further use. But, although we were unable to visit the Mission, we drove through this country of vineyards and ever-blooming gardens and orchards, flowers and fruit, obtaining a splendid view from the old fort, whose environs are said to resemble those of Damascus, with the surrounding orange groves, vineyards, lime, lemon and fig trees, olives and pomegranates, and here and there a palm to impart an oriental character to the scene.

For many weeks from this date we had an abundant supply of every kind of fruit; rich, ripe, and remarkably cheap withal.

From San Angelo to San Francisco the country was beautiful all the way, but for the last hundred miles very different from that we had been traversing—mountains, yet well wooded, with wild, deep cañons, and sometimes bare rock devoid of vegetation, or, again, dark forests. As the evening shadows fell we could distinguish the dim outlines of higher mountain ranges in the distance.

There was also an unmistakeable fall in the temperature, and as our clothing had been regulated to suit the intense heat, and it was impossible to get at our luggage to obtain warmer wraps, &c., we arrived at San Francisco at 9.30 p.m., on July 3, two poor shivering mortals; even the effort of resisting the importunate hotel "runners," who had boarded the train during the last twenty miles, failed to restore circulation.

These "runners" are a perfect torment, but we managed to resist them all. Having a letter of introduction to an American gentleman from some friends in

England, we were advised by him to engage some rooms in Montgomery Street, thus being free to obtain our meals when and where we pleased ; an excellent plan, as we contemplated several excursions.

CHAPTER XIX.

THE YOSEMITE VALLEY—CHINESE QUARTER IN SAN FRANCISCO.

THE next morning we were glad of a good bath, the pores of our skin still feeling as if they were choked with sand. Our clothes were carried away by Mr. Wing Hing to be restored to their proper colour at his laundry in Stevenson Street. The size of the bundle failed to satisfy his expectations however; he pointed, gesticulated, turned out our luncheon basket, dived under the pillows and bed clothes, finally shaking his own apparel, with a funny jerk of the head. " No mor, no mor thimmi-daw ! "

The washing was " promptly delivered, with fluting and polishing neatly done " according to the card; on our return from the Yosemite Valley, Mr. Hing Wing reappeared, and on that occasion must have carried away with him many ounces of red sand.

Our friends arranged a pleasant party for Independence Day, when the City and all its inhabitants presented a remarkably festive appearance; the streets were thronged with processions, and in the evening fine displays of fireworks might be seen at the Golden Gate Park and other favourite suburban resorts.

A beautiful bouquet of red, white (stephanotis), and blue flowers being offered to me, I accepted it, thus incurring Didymusa's disapproval. To carry the American colours was a kind of disloyalty; and although I pointed out the difficulty and discourtesy of a refusal, reminding her that if one comes to Rome, one should act as a Roman, she still deprecated my conduct.

Not a day was to be lost in visiting the Yosemite Valley, as the volume of water at the Falls begins to decrease after the end of June. On the 5th of July we were introduced to two ladies who wished to share a private carriage, in preference to travelling by the ordinary stage, and at half past four the same afternoon, went on board the S.S. " Empire City." It was a lovely night for our short voyage on the Pacific, and after a comfortable sleep, we found ourselves the next morning in the Slough (pronounced "sloo"), a side channel or inlet from the sea, at Stockton, whence we railed to Milton. There we found the carriage and the two American ladies, who were governesses, or " school marms " in the vernacular. Miss Boorse and Miss Wainwright proved to be excellent companions, and relieved me of all bargaining over incidental expenses. Miss Wainwright was particularly expert in this regard, talking to the mule-guide a few days later on for about half an hour in her high-pitched voice, and finally agreeing upon a certain sum to include visits to all the Falls.

We went by the Calaveras Grove and returned by the Mariposa. The journey occupied ten days, and most of the hotels were comfortable. When we saw anything interesting it was delightful to be able to stop, and between us we collected a good many specimens ; too many, indeed, for the capacity of the carriage and the temper of our elderly driver, who described our treasures as rubbish, and, at last, revolting, turned out nearly all the huge cones, declaring that one apiece was ample.

I fancy he will never forget that trip and the way we all teased him in turns, in order to provoke his crabbed retorts. The horses were a fine pair of bays, but one being a slug we used to hum these two lines to cheer him on the way :

"The splendid bays that bear us along,
Are lazy Maize and smart Long John."

Whereupon Mr. Brassfield, our Jehu, would add :

" Ah, John will be so smart, he'll kill himself before this trip is over, if Maize won't pull better ! " A broad hint that we must not diverge too far from the main route.

We always started at six o'clock in the morning to avoid the heat of the day. The country was wild with deep, umbrageous cañons here and there, but the quantity of red dust proved a serious drawback to one's enjoyment.

Mr. Brassfield pointed out the oak-pine and the nut-pine, which are rare in comparison with the sugar-pine (*Pinus lambertiana*) ; and there were quantities of the smaller manzanita, or red wood, chaparral, and other evergreens, besides some banks of azalea in full blossom.

Our halting places were Calaveras, Clark's, Raymond's, Priest's, Hamilton's, Copperopolis, Chinese Camp, and Crocker's ; the drive from Raymond's, after visiting the Mariposa Grove, continuously beautiful through the timbered foot-hills to the valley.

The grove of the Calaveras contains about a hundred large trees and many smaller, one being 325 feet in height, one 319 feet, one 315 feet, and about a score of 250 feet each. The largest has a circumference of 61 feet. Both the Calaveras and Mariposa Groves consist of *Sequoia gigantea* trees, named in honour of Sequoyah, the Cherokee Indian who invented an alphabet for his people.

Calaveras has nothing to do with skulls, as its name might perhaps lead one to infer, being so called after

" Calaverite," a mineral—a telluride of gold—which was the first found in Calaveras County.

The Mariposa Grove includes more than 400 trees, none quite so high or so large in circumference as the biggest in the Calaveras. Some of the great red-wood trees (*semper virens*) so closely resemble these in size, bark, and foliage, as at Santa Cruz, California, that for a long time it was supposed they belonged to the same species.

At Copperopolis we rambled through an abandoned gold mine, carrying away specimens, distinguishing the various nuggets, as we chose to term them, by our own Christian names.

In Tuolumne County we paid a visit to Mr. Goodwin, a Lincolnshire man, who had been out there many years, and owned a large vineyard and extensive orchards, all well irrigated. We saw some gigantic fig-trees, and great quantities of peaches and other fruits, which were being packed for the market. Mr. Goodwin also took us over his cellars, where there was a good stock of excellent red and white wine. He seemed to enjoy a chat about the old country whilst we rested in his nice house, discussing his port and sherry, this entirely according with Mr. Brassfield's notion of varying the journey. The ascent to Priest's being extremely stiff, and our horses tired, we elected to walk the last two and a half miles up an incline of 1400 feet. The " school marms " gave out before they had climbed a mile, and some " drummers," who were going the same way, puffed and groaned, and eventually retreated to their carriage. On our arrival the landlord and visitors at Priest's greeted us with three cheers on account of our successful accomplishment. Descending by a zig-zag road ten miles long, we obtained our first view of the Yosemite Valley from Inspiration Point, where we arrived about noon, and put up at Barnard's Hotel. Colonel Hutchings called upon us during the afternoon and conducted us to the Yosemite Falls on foot. I did not mind the ascent, but when it came to descending those steep places I felt decidedly unsafe, and the following day preferred to come down on the back of a mule. The Yosemite is a wonderful fall, situated nearly in the middle of the valley, originating in the creek of the same name, and leaping in three cataracts down 2550 feet. The upper fall of over 1000 feet rushes through a gorge ; the second is a series of cascades, measuring 626 feet, after which comes the third fall of 400 feet, below which is a talus 200 feet high. Then for about half a mile the stream divides into three branches, edged with tall trees, which present a fine vista called Cascade Avenue, from the numerous little cascades in its course. In the cañon between the Upper and Lower Falls the wind blew in fierce gusts, which caught our breaths, whilst the spray fell in showers. This fall does not form part of the river Merced, which enters the valley from the south-east, and just before reaching it is broken by the Nevada and Vernal Falls. The Nevada is the largest, but the Vernal ranks next in volume of water, if not in height, owing its name to its peculiar green colour. Leaning over a natural battlement of rock, we could see this cataract to great advantage. Between the Nevada and the Vernal Falls the Merced makes a descent of 275 feet, forming many beautiful rapids and cascades. After supper we strolled through the valley by the light of a perfect full moon, which greatly increased the grandeur of the scene, throwing the sharp outline of the majestic, towering Capitan (Indian name, " Great Spirit ") into bold relief. Its height exceeded the width of the valley, a perpendicular wall more than

4000 feet.   The sides of the valley, chiefly formed of granite, run almost parallel ; they are occasionally vertical, and always steep—varying from 1000 to 4700 feet in height—and looking as if they had been torn asunder by some mighty convulsion.   At the base on each side is a talus, or sloping pile of boulders and fragments fallen from above.   The colour of the walls is yellowish on the north side of the valley, and bluish gray on the south.

Barnard's Hotel was charmingly situated, and, the pellucid Merced rippling close by, one felt so reluctant to turn in that only the prospect of an arduous to-morrow finally drove us to bed.

I may mention that the Merced is a fine trout stream, providing some delicious fish for supper.   The first item in our next days programme was a visit to Mirror Lake at sunrise.   In order to save some extra hours in the saddle, we coaxed Mr. Brassfield to drive us there in the carriage, although the horses were supposed to enjoy a rest during our stay in the valley.   At 5 a.m. we set forth, accompanied by Col. Hutchings and Miss Hall, who narrated many an Indian legend, and read the mountain pictures while we were waiting for the sun, which is not reflected in the lake until an hour after it has actually risen.   Col. Hutchings has spent many secluded years in the valley, seeing a great deal of the Indians in former days.   He possesses a valuable collection of curios, which he subsequently showed us at his house.   Amongst the natural pictures presented by the mountains were the " Spanish Cavalier," the " Sleeping Beauty," the " Hen and Chickens," a fine profile of poor Tesinek, the Indian princess, who on being driven from the Valley, washed her clothes in the Merced and hung them on the rock in token of her intended return.   An imaginative eye could distinguish lines in the granite with very white cross pieces representing these draperies close to the face—of a fine Egyptian type, almost in profile. We were only allowed to gaze at the reflection of the sun in the lake for a few seconds ; even after this brief dazzling glimpse, everything we looked at appeared rainbow-hued for the next half hour.

To gaze for any length of time would be to incur total blindness.

Having returned to the hotel at nine o'clock and breakfasted, we set forth on mules, with a guide, and began to climb to Glacier Point, which commands an extensive view (snow being visible in many places), including Nevada Fall, "The Cap of Liberty," "The Half Dome," and the "Royal Arches" of Capitan. We visited all the Falls except the "Bridal Veil," which is, I believe, impracticable for riding ; but we obtained an excellent view of it both on entering and leaving the valley from the opposite side. The Bridal Veil Fall makes a descent of 1000 feet, and beautiful rainbows can sometimes be seen in the afternoon on its "leaping mists and flying shreds." It was tinged with a faint apple-green lustre, beautifully transparent, and occasionally edged with a curling misty vapour as it caught the full force of the wind. "Cloud's Rest," 10,150 feet above the sea level, was the highest point we reached. As we had loitered on the way, the time of our stay in the valley was necessarily curtailed, and, though I pitied Didymusa and the "school marms," who suffered terribly from the twelve hours' climb in the saddle, Mr. Brassfield said we must be off if we wished to complete the circuit in time. Although the visit ended all too soon, it will ever remain green in our memories—a most delightful reminiscence.

N 2

We returned to San Francisco on the morning of July 14, to find the city again *en fête* in celebration of the Fall of the Bastille. There was a march past of the French inhabitants, whose shops were very tastefully decorated. In the evening Mr. V. escorted us to the Chinese quarters, which we saw to great advantage under his able guidance whilst we felt safer than we should have done with a police officer, in threading our way through the intricacies of China Town and its opium dens.

China Town contains about 25,000 inhabitants, 13,000 being factory operatives, 5000 house servants, 3000 laundry men, 1000 merchants, storekeepers, traders or pedlers; together with about 2000 women and a few hundred children. Chinese notions are very exclusive regarding women, and the opposite sex is excluded from their apartments, which are quite sufficiently overcrowded. Their time is occupied in needlework, and the manufacture of fancy articles, varied by visits from ladies connected with the Chinese Missions. Walking through the quarter, you seldom meet a woman, or at the most one or two together holding children by the hand and looking rather guilty as if they had no business there. The peculiar dress renders it difficult to distinguish one sex from the other. The principal ornaments of the women are worn in the hair, which in front is oiled and plastered close to the head, sometimes being rolled and puffed at the back and sides, and decorated with gilt ornaments and high combs. The coiffure indicates their condition, whether married or single, and is changed at different ages. Bracelets and anklets of bone or ivory are worn as well as earrings and finger rings. The shaving of the men is an elaborate process, the skin being scraped from the shoulders upwards, excepting only that portion of the scalp from which the queue depends. The queue is washed, combed, oiled and braided, the eyelashes being trimmed and sometimes tinted. The Chinaman is extremely particular concerning his ablutions and his personal appearance generally.

There is a constant sluggish kind of activity in China Town by day, but to see the place in all its glory, you must visit it at night, when one is transported to quite another world.

We bought some quaint back scratchers, coins, and other souvenirs, Mr. V. chatting freely to many of the pedlers whom he knew.

Having made our way through a labyrinth of dirty passages we arrived at an opium den; neither more nor less than a reeking cellar, with shelves or bunks arranged round three of its four walls. Upon these, lay those frequenters of the place who were already overcome, often one on the top of another, whilst some who had not yet succumbed to the fumes were occupied either in cobbling shoes, making cigars, working sewing machines, or sitting at small tables smoking. One man began and finished two pipes in our presence, and still retained sufficient sense to fill and manipulate a third.

The fœtid atmosphere of the den, with its peculiar, faint, acid odour would soon have taken effect upon us, and, the night being unusually free from fog, we took the opportunity of enjoying the fresh air and a splendid view of this " City of a Hundred Hills " from California Street.

John Chinaman is too practical a person to build himself costly places of worship in a land where his footing seems precarious, and many of the more wealthy possess idols, which they worship in their own private apartments. Some small temples are supported by trade companies or guilds ; the laundrymen, for instance, boast of one of their own, with a kind of benevolent society attached to it.

The Joss House which we visited in Waverley-place is the chief. It contains three alcoves, each with its god, forming a kind of Chinese Trinity. In the middle of the trio is Yum Ten Tin, or the God of the Sombre Heavens ; controller of the waters of the earth and above the earth, extinguisher of fire, and conqueror of droughts. On his right sits the God of War, Kowan Tai, whose image may frequently be seen also in stores and dwellings. He is the favourite deity in San Francisco, settling disputes and quelling riots. Nam Hoi Hung Shing Tai, the God of the Southern Seas, is the third person of this Trinity. His is the control of fire, and if a China-man or his worldly goods be rescued from the flames, this deity receives thank-offerings of meat, vegetables, wine, tea, &c.

In other alcoves we saw Wah Tair, the God of Medicine, who holds in his hand a large pill, and, being invoked, cures all kinds of disease ; and Tsoi Pah Shing Kwun, the God of Wealth, who carries a bar of bullion. This god has many very earnest votaries ! Coolies and capitalists alike make their genuflections before his shrine.

There are other images of wood and plaster—good gods to be worshipped, evil deities to be propitiated ; and they are never allowed to go hungry or thirsty. When their slumbers appear to have been unduly protracted, a huge bell (cast in China) and an immense drum are employed to rouse them. In front of the altars stand incense jars, in which sticks of sandal wood are kept constantly burning on sand or ashes.

In another joss house there are some copper screens

representing scenes from early Chinese history, donations from a wealthy Chinaman.

The Chinese betray a remarkable lack of reverence, or even of formality in their worship; they smoke and talk in the temples, approach their favourite deity without uncovering, perform their chin-chinning operations (bowing low three times) as rapidly as possible, deposit their offerings and go about their business.

The female worshippers are more devout, often completely prostrating themselves before their deities. These prayers are usually for some material boon; success in business or in gambling, protection during a journey, general immunity from calamity, or recovery from sickness.

They entertain a keen dread of purgatory, and the days of most devotion are those on which they pray the souls of their friends out of torment.

The priests live by the sale of paper money, incense tapers and other paraphernalia, and it is usual for white visitors to buy some trifle as a curiosity.

Sunday, perhaps, is the best day to visit China Town, the factory men and domestic servants all rallying thither for the day, although there is no cessation from toil.

At some large restaurants wealthy Chinamen will pay from $10 to $100 for a dinner to half-a-dozen guests: the larger price securing the entire upper floor for the use of the party. Such a dinner may last from 2 p.m. until midnight, the guests stepping outside to enjoy an airing or transact business between the courses. The principal delicacies are birds' nest soup, sharks' fins, Taranaki fungus (which grows on a tree in New Zealand), Chinese terrapin, Chinese goose, Chinese quail, fishes' brains, tender shoots of bamboo, various vegetables and arrack (a spirit distilled from rice) wines, oysters, poultry and sucking-pig.

The tables are decorated on one side with screens and draperies ; the balconies or smoking rooms are illuminated by coloured lanterns, while the charm of the entertainment is enhanced by the discordant strains of a Chinese band.

———oo;◊;oo———

CHAPTER XX.

FROM SAN FRANCISCO TO SALT LAKE CITY.

In spite of all that has been done to lessen the natural steepness of the streets, San Francisco still remains exceedingly irregular. Twenty million cubic yards of earth have been transferred from the town; nevertheless, it continues well to deserve its title, " The City of a Hundred Hills." But cable cars run everywhere, the highest point being 938 feet.

The city has developed from two villages, one bearing its present name, the other that of Yerba Buena.

The village of San Francisco covered about 150 acres near the Mission church at the corner of Dolores Street, the Mission having been founded by some Franciscan Friars on October 8, 1776, and overthrown in 1835 by the decree of secularization. In that year, W. A. Richardson, an Englishman, who had lived for some time at Sancelito, erected a tent to trade in hides and tallow. So began the village of Yerba Buena, which, in 1845, covered forty acres of land on the shore of Yerba Buena Cove.

The two villages were separated by three miles of sand hills, covered with dense chaparral, the only communication being by a horse trail.

The inhabitants of San Francisco were Spanish-American, and lived by the sale of hides and tallow; those of Yerba Buena were British-American, and mostly traders.

A great change occurred in July, 1846, when the American flag was hoisted, and San Francisco bay became the head-quarters of the United States navy in the Pacific. The following July the village of Yerba Buena assumed the name of San Francisco, and in July, 1848, six months after the discovery of gold, its residents numbered 500.

Every house beyond a radius of two miles from the business centre has been built during the last forty-five years, and those who were familiar with the site in 1848 no longer recognise it. Hundreds of hills and ridges have been levelled; ravines and vast tracts of muddy flats and swamps filled up.

The climate is remarkably bracing and equable; never very hot, never very cold. In July and August the thermometer generally registers between 60° and 70°. When there is a lull in the cool trade wind from the coast, and a strong northerly breeze sets in, a few hot days occur, but there is neither rain, hail, snow, thunder, nor lightning, though it often blows hard; and dust and sand-fleas are plentiful.

The wind being less strong in the early morning, this is the best time to visit the Sutra heights, and we arrived at Cliff House about half past eight to see the famous sea-lions. The rocks were covered with them, some asleep, others suddenly diving into the water, or climbing on to the islets, occasionally emitting a grand, deep roar, which suggested a rising tempest. These animals are protected by law, and the fishermen complain that they reduce the quantity of salmon. In Spanish they are called *lobo marino* (sea wolf) the name of the place being La Punta de los Lobos Marinos (the point of the sea wolves).

Having walked through the lovely grounds of Sutra

Heights, enjoying its extensive views, we drove back by way of Golden Gate Park, which covers over a thousand acres, and possesses many fine avenues of smooth well-made drives, extending for miles. Grand mountain and ocean views are obtained from several points. Much has been done to improve the naturally sandy soil, and eucalyptus trees, with Monterey cypress, pines, and over 250,000 shrubs have been planted. On the east side of the Park a small area is tastefully laid out with flower beds and grass plats, whilst the conservatory, 250 feet in length, possesses an orchid house, fernery, and a rare botanical collection.

The noticeable absence of liveries in the American parks imparts a certain monotony to the equipages, although there were hundreds of well turned out buggies. Whenever our engagements permitted we went to see the Fire Brigade drill at noon : the horses always stood in readiness, the harness being suspended above them, ready to drop into its place immediately an alarm is given. The men descended by poles from above, and it is said that their very bedclothes are switched off by electricity. We always took sugar and apples for the horses, who after a few visits were inclined to move from their places on our arrival, so that the officials thought they were being demoralized ; albeit they expressed regret when we paid our farewell visit.

One of our friends, Mr D. being a member of the Stock Exchange, persuaded us to pay it a visit. The building, erected at a cost of $900,000 is over 80 feet high, with a cupola rising 85 feet above the roof. The front is composed of granite, light and dark, with pillars of the same stone polished. The walls of the board-room are wainscoted with Black Belgian marble, above which is a border of carved primavera wood. The doors leading to the vestibule are beautifully carved in walnut and cost $1000.

During the boom in mining stock when excitement ran high the fee for membership was $30,000. A railing encloses the oval space, outside which are seats on the floor; spectators paying to occupy them. These are for the most part persons desiring to buy or sell stock. The brokers, shouting and gesticulating, resembled a violent mob rather than an assemblage of business men. It was difficult to distinguish a word, amidst the Babel, and we wondered how the "Caller" managed, in such an uproar, to note each transaction so accurately, that, though thousands of shares changed hands, when the list of sales was afterwards read off by the clerk, his decision was seldom disputed.

I was disappointed in the "Diamond Palace," which is neither more nor less than a large jeweller's shop.

The mint is worth a visit as also the Safe-deposit, where one can leave either money, jewels, or paper securities. The vaults are guarded day and night and contain more than 4000 burglar and fire-proof safes.

We attended the Episcopalian services at Trinity Church and the Church of the Advent, preferring the latter, where there was a mixed choir, the anthem being sung in a very florid style, whilst the congregation remained seated. The last time we had been inside a church was in London, at St. Ann's, Wardour Street, on March 10, and the Church of the Advent could not be compared with this; but I confess I do not like the American Episcopalian service. We heard some excellent singing at St. Mary's, the Roman Catholic Cathedral in California Street, and also a very impressive Requiem Mass at St. Patrick's, which contains a fine chime of bells and the largest organ in

California. The most historically interesting church is the Old Mission, founded in 1786, with adobe walls three feet thick.

Finding that glass, china, and many other articles, were considerably cheaper here than in San Antonio, and having our house at Junction City to furnish, we indulged in a day's shopping in Mission Street. My riding hat beginning to look the worse for wear, I had it re-blocked at the steam factory, when the maker's name and address on its cork lining aroused the curiosity of the manager, who asked a good many questions. The Angora skins at Marx's, the furrier's, were quite a sight to see, and we bought two for the floor of our new drawing-room. Whilst making our purchase we were treated with a pleasant freedom of manner, and probably respected none the less, although the orthodox " Madame," and customary shop palaver, which ceases when the door swings behind you, were omitted.

Mr. Cowan's niece, a remarkably pleasant girl, gracefully performed the part of hostess when her uncle sent her with us to a dinner given by him at a restaurant close by. The people were sorry not to supply me with the usual " cuspadores," as they called it, but more properly, the *escupidera* (spittoon), but I had no intention of encouraging this kind of thing in my new house ! The extensive fruit market is, perhaps, one of the most interesting sights in 'Frisco : where every kind of fruit, the ripest and largest that can be imagined, seemed to be displayed, except cherries, which I never saw. You can only obtain the fruit wholesale, but for ten cents we bought a box quite as large as we could conveniently carry, full of figs, peaches, plums and strawberries, besides some bunches of bananas, a quantity of grapes, and some of those delicious, small

Mexican lemons, which are about the size of a Tangarine orange and not very acid.

At the time of our visit, the Palace Hotel was the largest in the world, but I believe it is now eclipsed by that at Denver. We often lunched and dined at the Occidental or the Palace Hotel; the latter being seven storeys high, with a frontage of 275 feet, and depth of 350 feet—containing about 800 rooms, and accommodating over 1000 guests. It cost about $7,000,000, and more than 30,000,000 bricks were used in its construction.

Nearly all the houses are built of wood, and those in the suburbs are covered with charming creepers, fuchsias, and ivy geraniums, growing as high as the second storey. Although roses, geraniums, verbenas, and heliotropes flourish abundantly as the result of constant attention, the sandy soil, absence of rain and expense of irrigation cause the city to be almost treeless. It is said that the 'Friscans do not encourage the planting of trees in the streets and suburbs, as, their summers being cool, they like as much sunshine as they can obtain. Such trees as one sees are the Eucalyptus, Australian acacia, the Monterey cypress and pine, with various kinds of dwarf palm; but when they grow large enough to be shady they are generally felled. The horse-chestnut, linden, maple, Lombardy and silver poplar, also may occasionally be seen.

Tickets for several theatres (not very handsome buildings or highly decorated) were presented to us, and at Baldwin's, where Daly's Company was performing, I first had the pleasure of seeing Miss Ada Rehan.

At the variety entertainment at the Orpheum we saw some Samoan or South Sea warriors. They were naked to the waist, and showed great activity in their war dances, indulging in grotesque, fierce, and repulsive gestures, squatting on the ground and shrugging their heavy muscular shoulders almost to dislocation to an accompaniment of horrible grimaces and guttural sounds; then suddenly springing to their feet, and wielding their rude clubs and spears. We began to feel more comfortable when they made their exeunt.

Our time was now becoming limited, and after several weeks' sojourn in 'Frisco there still remained a great deal to see. But we gave up the idea of visiting the wonders of Monterey and Santa Cruz, though we thoroughly enjoyed two picnics which were organised in our behalf. One across the Oakland Ferry to Strawberry Cañon, and to Berkeley, with its many varieties of foreign trees and shrubs, over 200 acres of grounds and an extensive botanical garden; the other to Mount Diablo, spending one night at Martinez. The sky looked clear, and the air felt dry, but the atmosphere was not favourable to the view from the summit, a kind of haziness from the red dust, as is often the case, obscuring everything. After rain in spring is the best time; but though we were disappointed of our climb, the country for many miles around was fertile, and at Pine cañon we found shade, water, and pleasant scenery. Mount Diablo is nearly 4000 feet high, rising like a cone about thirty miles from 'Frisco. Among the most remarkable sights from the mountain is its evening shadow as it falls across the San Joaquin plain, gradually climbing from its base to the summit, ascending 8000 feet, and reaching to a distance of 100 miles. We also made a pleasant expedition to Mount Tamalpais (the country of the Tamal Indians). Our route lay by Ross Cañon, the hill sides being covered with rich green laurel, with a few traces of its lemon-coloured bloom. In early spring the air is laden with its perfume. The lilac flowers of the ceanothus, with pretty pink and white blossoms of the manzanita intermingling with its greyish green leaves, were luxuriant; and we saw the evergreen oak, the Christmas berry bush, light green madrona, and other evergreens, but few deciduous trees and shrubs. Yet there was the wild gooseberry in full bloom, with the buck-eye, and the hazel dropping its catkins. On leaving the cañon we ascended the eastern slope by a zig-zag course, covered with chaparral, hazel, California nutmeg, and scrub oak.

Sorry as we felt to leave 'Frisco, we wished to return to Texas during the early part of August, and determined to travel to San Antonio *viá* Denver and the Rio Grand Route, with short halts at Salt Lake City, &c. Finally leaving San Francisco at 3.30 p.m., the train began to climb the Sierra Nevada; up and up during the greater part of the night, drawn by two panting toiling engines; our heads being sometimes considerably lower than our feet, which was hardly conducive to comfort. Towards morning we began to feel the increased heat and presently passed between forty and fifty miles of snow sheds.

The building of these sheds cost about $10,000 a mile; they are of immense strength in order to resist the shock of, and guard the trains against, avalanches of snow from the mountain slopes. During an average winter 55 feet of snow will fall; and the sheds also prevent it from forming immense drifts. Before rounding the headland of Cape Horn, our train ran along a narrow track cut in the edge of a vertical cliff 1000 feet high, with a curve so sharp that we lost sight of the engines. The unsurpassed sharpness of this curve gave rise to the story of an engine-driver, who, scared one night by the proximity of two red lights on the track, jumped from his locomotive to escape the effects of a collision, though the lights were on the tail of his own train. After leaving Remo and passing the desert, we changed cars at Ogden at 7.15 a.m. Our companions were lively and sociable, interchanging the contents of their baskets and presently combining for a rubber of whist; amongst them being two intelligent Japanese, (to whom we gave lessons in English), a German Jewess and her pretty daughter, an embryo public singer, at present on her way to New York to consult an oculist. There was also a violin player from the Tivoli, going to visit his father in Kansas, who kept us all amused, but suffered badly when we made the ascent of the Sierra. When not bemoaning his afflicted state, he sang snatches of " If ever I cease to love." But on reaching Salt Lake City, we bade all our companions farewell.

The country had been brown and barren, with sage bush for its only vegetation until we reached the Utah and Jordan Valleys, where we came upon a wealth of colouring —bright green on the mountain sides, pure white on the peaks, blue in the dim distance. Fine sleek, black cattle were grazing in the pastures, and patches of yellow corn alternated with vegetable gardens. The whole a perfect vision of beauty, repose, and agricultural wealth ! The Valley comprises more than a thousand acres. Having put up at Cullen's Hotel, extremely comfortable but pro-portionately expensive, we took a carriage and drove to Fort Douglas, where a regiment is perched like a bird on the East Bench above the city. The quarters are built of red sandstone from the neighbouring Red Butte Cañon quarry From this elevated position we obtained a magnificent view of the valley ; the mountains lay behind us, and in front the buildings of the city peeped out amidst the foliage, while the River Jordan in the farther distance was now visible, now lost to view, till it joined the glistening lake in the north-west. The islands on the horizon rise 3000 feet out of the blue waters.

To the left, in the middle distance, we saw the trees of Liberty Park, about a hundred acres in extent, and southwards lay farms, meadows, and orchards, varied by clusters of shade trees—planted by the hand of man—amongst them the tall, slender Lombardy poplars standing out conspicuously, with a background of black smoke issuing in columns from the silver ore smelting works.

Facing us, the Oquirrh Range, dropping suddenly a mile or more to the level of the lake, the western portion of the valley being still unoccupied on account of the dearth of water.

On our way back we paid a visit to Mrs. Dye's pretty house and garden, where we saw some enormous strawberries preserved in spirit, as specimens of the capabilities of the climate. Mrs. Dye was reticent regarding her religion, but from various hints it appeared evident that she was not enraptured with polygamy, although insisting that women, as a class, were happier at Utah than anywhere else in the world. Poverty is far more frequent than discontent.

We paid a visit to the Tabernacle, the acoustic properties of which are marvellous, owing to the peculiar construction and festooning of its roof.

Supported by forty-six columns, this springs in one unbroken arch, being the largest of its kind in the world except that at the Grand Union Depôt, New York, which was built by Commodore Vanderbilt.

The Mormon Tabernacle is capable of seating 8000 persons, and the faintest whisper, a pin dropped on the floor, or even a sigh, can be distinctly heard from one end of the building to the other. The building is 250 feet long by 150 feet wide, the arched roof 65 feet high, and the fine organ was manufactured chiefly of home-grown materials.

Not far from the Tabernacle the Temple is situated. Although more than a quarter of a century has elapsed since its foundation was laid, much remains to be done and we heard six years spoken of as the time still needed for its completion.

It is 184 feet in length, by 116 feet, about 96 feet in height, whilst its spires will reach 192 feet; already the building had cost $150,000. Great care is taken to ensure perfection throughout, everything is thoroughly overhauled and superintended, the slightest flaw or imperfection being at once detected and made good.

We received two little cubes of white granite, speckled with black as a souvenir. This material of which the Temple is built is quarried from the Wasatch Range, more than twenty miles distant. Our attention was called to a strange-looking house, occupied by a mad Swede, and decorated externally with coloured pictures, flags and various ornaments. He had the misfortune to lose his *fiancée*, who was shipwrecked and drowned on her way to join him. They had been engaged for twelve years and the blow unsettled his reason. His house was situated in the "Gentile" quarter.

Our driver took us to the spot where Brigham Young used to wrestle in prayer, and also to his grave, though it is stated, on good authority, that his body was embalmed and laid elsewhere. Of course, we indulged in the orthodox "dip" in the Great Salt Lake, but the water was lukewarm, and, instead of proving invigorating, as far as we were concerned, caused such lassitude that we felt glad it was afternoon.

The water is remarkably buoyant; more so than that

at Droitwitch. You can swim with little effort, and float without any ; indeed, the difficulty is to regain your feet. Thousands of persons bathe in the lake every summer, and on its shores are dancing pavilions (having bands during the season), refreshment booths, and covered piers. We picked up some small blocks of salt beside an adjacent spring, the water of which was icily cold. The salt-making industry appears to be on the increase. When the lake is full in spring, or after a stiff north-west wind, a temporary dam is thrown across the neck, thus confining the overflow in lagoons on the south-eastern shore. Having waited for the water to evaporate, the saltmaker goes into the now dry lagoon and shovels out the residue of salt. If the water has not entirely evaporated, it is got rid of by means of pumps. The brine contains, besides common salt, a variety of sulphates, borates, and bromides, from which are manufactured Epsom and Glauber salts, soda-ash, bicarbonate of soda, caustic soda, &c.

CHAPTER XXI.

THROUGH THE ROCKIES TO FORT WORTH AND SAN ANTONIO.

———

AT Denver we had time only to take a hurried walk through the city, and could remark little beyond its fine solidly-constructed buildings. After leaving Denver the line follows the Front Range of the Rockies for 120 miles, through marvellously beautiful scenery, diversified by rock, elevated table lands and water. Leaving behind us Marshall Pass, that wonderful pathway over the Continental Divide, we began to ascend. At first the grade was only moderately steep, but presently the hills become mountains, and the climb began in earnest. The train was divided, the engines toiled and panted, crawling round sharp and frequent curves, till about an hour later we attained the summit of Mount Ouray, bare and lonely and high above its fellows. Away in the distance rose the continuous heights of the Sangre de Cristo Range, their crests white with everlasting snows, their bases hidden by dark forests; and beyond, the great San Luis Park sloped into invisibility.

As we took a more westerly direction, the character of the scenery changed; the heights becoming less formidable, their surroundings softer, more subdued, and even more beautiful. There was Tomichi Creek running through sylvan shades, and in the far beyond, the broad plateau on which stands Gunnison City.

A glance backwards as the cars rolled on gave one even a better idea of the great ascent, and we stood on the platform of the car, gazing at the vast, unobstructed view until our senses grew bewildered.

The Denver and .Rio Grande Western line had not at that time been long in use. At Gunnison, together with several other passengers, we changed into open cars, in order to obtain the best view of the Black Cañon ; a grand, deep, dark gorge, verdant in places, alternated with masses of red sandstone, cedars and pinons growing luxuriantly in the crevices. The green river coursed along, on its way to Cimarron Creek ; water fell from dizzy heights, rebounding in masses from the lower terraces, tossed about by the wind, and finally reaching the river in clouds of white spray, or trickling from the cliffs in small streamlets.

At the junction of Gunnison and Cimarron, the gorge is spanned by a bridge, and from this the beauties of the cañon may be seen to the best advantage. Indians ignited their council fires here long ago—one could picture the flickering flames illuminating their dusky faces, traversing secret, guarded paths to their grave and sober meetings.

Other points of interest were the Animas Cañon ; the " Rio de las Animas Perdidas," or " River of Lost Souls," the finest gorge of the Rockies ; and the Currecanti Needle, the highest pinnacle visible on the route ; abrupt, isolated, somewhat suggestive of a hewn obelisk.

On emerging from the Black Cañon, we climbed the Cedar Divide, passing the Uncompahgre Valley and its river, with the picturesque peaks of San Juan in the distance, the richly coloured Book cliffs to the north, and southwards the snowy groups of the Sierra la Sal and San Rafael, glistening in the distance ; between these the broken walls which mark the Grand Cañons of the Colorado.

Flowers were prettily sprinkled in some places ; little forests of sunflowers and columbine; in others, as in the Black Cañon, the rocks were entirely bare ; perpendicular granite cliffs, sparkling like silver, but smooth, and uncovered by tree, flower, or shrub. Those solitudes seem to be unvisited even by birds ; the huge crags might guard the entrance to Hades ; and turned one's thoughts to certain scenes in Dante's " Divine Comedy."

The moon being on the wane, the night shut out much that was worth seeing. Reaching Pueblo at 5 a.m. we dis- embarked for a stroll, but met only a few tipsy persons. The Salvation Army has a garrison here. There are silver and other mines in the district, and the place, which seems to be growing, is extensively laid out and well planted. Early in the morning the air was cool and pleasant enough, but towards noon the heat became intense and the atmo- sphere oppressive, and we were glad when the time came to start again at 1.55 p.m. After spending the whole night in chairs we arrived at Childress at half past eight the following morning.

Yes, we were again in Texas ! The odour of burnt coffee directly we entered the hotel for breakfast, the familiar gallery, with its inevitable drinking pail and washing basin, were quite enough to remove any doubt that we had returned to the Lone Star State ! On again after a short rest, reaching Sunset at 12.30, and Fort Worth at 6 p.m.

A good story is told by the railroad men about Mr. Jay Gould, " who was once tricked by the level-headed superintendent of a small line, and lost a pile of money by the operation." Of course everybody wanted to hear about the man who had successfully pitted his wits against those of the great railroad magnate ; so the speaker went ahead

" About ten years ago, the Central branch of the Union Pacific, now part of the Missouri Pacific system, ran out from Atchison, Kansas, for about 300 miles west. The road was doing a fairly good business, two good crops having been raised in succession along its territory, but still it was a dead expense to the stock holders. Negotiations were entered into with Mr. Jay Gould, and he went out to see the property. The superintendent got wind of his coming and " fixed " things accordingly. The ' passenger ' with Gould on board started out of Atchison, but at the first way-station was side-tracked to let an apparently heavily loaded freight go by. It was the same thing at nearly every stopping place, train after train of long box-cars, all sealed, flashed by the waiting ' passenger ' until the return trip was commenced, when nearly as many empties swept by. Gould was greatly pleased at the apparent prosperity of the road, and at once entered into negotiations for it, which was successfully consummated, and not until then did he find out how he had been ' played.'

"That rascal of a superintendent had issued his orders, and those supposed heavily loaded trains were composed of sealed empties, with here and there a full car which would be ostentatiously side-tracked for effect. Coming back, the operation was repeated from Atchison. It cost the road a good deal of money to work the scheme, but the sale was made, and they were a great deal richer by the operation." Having finished this story, the narrator boarded a street car for the Union depôt.

Although I had left what I thought would be a sufficiently wide margin for incidental expenses, these were so heavy, especially at Salt Lake City, that a vague suspicion, which had been oppressing me for some time, now became fully confirmed. We were to leave Fort

Worth at 10 p.m., and the conditions of our round trip excursion ticket required us to finish the tour by 8.40, two nights later, at San Antonio. So that we could not stay to telegraph to the banker there, and receive his answer, unless we forfeited our tickets, and paid an additional sum for the remaining portion of the journey between Fort Worth and our destination.

We counted out the contents of our united purses, and found to our dismay that they were insufficient, even with the closest economy, to pay for our meals during the remaining two days. I tried to obtain an extension of the " ticket," entirely in vain. What was to be done! We counted out the contents of our purses a second time, without increasing the amount; should we fast by the way, or forfeit our tickets?

In this emergency Didymusa came valiantly to the rescue. What was to be done? Did she not possess a watch and chain! There was no help for it; off we trudged in search of a pawnbroker, and having found one, obtained a loan of $40 on my sapphire-and-brilliant ring and Didymusa's watch.

Although the sum was more than we required, I could not succeed in calling up any sense of satisfaction, one could not feel very proud of the experience, whilst yet it was impossible not to be a little amused at this easy method of relief—a method which would never have occurred to my unassisted imagination.

Once more aboard ; our luncheon basket amply provided with material for an excellent supper ; a roast chicken, and some cakes and fruit which had tempted us at a restaurant, where the only sustenance we felt inclined for, whilst our financial condition remained precarious, was a cup of coffee.

But our troubles were not yet over. When the con-

ductor came round to check the tickets we discovered that
we had boarded a Central Line train, instead of one
belonging to the Southern Pacific, by which we had booked.

If we could only get back to Fort Worth in time, we
might catch the 6 a.m. train. Our predicament was
generally discussed—Americans always show plenty of
ready sympathy—and one passenger suggested that by
alighting at Burleston, a stage of about twenty miles, we
could sleep at an hotel which he strongly recommended,
and return very early in the morning to Fort Worth. So
it was decided. Seeing some lights a little later we
supposed we were approaching a town, until the conductor
undeceived us.   We were passing a cotton field, in which
hundreds of lanterns were burning to destroy the moth of
the " bole-worm " (*Heliothis armigera*), this grub being a
terrible pest and very destructive.

It was close upon midnight when we reached the
primitive depôt of Burleston, and our friend on the cars
instructed the porter to take us to the Railway Hotel,
where he was " sure we should be comfortable as he had
stayed there himself." We had only a few minute's walk,
crossing the line, through several gates, and on down a
grass walk with a ditch on each side, the porter swinging
his lamp so confusingly that we were afraid lest we should
tumble into the water. Although the house was in total
darkness and the people were asleep, all the doors stood
open. Leaving us in the obscurity of the gallery, our
guide entered without ceremony. " Missus, here's some
passengers wants a bed for the night," he shouted; and
presently a dirty looking woman appeared, and invited us
to sit down where we were while she prepared our bed,
which, in fact, had to be vacated by her daughter, and a
"sick " child, who had been sharing it with herself.

Tired of waiting at last, we crossed the entrance room and entered another, where she was making preparations for our reception. The two rooms were separated only by a canvas partition about six feet in height, with an opening minus a door. The furniture of the inner room consisted, of a bedstead a few pegs on the frame of the partition, from which hung a girl's white frock and other dirty, tawdry apparel, and a broken chair. In a corner by the window, some reversed boxes supported a mattress, on which lay a boy, whose head, shirt sleeves, feet, and a portion of his cotton pants, were exposed by the white sheet which formed the insufficient covering.

"There's a corpse," whispered Didymusa, aghast. I was about to institute inquiries when the hostess forestalled me.

"It's only my little deaf and dumb boy," she said, "he won't hurt you."

"But supposing your little deaf and dumb boy wakes up and sees strangers in the room," I suggested.

"Oh, he'll guess you're his sisters, and he's a very quiet sleeper all the time."

Although this was not reassuring there seemed no help for it, and the woman retired. Our bed stood close to the outer wall, leaving a space between. Not having had time to eat our supper on the cars, we decided to repair the omission before seeking repose in this comfortless apartment. So, settling down on the edge of the odoriferous feather bed, we attempted to spread the feast on a broken chair, which already supported the candlestick. But everything did its utmost to slip through the hole in the middle of the seat, and at last Didymusa cut some slices of bread and butter and in despair we tore off the wings of the chicken and hungrily devoured them, dispensing with plates, knives, and forks.

In the midst of our repast, up started the deaf and dumb boy, gesticulating wildly and emitting disagreeable groans. We tried to appear unconcerned, and presently to our relief, he fell back on the bed and put his legs out of the open window.

Having drunk some wine and replaced the remnants of the feast in our basket, we lay down just as we were, but although tired after spending the previous night in chairs on the car, we agreed not to close our eyes. Indeed there was little fear that we should fall asleep; the stuffy room, the humid heat, suggestive of a freshly syringed forcing-house, only not by any means so sweet, quite forbade slumber! We intended to burn the candle while it lasted, but swarms of mosquitoes, mantis, and moths invaded the room, and we were compelled to extinguish it. Then the " chintz bugs " awoke, with other denizens of that dreadful feather bed, and kept us busy until two o'clock, when another train passed, and somebody approached the house with a lantern, presently to appear in the doorless aperture.

" Are you there, Tilda ? " he inquired.

" No—strangers," we answered, and off he stumped up a kind of ladder to the upper storey.

All being quiet again, the rats and mice came out, tempted perhaps by the odour of our cold chicken, for something was certainly molesting the basket.

Didymusa was disinclined to set her feet on the floor on account of the rats and mice, but she crawled to the end of the bed, and perceived a great dog engaged in an attempt to carry off what remained of the chicken, which for that matter he was welcome to, if only he would spare the plates, glasses, &c. In order that these should not be broken, Didymusa hauled the basket over the foot of the bed, and there let it rest. As soon as we had settled ourselves once more, we were startled by a loud thud, as of something heavy falling upon the floor. The deaf and dumb boy had, in fact, tumbled off his mattress, and was now groping about the floor to find it again. This lasted for some time, till presently he crawled under our bed, where eventually he went to sleep again. On the whole we felt extremely thankful to see daylight at four o'clock, soon afterwards being called by mine host, who inquired whether we wanted breakfast. But as the meal in course of preparation did not smell very appetising, we decided to wait until we reached Fort Worth.

Mine host then performed his ablutions just outside our window, and when he had finished with the towel threw it into the room.

" There's plenty of water down here if you want a wash," he cried, but in all the circumstances we postponed this operation also, until we arrived at our destination, making haste to take our departure from this hotel which had been so strongly recommended to us.

The poor little deaf and dumb boy and his dog escorted us to the station, looking harmless enough by daylight, though they had not added to the comfort of the night. The boy smiled at us in quite a friendly manner, and we bestowed the remnant of chicken on the dog.

In due course we arrived at Fort Worth, and entering the right train this time, changed cars at Hempstead at 4.30, resuming the journey at two o'clock.

More than half the population of Hempstead seemed to be negroes. A " nigger " dance had recently taken place, and the ladies dresses were curious to behold, although not to be compared with their coiffures ; which uncomfortable and elaborate arrangements being once well " fixed " would be retained for a fortnight. Their owners sometimes spend the first few nights in chairs for fear of disarranging them.

The country about Hempstead seemed to be marvellously productive, but the moist, hot climate was very different from the fine dry air of the higher altitude in our part of Texas. They told us at the restaurant that quinine was always served with meals, and drunk as a matter of course by the inhabitants.

After another change of cars at Austin, where there was time only to get the baggage rechecked, we arrived at last at our favourite San Antonio. From the depot to the St. Leonard's Hotel we travelled by the new electric cars. The swiftly galloping mules have now disappeared, the whole system of street railways, more than forty miles in length, being driven by electric motors.

We did sleep soundly that night! So soundly and so late that we nearly missed breakfast the following morning.

———oo∗o∗oo———

CHAPTER XXII.

RETURN TO JUNCTION CITY — FLOOD — SETTLING
IN OUR NEW HOME—TARANTULA—WEEVILS—
SERENADERS.

WE devoted a day at San Antonio to the selection of furniture for our new house, not buying anything very elaborate;
chairs, tables, bedsteads; two or three hanging glasses, but
no dressing tables or wardrobes, as we had planned a small
room containing shelves and a cupboard. We purchased
one of the " Early breakfast " cooking stoves, a refrige-
rator, a " Paragon " freezing machine for making ices, and
to complete the list, a New England piano.

Louis, the former driver, had found more lucrative
employment in San Antonio since we were last on the stage.
There had been a serious flood during our absence, which
hindered the freighting of my lumber, and the last exploit
of Louis was to ride the fifty-five miles with the in-mail,
swimming his horse across the swollen creeks. The last of
these was so deep and dangerous that the mail bags were
taken across in a boat, Louis being compelled to pass the
night at a ranch on the other side.

I was acquainted with the new driver, H. M., of
Junction City, who, knowing that I liked to handle the
" lines," expressed his intention of taking things easily for
once, and insisted on turning the reins over to me.

I felt quite proud to drive the stage, but as the heavy
brake required to be constantly on and off over the broken
ground, it proved more than I could comfortably manage

with the full team, so that Didymusa clambered to the off side, and acted as a very efficient brakesman.

One of the passengers, who carried a baby in her arms, made some demur at this change of drivers, but seeing that we went along pretty steadily, became gradually reassured, especially when the deposed driver, being fond of little children, relieved her of her burden from time to time. Some Mexican freighters, who passed us on the road, seeing the driver inside the stage, and the lines and brake in the hands of two señoritas, reported on their arrival that he had either broken his arm or become seriously ill.

Owing to the detention of our lumber, and the soaking it had received in the flood, the building of the new house had been retarded, and we took up our quarters at the City Hotel. Tony had drawn the cedar poles for the lot and granary buildings, and, these being so far finished, was helping to nail on the shingles ; but three weeks passed before the house was ready to receive us.

There was a pump in the lot, with an ample supply of water ; but this was " real mean," a term applied in Texas to anything disagreeable or not quite as it should be. Even the horses refused this water, unless they were starved into drinking it, and it subsequently proved utterly useless for culinary purposes. Potatoes boiled in it came out black. Tony had been compelled to cart water every day from the river.

Many domiciles being provided with wooden rain-water tanks or underground cisterns supplied by troughs from the roofs, &c., I decided to have one of these, and Mr. Archer undertook to build a stone and cemented cistern underground, capable of holding some thousands of gallons, supplied by large troughs which carried off the water all round the house. This cistern certainly proved a " joy for

ever." We soon acquired a taste for soft water; it was
deliciously cold, even on the hottest summer's day, and, as
there were no sooty chimneys, it ran from the roof as clear
as crystal. We always used to lower butter, melons, &c. to
cool in the underground cistern.

Being told that the water of the despised well possessed
valuable alkaline properties, I sent a specimen to Dr.
Kennedy, of San Antonio. But as his fee for making a
quantitative analysis was $100, and I entertained consider-
able doubts as to the actual medicinal virtues of the water,
although it tasted certainly not unlike Vichy or Contrexe-
ville, I preferred to let the money go towards the cistern.

We had not long to wait for its filling, as a few weeks
later there was another extraordinary flood. If it had
arisen from both the North and South Llanos, the
lower end of the town must have been carried completely
away. In this case, as in the last, it fortunately only came
from the South Llano—above Paint Rock, whence, after
very heavy rains the water pours down as if a reservoir had
suddenly burst in the sky; filling the dry ravines, and
carrying everything before it.

I felt thankful to find that my land was sufficiently
high and dry and far from both rivers to escape inundation,
but in the lower parts of the town, a perfect panic set in.
All kinds of vehicles were made ready to transport the
unhappy owners of the threatened houses, with all their
worldly goods, to the higher ground amongst the mountains, whilst men anxiously watched the rising waters.

Some had been already washed away with their shanties
one poor old man being saved by climbing a tree, on which
he remained for twenty-eight hours, when Tony swam out
to it, and with help, succeeded in rescuing him in a state
of extreme exhaustion. Tony himself was the principal

P

sufferer in consequence of this exploit; being liable to chills and fevers from that day forth; never in fact entirely free from them.

The country below us presented a curious panorama; one huge lake, with all kinds of debris floating on its surface; tree tops and house-roofs just visible above it. A nearer view showed the rushing turbulent waters, bearing along large trees, tables, bedding, dead cattle, and an empty cradle! The flood did not rise to the principal plaza, although our friends at the Stores were expecting it; having piled their goods upon the highest shelves, and taken every precaution in case of the worst. Such a flood had not occurred within the memory of man, and another so serious might not be experienced in a century. It made a deep impression upon the dwellers of the lower part of the town near the creek on the Kerville road, and those who could afford to do so, immediately entered into negotiations for plots at the western end of the town, and set to work to remove their houses.

Before many weeks, open spaces on the opposite side of the road in front of us, were occupied by the Recorder and several of the most important inhabitants. It was curious to watch the removal of the houses, the great expense being " gitting of it thar."

It would be raised by means of levers, and shifted on to a kind of raft upon wheels, drawn by forty yoke of oxen, mules, and horses combined, the moving houses looking curiously comical. Nothing inside them was disturbed, and on arriving at their new sites they were simply placed on wooden or stone blocks previously erected to receive them.

Simultaneously with the completion of our dwelling-place arrived the crockery, &c., from San Francisco, and the furniture from San Antonio; fortunately everything was safely bestowed before this second inundation.

So marvellous are the recuperative powers of Texas that, beyond the loss of some fine timber, and the alteration in the course of the river and creeks, all traces of disaster soon disappeared, log huts occupying the sites recently vacated by the wealthier citizens.

The most serious result of the flood, as far as I was concerned, was the cutting off of irrigation, the dam having been carried away. This had been built in the form of a horseshoe, which the Boss said was a mistake, since the water had more power to carry the dam away as it rushed in. The reconstruction of the dam was a considerable expense to the town, and a good deal of difference of opinion existed as to its most desirable form.

Camp meetings were now in full swing, and the builder, Mr. Lightfoot, expostulated on account of my abstention. He was one of the preachers at Union Church, and evidently regarded me as a shocking reprobate. The Boss of Lechuza Ranch was hastening the building of an Episcopalian church, to the expense of which he had largely contributed, and Mr. Lightfoot could not understand why I did not attend his services until this church should be completed. When I offered reasons he demanded whether we should not all meet in heaven. I replied that such was my hope, but silently prayed that the angels might wave their wings over us, and cry: " Circulez, circulez, messieurs!" if ever Messrs. Lightfoot and Company and I found ourselves together in Paradise !

He did not believe, he said, that either niggers or Mexicans had souls; an excellent illustration of the estimation in which the latter are held in Texas !

I could not help retorting that his own chance of heaven might be problematical; whereupon he informed the city that the Episcopalians entertained some "mighty queer notions—especially Miss Jaques!"

A few mornings after we were settled in our new abode, Didymusa calling me rather frantically. I hurried to the spot to find her in pursuit of a snake with brilliant red and yellow markings—the king snake, venomous, but possessing the merit of being a mortal enemy of the rattlesnake. Seizing some splintered wood, which remained from the lumber used in building the house, we succeeded in beating in the snake's head till it was killed. When Didymusa skinned it, she found it had recently swallowed a rattlesnake. Glued upon a board and varnished, the skin made an excellent specimen. We never saw another king snake at "The Field," but later on the same day, walking with Tony to the maize patch, where harvesting had begun, we came across the dreaded tarantula (the Texan *Mygale Hentzii*). We had frequently seen the *Nephila plumipes* (silk spider) and had heard that this hairy monster, the tarantula, was often found in Texas, though we had never met with one till now. They seemed abundant under the fruit trees and amongst the weeds, and, not having a particular affection for any kind of spider, I betrayed some concern, till Tony assured me they were not likely to make their way into the house. But he considered the bite of the tarantula almost as bad as that of a rattlesnake, although a thin shoe or even a glove affords protection against it.

Tony was very intelligent; anxious for any kind of information, and I told him of the origin of the name at Tarentum in Italy, and that formerly, the bite was believed to cause a malady comparable to hydrophobia. I explained that the Italians used to place implicit faith in music as a

OUR WAGGON AND TEAM.

sovereign remedy, and how that the learned Boglivi wrote a treatise wherein he gravely designated the particular airs to be played for each symptom as it was exhibited by the victim of a bite.

I often played Heller's Tarantelle from memory, and Tony, who was fond of music, would repeat it on his French harp.

In Texas they prefer whisky to music as an anti-dote, though the spirit sometimes causes a worse smart than the tarantula! As there were a number of large wasps (*Pompilus formosus*, or tarantula killer), we hoped these would keep the tarantulas under.

A smaller kind of wasp, a species of *Pepœus*, formerly known as "mud-daubers," soon began to form their nests in the corners of the rooms and on the woodwork of the gallery. The cells were constructed of mud and grouped in large masses; the female first paralysing spiders with her sting, and afterwards giving them as food to the larvæ. A mud-dauber will not attack a taran-tula.

Tony had kept my team in "fine fix" during our absence, but whilst admiring Dandy, regarded him as an indifferent worker. Dandy had "cut up" on one occasion when Tony was going to ride him, and given a display of his pitching powers, so that Tony looked very doubtful the first time he was called upon to saddle the horse for my own use, until, seeing how well he carried me, he came to the conclusion that Dandy ought not to be employed for heavy draught purposes. Eventually, I bought other horses to take his place and kept Dandy entirely for my own use. I became the owner of "Monte," a flea-bitten brown, who took the wheeler's place with Button. Monte was young, and had never been in harness, but after being hitched up in the waggon by Tony and his brother, he gave very little trouble.

We derived some amusement in trying the various animals offered to complete our team, these being loaned before the completion of an actual purchase.

The Texans are sensible enough never to use their saddle horses for collar-work, unless this is very light, knowing that it often causes stiffness, whereas flexibility of the shoulders is absolutely essential in a cow-pony.

Mr. J., an experienced ranchman, warned me against using Dandy for draught purposes if I intended to ride him myself. The animal was far too good for slow work, and it was amusing to see Tony on one occasion (before the horse was taken from field work) trying to harrow in a patch of rye which he had planted for winter fodder; Dandy pacing along at about seven miles an hour; poor Tony's long legs moving almost at a run, in his efforts to keep up.

Besides the rye and wheat we grew a patch of millet, some of which was cut and dried and stored in the granary, proving extremely useful as fodder during the winter.

There are several kinds of weevils in Texas: the plum weevil, the nut and grain weevils, &c., all great pests, infesting everything and destroying a good deal of Indian corn. An excellent means to circumvent them is to gather early, pulling the shucks with the corn, using plenty of water and at least one and a-half bushels of salt to every hundred pounds of grain, pressing the whole tightly into the crib to form a compact mass. The water generates sufficient heat to kill the imprisoned weevils, whilst others are unable to penetrate the bulk of corn unless rats lead the way. All corn cribs should be rat-proof. Moreover, the salt is by no means wasted, as cattle and horses eat the

"THE FIELD"—OUR NEW ABODE.

shucks, which should be pulled to pieces, and are more nutritious than fodder.

A lot of work had to be done in " The Field " before the busy pruning time. Mr. Taylor, having left the Lechuza, became one of our hands to assist Tony. When once fairly settled, of course, we gave the customary house-warming, causing offence by extending our invitations to a Mexican family of good birth. But this breach of Texan etiquette was apparently condoned before many weeks, or we should not have been favoured with a serenade, which is always a sign of great popularity.

We generally retired about ten o'clock, and it was mid-night before the buggy arrived with the night warblers and their banjoes and lanterns. It is the custom to invite the serenaders to enter and offer them refreshment, but on first awakening we could not imagine what was happening, and before we had time to decide how to act or make our-selves presentable, the music ceased and the musicians departed.

All the ditties were of a sentimental character, some being very pretty and remarkably well rendered. The following are favourite songs on such occasions :

ONE TOUCH OF THE HAND.

Thine eyes, like the stars that are gleaming,
  Have entered the depths of my soul,
And my heart has grown wild with its beating,
  And my feelings I cannot control.
Still, still do I love, do I fear thee,
  Would keep thee, yet beg thee to go,
One touch of the hand makes me tremble
  And recalls all the sorrows of yore.

Why once again have I met thee ?
  Why is this sorrow now mine ?
In vain do I strive to forget thee
  But my soul is enslaved into thine.

Still, still do I love, do I fear thee,
  Would keep thee, yet beg thee to go,
One touch of the hand makes me tremble
  And recalls all the sorrows of yore.

THE SPANISH CAVALIER.

A Spanish cavalier stood in his retreat
  And on his guitar played a tune, dear,
The music so sweet, they'd ofttimes repeat
    The blessing of my country and you, dear.
    Say, darling, say when I'm far away,
      Sometimes you may think of me, dear,
    Bright sunny days will soon fade away,
      Remember what I say and be true, dear.

I am off to the war, to the war I must go,
  To fight for my country and you, dear,
But if I should fall in vain I would call
  The blessing of my country and you, dear.

And when the war is o'er to you I'll return
  Back to my country and you, dear,
But if I be slain, you may seek me in vain,
  Upon the battle field you will find me.
    Say, darling, say, when I'm far away,
      Sometimes you may think of me, dear,
    Bright sunny days will soon fade away,
      Remember what I say and be true, dear.

Her eyes as bright as bright can be
Like sun rays on a summer sea.

Her hair is like a sunset crown
O'er fields of wheat just turning brown,

And in her lips the mantling blood
Is like a pomegranate bud.

Her heart is true as true can be
Like some staunch oak beside the sea.

And her small hands are pearl and pink
Like peach blooms by a river's brink.

Her voice is like a gentle breeze
Borne through the languid laurel trees.

But oh ! her soul, that few may know,
Is strong as fire, and pure as snow.

CHAPTER XXIII.

DOMESTIC LIFE AT "THE FIELD" — "FURIOUS RIDING THROUGH THE TOWN STREETS" — MASONIC FUNERAL — PREPARATIONS FOR CHRISTMAS.

As the lumber of which the house was built had been saturated during its freightage, to say nothing of the effect of the subsequent heavy rains, we decided to leave the interior varnishing and exterior decoration until all became thoroughly dry. But everything in this regard was ready for the finishing touches a few weeks later, when Mr. Lightfoot arrived with " a colour sheet," from which the " trimmings " (outside painting, &c.) were to be selected.

Then our cosy home began to look very pretty, and the various domestic arrangements afforded ample occupation. Instead of dressing-tables, we placed our own trunks upon reversed crates, decorating them with chintz. Mrs. Boss was kind enough to stitch the light counterpanes, sheets, tablecloths, art muslin window curtains, &c., with her sewing machine, whilst we fixed shelves, supported by small brackets, in the corners of the rooms beneath the hanging glasses.

Although we made one batch of yeast-cakes, we found the " Twin Brother " or " National," which we bought at San Antonio, better and lighter. As the late peaches were still ripening, we preserved a quantity, and not yet having received our " early breakfast stove," boiled them in the open, in a copper cauldron lent for the occasion by Tony's mother—the " Groszmütter," as we named her.

It was a somewhat difficult process ; the preserve *would* boil too quickly, and the strong breeze fanned the flames so fiercely that we were compelled to remain at a respectful distance from the cauldron and to stir its contents with a long pole.

The Groszmütter waxed excited when the flames rose from the fiercely-burning cedar logs, but, although my German is not very good, I succeeded in calming her to some extent, and, notwithstanding that the increasing power of the sun towards afternoon made the general heat almost unbearable, she snatched the pole from me and Didymusa, and with cries of " Cocket, Cocket ! " valiantly took her turn at the stirring.

Tony's mother was unable to read, but listened with great enjoyment when I read aloud from the devotional books she lent to me. I could read quite fluently and hope that she translated them for her own benefit ; at all events she complimented me upon my " pretty accent," and declared I was a " booful reader."

During the evenings, we always had music or a rubber of whist ; friends constantly looked in from the city, or if they failed, we could make up our own set. Tony taught us a German game " Sixty-six," at which he was an adept ; also euchre, poker, nap, monte, and others ; we reciprocating by teaching him whist, at which he " caught on " at once and soon became an excellent player. The Groszmütter, also, we initiated, but on joining our party, she grew so excited that it was advisable to make Tony her partner, he being more successful in subduing his mother. On one occasion when she held a fine hand of trumps and he persistently ignored her signals, so that she could not obtain the lead, she could restrain herself no longer, but throwing up her arms, exclaimed: "Toany, Toany, spielen sie trumpen, Toany!"

Being a staunch Catholic, she looked upon the proceedings at the camp-meetings with profound dislike. We could hear the incessant singing and praying, and the high-pitched voices of the preachers quite distinctly at the house. Entering the field at her side one evening we saw the Groszmütter flitting about amongst the shrubs in a white, or at least, a very light dress, and told her she looked like a ghost. Not quite understanding, she shook her head with a determined:

"Nein, nein, kein Heiligen Geist dahin": referring to the camp-meeting.

A kind of tournament was to be held at Christmas, and, there being a hint of some ladies' races, Mr. Taylor and I used to try our horses on a nice little track "back of" the town; whereupon I received the following letter from Mr. J. R.:

DEAR MISS JAQUES—

I have heard from two or three people this morning that you are liable to be arrested for furious riding by galloping and racing through the town streets. The Sheriff's attention has been called to it, and I thought I would inform you, so that it would not come as a surprise when you did it again.

Yours truly,

J—— R——.

It is against the laws to ride furiously through the town streets or a public highway; in the country lanes it does not matter so much.

So our trial track was a public highway! Well, we had entirely failed to distinguish any difference between "highways" and "country lanes!"

Mr. Taylor pooh-poohed the warning and felt sure no one would appear as a witness against me; but I never repeated our trial races behind the town.

On the first day of the Court sitting shortly afterwards, Mr. Taylor and I rode to a ranch about ten miles below the city to bring up a cow with a week-old calf. Now nothing is more tiresome to drive than a single cow and calf. In the first place the calf gives a lot of running, until it becomes thoroughly exhausted, then it generally " sulls " (sulks), and the fun gives place to a dreary exercise of patience, as you crawl to your destination, riding one on each side of the cow, which creates occasional diversions by turning backwards and frequently taking a wire fence by the way.

We were in the act of passing the city, intending to turn down a side street, when off started the cow, tail in air, at the top of her pace, across the square. It was my business to cut her off and that quickly, as, once give her time to turn, she would soon be back at the river ! After a moment's consideration, off I dashed across the plaza in pursuit, turning the opposite corner and the cow very neatly.

Of course, I was again " riding furiously on a public highway," and right before the eyes of outraged justice ; for I observed persons peering through the very Court House windows. But Judge Martin was immediately " stuck " on my horsemanship, and charged Mr. J. R. (who happened to form one of the jury), with numerous complimentary messages, which were faithfully delivered in due course. The Judge was to be brought to my house and introduced, or I was to go to the Court the next morning and hear him. Alas ! before the next morning judge and jury were under the tables, half seas over ; the usual state of affairs during the opening week. I never met the judge or heard any more about my threatened arrest !

In travelling through the United States I saw no

mendicants, and met with few so-called " charities." The country is remarkably free from pauperism. Mexico, on the other hand, swarms with beggars ; one meets them at every turn and corner.

However poor a Texan may be, he scorns anything in the form of " charity ; " resents all help which is not born of friendly feeling, and offered as from an equal. There is nothing servile about the Texan, and one can but admire their independence of speech and conduct; nor, on the other hand did I perceive the slightest lack of generosity.

As one instance of kindly sympathy and consideration, take the case of a stranger who arrived at Junction City in an advanced stage of consumption. For the first few weeks the fine, dry air worked wonders, but it was only a fitful rally ; to restore the invalid's strength was quite beyond the power even of that fine climate. He was utterly alone, but yet lacked nothing ; every want being satisfied, every luxury provided. Being a Freemason, the brothers of the Lodge (instituted at Junction City only the previous year) took it in turns to sit up with the lonely man till he died. He had not attended the Union Church, and unaware whether he was a member of any particular denomination, they buried him with Masonic rites ; the whole City and the school turning out in gay attire to honour his memory.

We were occupied in clearing away the dinner things as the crowd went on its way to the quiet little graveyard at South Llano, and ran to the gallery to see what was happening. Didymusa and I thought we might as well join the throng, but Mr. Taylor preferred staying at home to wipe up the plates and dishes. After our departure he stood on the gallery watching the crowd for a few minutes, and subsequently told us that it reminded him of a Derby day. The people were riding, driving, walking, running, shouting and pushing, and some, seeing him, shouted " Come on, Taylor. Be quick, hitch up and we'll wait for you."

And the behaviour at the graveyard, to our English eyes, appeared even more unseemly, albeit the scene was extremely picturesque ; the women in their large sun-bonnets, and simple costumes, others in every variety of colour, all prettily grouped about the grave.

It is the curious custom in Texas to let a piece of glass into the coffin, lid in order to afford a last look at the deceased ; who is, of course, buried the same day on which he breathes his last.

The grave was enormously broad, and whilst we stood looking on somewhat bewildered by the surrounding scene, a huge shell was lowered into it, previously having been turned topsy-turvy, with a rattle and bang as it righted itself again. Into this shell the coffin is subsequently lowered.

" Oh, I hope I shall never be buried in Texas," said Didymusa in a subdued whisper.

But at that moment a sudden hush fell upon all the throng, and the cortêge approached the little gateway. The beautiful and impressive hymns and funeral address were somewhat marred by the nasal tones of those who officiated. The coffin was passed under the crossed rods, all the Masons following in procession, each individual afterwards walking round the grave repeating a text from Ecclesiastes xii. v. 7.

" The body returns to the earth as it was; and the Spirit returns to God who gave it."

As we stood about the grave talking, while the crowd dispersed, I mentioned that my father had been a Mason, whereupon some of the brothers joined hands and said, " Hitherto it has been our pleasure, now it is our duty, to protect you."

There was some discussion as to the desirability of instituting a branch of the " Eastern Star," at Junction City, for women. The wives, widows, and daughters of Masons, only, are eligible for this order, which, without making women Masons, communicates, under a solemn pledge of honour, the secrets of the Eastern Star degrees. Thus they make themselves known to Masons—an advantage all the world over in time of need.

Already I had been introduced to some ladies of this order at San Antonio, and regretted that I could not join it, but this was impossible without access to private papers in England, to prove that my father was a Mason, although I believe the Secretary wrote to Madras, where he was initiated and took the order of Royal Arch.

December and a temperature of 90°! It was difficult to realise that the cakes, plum puddings, and mincemeat were actually intended for Christmas! Our willing helpers were many, but, the materials being difficult to manipulate during the heat of the day, we generally left the stoning of plums, suet chopping, &c., until evening.

Our great cake (8lb. weight) had an icing of pecan, instead of almond : chocolate surmounted by white, with designs in small sugar-plums—undertaken by Mr. Taylor.

Didymusa railed at us as untidy and easily-tired workers, but if the boys once began she made them stick to it, turning a deaf ear to all hints concerning music or whist by way of a change. The groceries were mostly freighted up from Kerville, sugar crystalised in large barrels costing ten cents a pound. It was difficult to keep the large red ants out of it, and the only effectual barrier was water, which they never care to cross. Their bite is a thing to remember !

Amidst our preparations for Christmas, Tony came in one day in a state of high excitement with news that his brother had seen some deer and numbers of wild turkeys. A hunting expedition was hastily organised, and as the deer had been seen in the neighbourhood of San Saba, whence we had received an invitation to a ranch, we persuaded our friends to meet us on the road. The prospect of camping out under the full moon appeared delightful ; so we locked up the house, packed the necessary provisions and utensils to cook them, with guns and ammunition, in the waggon, which, for the first time, carried its bows and full white sheet to protect us in the case of a Norther. Didymusa, who, being liable to rheumatism, was allowed a mattress, went in the waggon with Tony, whilst Mr. Taylor and I rode.

Tony, being the huntsman, crept off quietly alone the first evening, and lay concealed for a time near some water, but returned without seeing the deer. However, he intended to try again the next morning ; and before day-break we heard him release the horses, which were staked close at hand. As the birds began to twitter with the earliest dawn, we distinctly distinguished the report of a Winchester. Knowing that Tony would not return just yet, we postponed lighting the fire and preparing breakfast and set forth in an opposite direction bent on quail shooting. On and on we walked, wishing for a good dog to retrieve the quail, which are nearly the same colour as the ground and often run some little distance before dropping.

Suddenly it occurred to us that we ought to be return-ing to camp ; also that we had completely lost our bearings ! We were now in a locality strange both to Mr.

Q

Taylor and myself ; Menard County, wild and desolate ; each mountain looking much the same as any other to our unfamiliar eyes. Although our cartridges, both for the Winchester and the shot gun were running short, we thought we would have a little practice in the hope of attracting Tony's attention. Mr. Taylor threw up his large sombrero for Didymusa and me to shoot at, and the one kind of cartridges exhausted, we placed a white stone in a dead tree and fired at that. After this long-range practice, there was a pause. Didymusa offered her little charm (a compass) to Mr. Taylor, and when he declared that such a toy was useless, lay down at full length under the tree, which was not a juniper.

"Oh, I do wish I had had my breakfast before we started!" she cried, when, as she ceased her lament, Mr. Taylor, who had climbed to the topmost branch, announced that he saw an approaching object. Tony, for Tony it proved to be, coolly told us that we had been walking straight away from the camp ; and although some excuse might have been made, as the morning was dull and the sun invisible, he evidently regarded us with not a little contempt.

Having been bred in Texas, he knew every stunted bush, blade of grass, stick, and stone on the prairie for two or three hundred miles around. We retaliated by chaffing him about the deer which he had missed ; but he had made a good bag of wild turkeys, and one of these was over the camp fire instead of the promised venison steak— a capital breakfast and thoroughly well earned, as Didymusa thought. Before the meal was over, we began to feel an approaching Norther, and, hastily packing up our things, got under way, not having gone far before sleet fell, accompanied by intense cold. We should have been frozen in our saddles, so Dandy was tied behind the waggon with Mr. Taylor's pony, and creeping under the hospitable tilt, we were glad of the protection of rugs and blankets, brought for such emergency.

There were several miles to drive before we reached the Los Moras ranch, where we ultimately arrived, half frozen, to receive a hearty welcome and enjoy hot toddies by the blazing cedar logs.

Our kind host and hostess were French, as also their partner, who played the mandolin. As night fell the Norther ceased, and the morning was as genial as usual.

This ranch was beautifully situated, well watered, and near some fine timber. There are said to be oysters with pink pearls in the San Saba river, by which we had a picnic ; but the large kind of bivalve with a pretty shell, found on this occasion, contained a pearl of a yellowish-white tint.

We returned home by a different route, and, though we saw little game, were blessed with two ideal nights for camping, played whist by moonlight, eked out by that of the camp fire, and were joined for a little while by a posse of cowboys, one of whom possessed a fine tenor voice. He threw a great deal of pathos into the simple ditty, in a minor key, which seems to be the cowboys' favourite. I am sorry I could not succeed in obtaining a copy of the music.

" Oh bury me not on the lone prairie,"
  Those words came low and mournfully
  From the pallid lips of the youth who lay
  On his dying couch at the close of day.

He wailed in pain till o'er his brow
  Death's shades were fast gathering now.
  He thought of his home and his dear girl nigh ;
  And the cowboys gathered around to see him die.

22822

" Oh bury me not on the lone prairie,
 With the turkey, buzzard, and coyote,
 In a narrow grave six foot by three,
 Oh bury me not on the lone prairie.

" In fancy I listen to the well-known words
 Of the free wild winds and the song of the birds;
 I think of home and the cottage in the bower,
 And the scenes I loved in my childhood's hour.

" It matters not, so I've often been told,
 Where the body is laid when the heart is cold;
 Yet grant, oh grant this boon to me,
 And bury me not on the lone prairie.

" I had hoped to lie in the old churchyard,
 Down by my native home on the green hill side;
 By the side of my father, oh let my grave be,
 And bury me not on the lone prairie.

" Oh, then, bury me not on the lone prairie,
 In a narrow grave, six foot by three,
 Where the buffalo paws o'er a prairie grave,
 And the wild coyotes will howl over me.

" Let my death slumber be where a mother's prayer
 And a sister's tear will be mingled there,
 Where friends will gather to help bury me;
 Oh bury me not on the lone prairie."

" There is another whose tears will be shed for him
 Who lies on the prairie bed in the hour of pain.
 She is the joy of my heart while I speak of her now;
 She has curled these locks, she has kissed this brow.

" These locks she has curled, shall the rattlesnake kiss?
 This brow she has kissed, shall the cold grave press?
 For the sake of the lov'd ones that will weep for me,
 Oh bury me not on the lone prairie.

" She has been in my dreams" — but his voice fail'd
   there;
 And they gave no heed to his prayer.
 In a narrow grave, six foot by three,
 They buried him there on the lone prairie.

Where the dew-like wings of the butterfly rest,
And the wild flowers bloom o'er the prairie's crest;
Where the wild coyotes and the winds sport free,
On a wet saddle blanket lay a cow-boy-ee.

Shortly afterwards we were sorry to hear that the singer had been struck by lightning and killed whilst riding with the herd.

Our round of Christmas festivities lasted more than a fortnight. "Santa Claus" appeared at about three o'clock in the morning in the form of Tony, staggering under the weight of two large linen-baskets. As he was surreptitiously conveying them to the dining-room, Didymusa arrived on the scene in night attire, candle in hand, to ascertain the time, but Tony crept out without a word.

Honour forbade us to examine the linen-basket at once, but on rising early to prepare for our large dinner party at noon, one basket was found to contain fireworks, the other a beautifully painted breakfast service, a case of Atkinson's perfumes, champagne, bonbons, with nicely arranged baskets of candies, besides sundry scarves, shawls, and "fascinators."

The Groszmütter and Tony joined us at dinner, curious to taste the Christmas pudding, which they had seen in embryo. "Gut!" was their verdict; and besides the pudding we had a fine turkey and roast sucking-pig— neither of them wild.

Needless to say, we remembered our friends in the old country. At Junction City time is nearly seven hours later than in London, so that we pictured those at home still sleeping soundly in their beds, presently to turn out on a cold, raw, frosty morning; while we in Texas were revelling in glorious sunshine.

At two o'clock began the races, of an amusingly nondescript character—horses, ponies of all ages and sizes, carrying any weight, and ridden with or without saddle, as the case might be. " Lifting the rings" afforded an opportunity to display some neat horsemanship, but our champion had drunk not wisely, but too well, and, actually seeing double, remained under the impression that he had all the rings on his pole, when there was but one. Expostulation regarding his condition provoked the retort that he was not " quite gone ; only seven-eighths ! "

Another dexterous feat is to pick up a hat, a handkerchief, or even a dollar, from the ground at full gallop. The ladies race fell through as there were too few entries.

Before tea and the subsequent display of fireworks, we all set to work clearing away and washing up the dinner things ; surely there was never before so merry a party of butlers, cooks, parlour maids, and footmen !

The fame of our Roman candles, rockets, and fire-balloons spread in due course as far as San Antonio. But after the display, when our friends went to prepare for the dance at the court house, leaving us to obtain a little rest before doing the same, we discovered that the roof of the gallery was on fire. We tried to extinguish the flames with wet towels, and fortunately our shouts for help were heard by Tony and also by a neighbour on his way to the dance ; who handed up pails of water to Tony on the roof, so that between them they put out the fire without much damage.

CHAPTER XXIV.

PRUNING FRUIT TREES—MR. TWOHIG'S IMPRISON-
MENT AND ESCAPE—COST OF FUEL—STOCK
YARDS, &c., AT SAN ANTONIO—SURVEYING AND
ASSESSMENT—PELON DOG—CATAMOUNT AND
OTHER PETS—TEXAN AND MEXICAN WEDDINGS.

———

THE pruning began with the New Year and lasted for
several weeks. It ought to have been wisely done—there
being assuredly a multitude of counsellors. We had
several volunteers to help us, superintended by Mr. Bolt, a
young Englishman of great experience in the old country ;
Mr. Van Buren (from Rochester, New York), who had seen
a good deal of fruit-growing, cautioned him not to prune
too *hard*, shade being desirable in so hot a country, and
also advised the application of linseed-oil wherever the
pruning-knife had been used, to prevent canker. Didymusa
and I, accordingly, followed the pruners with brushes and
oil-cans.

Whilst using his left hand to an awkward branch,
Mr. Taylor's knife slipped, inflicting a terrible gash across
his right knuckle. Once more our Ambulance knowledge
proved useful, although for the first few days we had a very
anxious time, and Mr. Taylor could not use his right hand
for several weeks. He was extremely apt with his left, however, and happily our fear of a stiff joint was not realised.

Mr. Grantham, the clergyman of the Episcopalian

Church, came our way every three months, having the use
of Union Church until his own should be finished. The
Holy Communion was celebrated in our drawing-room at
" The Field."

Having enjoyed our first experience of camping, and
there being nothing in particular to detain us at home, we
determined to spend Easter at San Antonio, driving all the
way in the waggon, and resting the team two nights at
Kerville.

The cotton season extends from August to April, and
the roads were alive with wool-freighters, San Antonio
being the most important primary wool market in the
Union. Its average receipts amount to 9,000,000lb. a
year, or about 15,000 bags.

Between Boerne and Leon springs we found very
picturesque sleeping places—one near the Aransas Pass
railroad and a bridge. When the evening train passed,
the young horse Monte was so terrified that we thought
he would break away from the picket, in spite of all
attempts to quiet him. He managed to cut his fetlock
with a rope, and went lame the next day ; but fortunately
we were not far from our destination. Button and Dandy
had enjoyed previous experience of trains at Kerville.

The ladies of the " Eastern Star " were extremely
courteous, and amongst other pleasant expeditions we
undertook one to the old aqueduct, about four miles from
the city, which now forms a picturesque ruin.

The aqueduct was constructed by the Fathers of the
Order of St. Francis, in order to supply the missions and
the fields and gardens cultivated by the Indians under the
directions of the friars, who were astute enough to perceive
that these people must be taught to work before they
could be converted. The irrigating ditches, which reticu-

late the river valley, offer ample evidence of the practical nature of the teaching of these missionaries.

The Alamo Monumental Society aims, as I was deeply interested to learn, at restoring the Alamo Church to its original form, and adorning its walls with fitting memorials of those who died beside them. First-rate artists are to be employed, and the incidents of the massacre of the Alamo and other contests during the rising against Mexico are to be commemorated by a shaft of granite or marble.

Stirring stories abound of Indian raids and the Mexican feuds and revolutions which attracted to Texas the bold, lawless, and restless spirits of the South-Western border of the Union, together with numerous adventurers from foreign parts. Mr. Twohig, a prominent banker, still survives to relate the following story, for the most part from personal experience as an actor, not merely an eye-witness.

Before the uprising of the Texans, Mr Twohig, then a storekeeper at San Antonio (the city being held by the Mexican general Cos against the patriot army of Burleston), was imprisoned and sentenced to be shot, together with Maverick and Cox, for signalling to the besiegers. The gallant Milam (himself cut down in the heat of the conflict) and his comrades, saved the condemned men from the consequence of this " pernicious activity " in the cause of freedom. Those familiar with the story of Texas can easily recall the fact that even after it secured independence, its inhabitants were frequently harrassed by Mexican raiders.

Mr. Twohig was one of those abducted and spirited over the border by General Woll in 1842. The ancient enemy was perhaps the more incensed because he had deliberately blown up his store, thus destroying certain hopes of booty. Mr. Twohig, therefore, with Maverick and others, was carried to Vera Cruz in chains and immured in the castle of Perote—a sufficiently tragic experience, no doubt, but, in the manner of their escape, not devoid of an element of comedy. The prisoners were kept at hard labour, an indignity which Mr. Twohig resented so vigorously that the result was solitary confinement.

Now he began to form his plans to obtain freedom, not for himself alone, but for all his fettered companions. While the others were rigorously kept to their appointed tasks, he tunnelled with infinite pains and patience the massive walls of the fortress, only to discover at the last moment that the opening was much too small to allow one of the prisoners, Major Colquhoun, whose captivity had only served to increase his natural girth, to pass through. Once more the tedious task was resumed, the opening at length became sufficiently large and the escape was finally accomplished. Mr. Twohig evaded his pursuers in the guise of a native pedlar, bearing upon his head through the streets of Vera Cruz a tray of *tamales* and *peloncillos*, and at length made his way to New Orleans with safety on the same ship as the officers sent out to recapture him. The better to guard against arrest, after his escape from Castle Peroto, he joined a company of Mexican bandits, a gentry whose influence in those adventurous days was considerable.

Into the treasury of this fraternity he paid the regular initiation fee of 750 dollars, but on severing the connection about a week later, the money, contrary to custom, was returned. The explanation of this unusual act of generosity Mr. Twohig laughingly leaves to the imagination of his hearers.

When the state was admitted to the Union and all the tribulations of the Texans were ended by annexation, he scaled the tower of the old Cathedral of San Fernando, and was the first to fling to the breeze at San Antonio the starry emblem of Liberty and Union.

For over fifty years as merchant, banker, and citizen, he has evinced an unswerving loyalty to the principles of progress, whether its manifestations were merely material or that more sublime inspiration which has made the brief history of the Lone Star Republic that he helped to make " an epopee of ages."

A fire is required only during two or three months in the year at San Antonio (and then but occasionally), yet the cost of fuel for cooking purposes is a matter of great importance, the price of wood being higher than in many backwood towns, although moderate compared to that charged in St. Louis, Chicago, or Milwaukee. Oak is delivered to the customer at five dollars fifty cents to six dollars the cord. Cut and split stove wood, dry and good, was to be seen in enormous quantities in Burleston Street, near the Southern Pacific depôt, where we saw it being carried from the splitter by elevators into boxes, which hold from one to two cords each. These boxes are elevated so that the delivery waggon can be driven under and loaded in a few minutes. With this cutting and splitting plant the firm can deliver to consumers from fourteen to seventeen cords of stove wood a day. The wood yards are only busy about four months in the year, during that time about 150 cords of wood per day are being consumed in the city. Coal is consumed to some extent and is brought from the Lignite Company at Lytle Texas, where there is a vein of pure dry lignite five feet thick and seventy deep. Its heating power is considerably less than that of the coal from the Indian Territory, a ton rendering the same service as a cord of the best dry post oak wood. Anthracite coal also comes from the San

Antonio and Indian Territory Fuel Company, but is not so extensively used.

Mr. Taylor bought a pretty pair of young sorrels at the enormous stock yards, which are well worth a visit. No other market in the South-West can boast of so great a traffic in horses and horned cattle, San Antonio being the central point for all Southern and Western Texas. The average sales include 100,000 head, while some transactions (not requiring the intervention of a middleman) do not figure in the books. In 1890 the shipments by rail for all kinds of live stock were 91,058 head.

We found quite a curiosity shop at Mr. Whichel's, the English bootmaker, who made me a smart pair of riding boots, much to my satisfaction, as those I brought with me were really giving out. Mr. Whichel was also a taxidermist, and besides stuffing and mounting many of our trophies, made up some of the snake skins into belts.

He was in the habit of keeping live rattlesnakes in a basket until he wanted them, and used to be very venturesome in handling the reptiles, until one day his head came within reach of their strike, and he was ill for several days.

At Harnisch and Baer's, besides a very cordial welcome and the best ice cream shake they could mix for us, we were favoured with their best recipe for ice creams in return for the pleasure afforded by an account of our travels in California—though it was a second edition !

The pleasant Zoological Gardens include an interesting museum, but not a large collection of animals ; a catamount or lynx had recently been captured with four kittens; she was very fierce and flew savagely at the bars of the cage on our approach. I bought two of the kittens and as we were leaving early the following morning, arranged to pick them up as we passed. The keeper had not previously told us that the kittens could not feed themselves, but, progress being slow through the streets of the city, Mr. Taylor ran back to buy a baby's feeding bottle at a chemist's shop. On the way home we lost one of them, not being able to obtain fresh milk and the kittens refusing condensed milk.

But when Mr. Taylor offered the survivor a bird, shot for the purpose, and laid on the top of its box, it was immediately seized and dragged through the opening, and on this kind of food the kitten seemed to thrive.

The sorrels, which were said to be broken to saddle and harness, were led behind the waggon, behaving at times in a rather startling manner. When Mr. Taylor hitched them up on our return, they upset the waggon and broke the pole. They proved extremely fractious, and not at all a good bargain, inasmuch as Mr. Taylor eventually sold them at a loss.

About this time the surveyors were busy in all directions, partly in connection with the proposed extension of the railway from Kerville, and partly on behalf of various settlers; the lands subject to pre-emption must be surveyed and recorded at the general land office, the settler agreeing to occupy and improve them for three consecutive years. The whole cost of surveying and land office fees is about $11. The lands available for settlement in Texas are: First, those open to pre-emption; second, railroad and State capital grants now in the market; third, the State school-lands; fourth, those of private owners. Within the first three of these classes some 64,000,000 acres are comprised. By the terms of her admission to the Union, Texas reserved all her public lands, of which she has disposed of some 32,000,000 acres in aid of railroads, and of 3,000,000 acres to the syndicate that built the new

Capitol at Austin. The State, says Land-Commissioner Hall, has about 25,000,000 acres of common school-lands for sale, of which, perhaps, 500,000 acres are valuable for the standing timber; 4,000,000 acres being subject to pre-emption. The assessment on personal property afforded us much amusement on account of the fabulous value given to some articles—the insignificant value to others; the balance at the bank, rings, watches, pianos (exempt for professional players or teachers) cows, horses, pigs, poultry. Mr. L. asked the average number of eggs we had, and reckoning the total for the year, made quite a splendid return; the fact that hens do not lay every day in the year never appearing to occur to him! He also worked out my future crop of millet in a marvellous way. The State and county taxes on real estate of $3000 would run thus:

State *ad valorem*	$4·50
School *ad valorem*	3·75
County *ad valorem*	7·50
County (special)	12·00
District School	6·00
Total tax	$33·75

Property is supposed to be assessed at half its actual value.

We were beginning to acquire quite a menagerie! Besides the domestic cat brought in by Mr. Taylor one evening, slung across his pony in a sack (which for a few days would live nowhere but up the chimney), there was a wolf, the catamount, a pair of squirrels, a pair of raccoons, two long-haired kids, horned frogs, all at large, besides several of the mongrel dogs, and last, but not least, Didymusa's "pelon" (hairless in Spanish.) This dog was given to her by our kind friends at Roca Springs, as a charm against

rheumatism. She certainly suffered less after he became
her constant companion, although I attribute her immunity
to the climate. He was perfectly devoid of hair, blue-black
in colour, Gerino by name ; and at first actually repulsive
as far as I was concerned. But his beautiful symmetry
and great muscular activity gradually won my admiration.

These dogs are described by Humboldt, and were found
by Columbus in the Antilles, by Cortes in Mexico, and by
Pizarro in Peru, under the name of " Perros chinos." It

GERINO.

suffers from the cold of the Cordilleras. It is identical
with the Japanese edible dog, and the Mexican " tamale,"
also, is said to be largely composed of its flesh—a fallacy,
as we never saw a pelon in the City of Mexico, and seldom
when passing through the Interior.

There is another kind, called by Dr. Duncan "Canis
ingæ," having pointed ears and nose, and in the old Peruvian
graves the skeleton of this dog is sometimes found resting

at the feet of the human mummy, presenting an emblem
of fidelity, frequently employed by the mediæval sculptors."

This breed is distinguished by great ferocity, and will
bite strangers upon the slightest provocation, and even
without any provocation at all—with their masters, too,
they are often surly.

Our pets were all very tame and tractable ; Danger, the
wolf, often following me when riding with the dogs, or to
the meat market, where he was not scrupulous in helping
himself.   At the sight of a stranger, he always disappeared,
making burrows to hide himself in the day-time, and at
night coming out to gambol about the house and gallery,
inflicting white scratches upon Gerino's back, and frequently
stealing honey or butter from the table.   A favourite pastime
of Danger's was to play with one's feet, and, as I often
went about the house stockingless, wearing light sandals,
I hardly enjoyed the game—however, he never hurt me.

The " Mounte " cat grew very handsome.   She always
slept with Didymusa, and gave forth a rich, sonorous purr.
Many persons thought we ran some risk, but she was
extremely affectionate, albeit rather fierce and assertive
where raw meat was concerned.   Occasionally, I brought
up a bag full (costing about ten cents) on Dandy,
" Mounte " meeting me with savage cries of " whack,
whack "—not by any means a " me-ow."

Dandy " knew that sound," having been terrified the
first time " Mounte " tried to climb up his legs ; so I was
in the habit of throwing down the sack and riding off, to
venture near again after she had satisfied her craving.

On one occasion when it was too hot to kill a " beef,"
birds also being scarce, " Mounte " had fasted several days.
We had provided a roasted chicken for dinner, and
happened to turn our backs after it was placed on the table.

" By Jove, our dinner's gone ! " exclaimed Mr. Taylor, and there was " Mounte " walking off with the whole chicken in her mouth !

The squirrels, " Twiddle " and " Twaddle," were very tame, and would carry the pecans from the table and hide them in all kinds of corners ; sometimes filling the large pockets of Mr. Taylor's ulster.

About this time we were invited to two weddings, one bride being a Texan girl with an Englishman for groom, Mr. Ernest W., one of the Lechuza hands, at present filling Tony's place at " The Field " ; Tony having had to give up on account of continual fevers, dating from the rescue of the old man from the tree-top in the flood. Ernest was to take possession of the cottage a few days after the wedding.

The ceremony took place at 8 p.m., a civil marriage, before Judge Aley, who merely asked a few questions and straightway declared the couple " united in the holy bonds of matrimony "—a short and simple process !

Judge Aley was a man of many occupations : performing marriages, making coffins, acting in a judicial capacity, running foot races, selling corn, and " handling " a flourishing store.

It was a beautiful night for the wedding, and, the assembly being large, we all stood round the gallery while the happy pair came forth from the house attended by a bridesmaid. The short ceremony over, they sat down to receive congratulations ; most of the ladies kissing the bride and shaking hands with the bridegroom. After this there were dancing, cards, and supper.

Instead of participating in this gaiety, Didymusa lay stiff and bruised in bed, having been rather severely cut about the eye and ear in a buggy accident the previous

R

Sunday. Mr. J. R. was taking her for a drive, when the gallant greys (from the livery stable) ran away; rather a joke, in the face of her assertion that this pair was " so much nicer and more reliable than my half-broken young team." The buggy was overturned and smashed; Mr. J. R. sprained his foot, he and Didymusa being compelled to wade through a creek and to despatch a messenger to the town for another carriage. Mr. Taylor and I had driven to the wedding, with Dandy in the buggy, through thickly-wooded, rough, rocky country. Over the worst ground we were preceded by two horsemen, holding handkerchiefs as a guide, Judge Aley bringing up the rear in his buckboard. On reaching home, after the ceremony, we found Didymusa in a state of great agitation. The piano had begun to play of its own accord; manifestly an ill omen! However, having laughed at her alarm, we did our best to soothe her.

What with our absence at San Antonio and my extra occupation during Didymusa's illness, the piano had not been opened for more than a month. Well, one evening shortly afterwards, Mr. J. R. limped up to the house as gracefully as his sprained foot would permit, bringing some sweetbreads, which he insisted on frying himself. He was inclined to " boss " all domestic operations when he had the chance, and somewhat to Mr. Taylor's delight the pan caught fire, and its contents were deposited on the floor, a sad degradation for Mr. J. R. !

Didymusa, being *hors de combat*, only heard of these goings on; but on getting up again she perceived on her snowy boards a queer looking mark like the sun in a fog, or a comet with its tail; and yet Mr. Taylor had gone down on his knees and scrubbed the floor quite recently. Didymusa declared that we did not know how to scrub,.

and that night the piano played again ! Determined to investigate the mystery we removed the front and key-board, heard a feeble squeak and scuffle, and beheld a sweet little nest of green fluffy felt, containing four wee baby mice ! The piano was none the worse, though I paid Mr. Nordmann twenty - five dollars for coming from San Antonio to make it mouse-proof by lining the bottom with tin.

The other wedding to which we were invited was that of a daughter of Señor Morales, a Mexican, but we had not understood that it included the honour of being Pauline's bridesmaids. Tony was the only Texan guest, the rest of the company being English and Mexicans. Señor Morales was of good family, and rumour had it that an interesting history was connected with his migration to Texas. Judge Aley was not required to tie the knot on this occasion, there being a Roman Catholic priest to officiate before a temporary altar. The little dark-haired bride looked very sweet in her white silk and orange blossoms, and the first pair of white kid gloves she had ever possessed—a source of great delight to her.

I had some difficulty to persuade her to take them off in order that the ring might be put on her finger, her English being little and my Spanish less. Happily one of the groomsmen—an Englishman—proved an ·efficient interpreter. All passed off well, and the young bride was overjoyed to be attended by the English señoritas. Her eldest brother afterwards married an English lady, greatly to the disgust of the Texans.

—––∘oo∘—––

R 2

CHAPTER XXV.

THE CRYSTAL COLUMN CAVE — CAUGHT IN A THUNDERSTORM — BUGGY CAPSIZE — NIGHT AT STEWART'S CAMP—VISITS FROM "DRUMMERS" —INDEPENDENCE DAY—THE LOVER'S LEAP— CAMP MEETINGS.

————

A WONDERFUL cave had recently been discovered in Sutton County by Mr. Richard Ruth, otherwise Buffalo Dick, a renowned hunter, who had taken 15,000 buffalo hides and shot 4000 deer. Our friends at Fort Territt, Mrs. Trainer and Mr. Van Buren, kindly invited us to accompany them on a visit of inspection. Fort Territt was a very interesting ranch, built of stone from the old forts, which were used in the times of the Indian raids. Many stones engraved by the Comanches and arrow heads might be found.

We set forth early from Fort Territt, with a buggy and a hack; Buffalo Dick, in a buck-board, carrying the commissariat and a number of lanterns and candles. After unharnessing and hobbling our horses, we prepared the lanterns and started towards the mouth of the cave. After a few minutes' walk we reached a large round hole in the rocks, about six feet deep, and although Mr. Van Buren chipped out a little ledge which was of some help, Mrs. Trainer and Didymusa and I found some difficulty in dropping to the bottom, where we found an opening just large enough to crawl through one by one on our hands and knees, Buffalo Dick having gone first and struck a light. Then we were within the cave itself, all carrying candles, which we deposited at intervals and lighted others. Descending gradually amongst piles of broken rock and sharp boulders for several hundred feet, we came to the main chamber of the cave, at between thirty and forty yards below the surface of the earth. Throwing the light upwards, the roof appeared at least fifty feet above our heads. In some places the stalagmites were so sharp that it became difficult to walk over them. There were no traces of fossils, and this enormous calcareous formation had probably never been entered by man or beast or reptile until Buffalo Dick penetrated to its recesses a short time before our visit.

Continuing our way we came across an almost perfect representation of a graveyard, with white tombstones below, and above beautiful representations of a coral island twenty feet square. Wonderful snowy bunches of stalactites and stalagmites formed the whole side of the cave, and near the top of these was a picture of a German castle with towers and small windows of remarkable verisimilitude.

Our unassuming guide assured us that we had not seen "all de pretties yet"; and, indeed, the beauties of the cave were alike too numerous and too remarkable for any adequate description. In one chamber, which we named the "Throne Room," stalagmites rose to a height of five feet, and resembled prows of immense ships. The throne was of a dull brown colour, the roof of dazzling brightness, and as we held up our candles it appeared to be studded with thousands of glow-worms, or to vary the simile, resembled a starlit sky. In another chamber hung a long cluster of stalactites in the form of an alabaster chandelier ; in yet another stood a solitary figure which I named Ariadne, and Mr. Van Buren Varuna, it having a kind of double hand with a coil like the Indian Neptune.

Although on returning to daylight and the camping ground we were hot and tired, our boots and dresses presenting a somewhat bedraggled appearance, whilst Mrs. Trainer had injured her ankle, we all felt that our pains were amply rewarded. After supper and a long rest we drove back to Fort Territt with a brilliant moon to light the rough road, and during the evening Mrs. Trainer sang to the accompaniment of her own guitar, her elder son surprising us with the music he produced from a French harp, whilst John, the Chinese cook, after considerable persuasion, gave us a couple of songs, which were amusing if they did not tend to edification. In the morning we saw some freight waggons unpacked and their contents placed in the fine store attached to the ranch, also visiting the forge, Dandy having cast a shoe. Afterwards there was a pleasant row on the river to the head of the North Llano, where the pecan trees are a sight to see.

The weather was sultry and on the day fixed for our return threatened a storm, but we disregarded the warning of our friends and the elements, and Dandy was led up behind the waggon so that I might ride a part of the way with the Trainers.

The distance to Junction City was about thirty miles, and after halting half-way and bidding good-bye to our friends, we had scarcely resumed the journey when a cloud burst over us. In a minute our thin garments became saturated ; Didymusa fainted and slipped to the floor of the waggon, whilst Dandy, whose rope I just managed to clutch as it fell from Didymusa's hand, pitched violently by its side. A vivid flash, a peal of thunder, and round spun Joe and Button; the waggon lurched and would undoubtedly have capsized, if Dandy had not charged the team in the nick of time and saved us!

Didymusa recovered sufficiently to relieve me of Dandy's rope and, remembering that Baker's little ranch was near at hand, I drove on as fast as possible. The accommodation was poor, but we went to bed while our clothes were dried and were able to set forth again the next morning none the worse for the wetting.

Approaching Calf Creek we saw a polecat with six kittens, all carrying their tails erect and waving over their backs exactly like the mother. Having heard that they make pretty pets if their scent-bags are removed early, Didymusa alighted as the mother cat disappeared down the cañon with one kitten in her mouth. The rest ran towards Didymusa, who secured a pair in the luncheon basket, whilst, heedless of all remonstrances, she returned for two more. But the smell was so overpowering, we were compelled to leave the kittens behind. Didymusa's gloves had to be burned, as also the famous luncheon basket, which no amount of washing and scrubbing could make agreeable. To this day, however, Didymusa insists that the kittens were "*sweet* little things," and wishes that she had kept them!

The following Sunday, Bishop Johnstone, of San Antonio, Missionary district Bishop of Western Texas, held a confirmation, Mr. Van Buren being the solitary candidate. The Bishop promised 100 dollars towards the new edifice and preached two excellent sermons to overflowing congregations in the Union Church.

With other friends, he came to tea and seemed curious concerning the future career of the catamount. " Mounte " did not offer him a very cordial welcome, and the Bishop foretold that we should have trouble in training this child in the way it should go, hoping that the next time he came there would be iron bars between. We received a cordial invitation in the event of our again visiting San Antonio.

It was not long before we made another trip to Fort Territt, this time on the invitation of Mr. W., joint owner of the ranch, who was frequently absent. Mr. W. possessed an excellent library, and besides giving me much valuable information, lent me the best histories of Texas and Mexico, together with the prose works of Ralph Waldo Emmerson, the following extract from whose Essay on Friendship made a great impression upon me :

A man's fortunes are the fruit of his character—a man's friends are his magnetisms. Ask what is best in our experience, and we shall say, a few pieces of plain dealing with wise people. Our conversation has once and again apprised us that we belong to better circles than we have yet beheld, that a mental power invites us, whose generalisations are more worth for joy and for effect than anything that is now called philosophy or literature. In excited conversation we have glimpses of the universe, hints of power native to the soul, far-darting lights and shadows of an Andes landscape such as we can hardly attain in lone meditation.

Here are oracles profusely given, to which the memory goes back in barren hours—add the consent of will and temperament, and there exists the covenant of friendship. Our chief want in life is somebody who can make us do what we can. This is the service of a friend. With him we are easily great. There is a sublime attraction in him to whatever virtue is in us. How he flings wide the doors of existence ! What questions we ask of him ! What an understanding we have ! How few words are needed ! It is the only real society.

A friend is a person with whom one may be sincere. Before him I may think aloud, and may drop even those undermost garments of dissimulation, courtesy, and second thought, which men never put off and may deal with him with the simplicity and wholeness with which one chemical atom meets another.

Ernest met us with a long face on our return, some of our pets having come to grief, in spite of the greatest care on the part of himself and his wife. The raccoons had refused food and died; the squirrels had been killed, for their untimely end Didymusa blaming " Mounte," while I accused " Gerino."

Mr. J. R. brought us a stuffed peba which had been killed near the city, a kind of armadillo (*Tatusia novem-cinta*); but although we had not seen one before, I heard that the *tatouhou*, as it is sometimes named, is common in some parts of Texas.

Monte not having been in good form since the long journey of 250 miles to San Antonio, I borrowed a horse from Ernest and turned my own out to grass; but he jumped the fence and wandered at his own sweet will.

We had invited our little friend Mattie Bradley to pay us a visit, and on the way to fetch her in the two-wheeled buggy, fancying I saw Monte's silvery main and tail as I passed his former range, I turned my head to obtain a better view. The next instant the wheel ran up a high stump and the little light trap seemed to turn a somersault. I suppose Dandy had swerved, at all events, I found myself on the ground, saw fireworks first, then nothing but darkness, and was nearly strangled by the strings of my sun-bonnet as I rolled over. Righting himself quickly, Dandy broke away at a gallop: fortunately, I had retained my hold of the reins, and sometimes dragged along the ground, sometimes running by his side, at last, taking both hands to the right rein, I managed to bring the horse to a standstill.

Except a slight graze on the left wheel no harm was done to the trap, upon which I congratulated myself as Didymusa would have declared that the accident happened because she was not with me. But when night came, I was obliged to confess. Either the axle or the step had struck me when I was thrown from the buggy, and now I found that my ribs were slightly injured, so that during the ensuing two or three weeks the most comfortable place was the hammock.

We took Mattie home in the waggon with Dandy and Button for team, and on our return journey, Dandy refusing to hold back at the last creek, went down the steep pitch in advance of Button, and snapped one of the single trees. Slipping off her shoes and stockings Didymusa began to wade, but I succeeded in reaching the opposite shore, and with two small pieces of wood and some twine we made the broken bar good.

We had another adventure on the way home from a brief visit to the Groszmütter's married daughter. The heavy rains had swollen the creeks at Roca Springs, but being due at home on Saturday, as the weather began to clear in the afternoon, we started, finding the journey extremely tedious on account of the wet slush. Night began to fall as we approached the last creek. At such times the bed of the river often changes, and I began to feel alarmed as we drew near the ford. Ernest had once been carried away in the Llano; losing his waggons and their contents and saving himself only by " the skin of his teeth." The Groszmütter grew frightened and excited; Didymusa urged me to drive through—anything rather than turn our faces away from home in the increasing darkness. Aware that the water was shallow a little way above the usual ford, I drove some distance along the steep bank, only to find things looking worse than ever. Unhitching Button, I rode barebacked into the river to test its depth, but losing his footing, the horse began to swim, naturally making for the opposite side—the way home. We were carried a few yards down stream before I could overcome his objection to return to the Groszmütter and Didymusa; who were both afraid lest the strong current should bear me away.

To cross being manifestly impossible, what was to be done! Although the waggon stood in an extremely awkward position, by dint of backing and manœuvring, we pushed it round and regained the road, but there was no ranch within ten miles, the only place of shelter for the night being Stewart's Camp, about three miles distant.

For Stewart's Camp accordingly we made as fast as the circumstances permitted; rain was falling again, and I felt some uncertainty which direction to take. Didymusa walked in front to avoid driving through the wire fence which I knew to be somewhere ahead of us in the pitchy darkness. Presently she ran foul of something and shouted.

"Who's there?" cried a voice, a few minutes later; then dogs began to bark, and a man appeared, who, having heard of our forlorn condition, "guessed he'd better unhitch the horses."

"Mees" Hurn and "Mees" Stewart were roused from their slumbers, as the man had previously been, and we found that the two families with six or seven children between them, occupied this log hut, about twelve feet by twelve, with a mud floor!

The prospect was hardly inviting, but refusing to let Didymusa and me sleep in the waggon, these hospitable people rekindled the dying embers, prepared coffee and would have made some hot biscuit also, if we had not preferred the "light bread" which the groszmütter had fortunately brought.

Candles or lamps there were none, and the hut presented a very rough appearance by the flickering fire-light;

its contents two bedsteads, a small table, the stove, the wooden form on which we sat, and a broken chair.

Didymusa had brought Gerino, who lay between us on the floor, where we had a roll of something for a pillow. How the rest of the ladies and gentlemen disposed of themselves is still a matter of wonder, but the Groszmütter solemnly donned her sleeping gear even to the crochet-work night cap with its elaborate tassel. She then crossed herself like a devout Catholic, and squeezing herself in somewhere, found repose as her heavy snoring soon proclaimed. No sleep fell to our lot that interminable night. The fowls had free access to the shanty, and the vermin they left behind tormented the dog, to say nothing about our own sufferings ! How ardently we longed for daylight, how intently we listened to ascertain whether the rain still continued, in which case, if the upper creeks proved as impassable as the lower, we might be prisoners another night.

Not liking to talk, our only relief from the monotonous darkness was a chorus of snoring, with an occasional solo from amongst the babies, one child of about two years old rolling off its bed, to spend the remainder of the night stretched across Didymusa's head.

With the earliest dawn we crept forth and, glad to be in the air once more, strolled to the river, which still looked swollen and rapid. The camp was all astir on our return, and breakfast, consisting of hot biscuit, fried eggs and bacon, and the inevitable coffee, was partaken of beneath a canvas awning which projected from the hut.

The cups lacked handles, the plates and forks were strictly limited in number, and though I was honoured with an ample service, the Groszmütter and Didymusa had but one plate and fork between them.

Observing that Didymusa sipped her coffee with anything but zest, the Groszmütter held the cup to her lips.
" Trinken, trinken," she cried emphatically, but still
Didymusa seemed reluctant. Afterwards I learned the
reason : " Mees " Hurn, it appeared, had hurried her
husband's ablutions in order that she might use the bowl
in which he washed to mix the flour, &c., and in her haste
had omitted to rinse it ! Truly " what the eyes do not see
the heart does not grieve over."

About six o'clock we bade adieu to these friends in
need, escorted to the creek by Mr. Hurn and Mr. Stewart,
who, first riding into the water, decided that we might
cross in safety if we kept in a line between them. Thankful enough we were to touch dry land the other side, to reach
home and remove our bedraggled white dresses, the bottom
of my own having been drawn through the water.

Now and again we were entertained by visits from
drummers (bagmen) ; but of one, who " travelled in
lightning rods," I had been forewarned. In fact, he had
swindled Mr. Cowsett ; his method being to insist, despite
protests, upon fixing his rods without charge, and afterwards to demand seventy dollars in payment.

The same little game was tried upon me, but I ordered
him not to meddle with my house. His lightning
conductors being merely fixed to the roof and not connected with the ground were obviously a great deal worse
than useless. I plainly told him that I would rather trust
in Providence. For three hours we wrangled, he now
flattering, now threatening me with all kinds of disaster,
whereupon I declared that I loved the thunder and enjoyed
seeing the lightning play about my wire fence.

Oh, he could stop all that, and then, what a showy
appearance the rods would impart to my fine house, which

would otherwise look conspicuous as the only one in the neighbourhood without a conductor

But I told him I did not care to be like other people, and would not miss the play of lightning on the fence for all he could give me : to see such lightning was alone worth the voyage from England.

Didymusa and Mr. Taylor supported me nobly, and at last the drummer left us with a parting sarcasm : he had been given to understand that I was a smart woman.

The 4th of July was quite a gala day ; people flocking to Junction City from every neighbouring county. The Declaration of Independence was read, and an address delivered, but I was not near enough to hear much of either. All kinds of games were provided : round-abouts, dancing, &c.

A committee superintended the provisions, which were served on trestle tables. This kind of feast is often known as a barbacue, from the mode of preparing the meats, which I have described in a previous chapter. In the evening there was a ball at the court house, everybody putting in an appearance.

And here let me pay my tribute to the invariable gentle behaviour and courtesy one meets with, not only at these meetings, but throughout the country. The cowboys are chivalrous to all women, and Americans generally are assuredly nature's gentlemen, displaying an ease of manner, an independence of mind, and a politeness, which, if not in complete accordance with the usages of English society, is exhibited both at home and abroad, and being due to innate kindliness, is not thrown aside and resumed to suit a passing whim.

Mr. Harby, in *Harper's Magazine*, well describes the cowboys as a class : " Bold, fearless, and generous ; a warm-

BAPTIST IMMERSION IN SOUTH LLANO.

hearted and manly set, and Texas need not be ashamed of the brave and skilful riders who traverse the length and breadth of her extensive prairies."

In the early days of August we began to harvest our fine crops of sugar-cane and maize, employing four extra hands to cut the sorghum. On still, moonlight nights we used to stroll near the sugar-cane, which stood from seven to eight feet high, while the breeze rustling through it reminded us of waves receding from a shingly shore. Or the sound recalled a scene in the "Bells of Haslemere," where the unfortunate hero, hunted down by his pursuers, forces his way, breathless and exhausted, through the tangled plantation, and listens in imagination to the village bells at home.

Towards home, too, our own thoughts often turned, and yet one would not willingly leave this sunny climate, with its warm-hearted people! East and west we looked upon the beautiful mountains, soon to see the sun set in a glorious blaze of red and gold over the spur for the last time. Or on pleasant evenings we sat in full view of the beauties of the South Llano, listening to romantic stories of the place in the moonlight, not entirely without suspicion that some of these were made to order. The lover of Leona, a beautiful Indian girl, having been sent on a distant raid, she promised to light a beacon fire on the cliff each night of his absence. But alas! weeks grew to months, he didn't return, and the old chief, her father, ordered her to marry "another." In despair one night Leona threw herself down the precipice, ever after known as the "Lover's Leap." The gorge below is still haunted by her restless spirit!

We could not resist attending the camp-meetings, which were again in full swing; besides it was the proper thing to do! They were held near the river, where a partly-natural arbour received the addition of a roof of interlaced boughs and twigs to eke out that which already existed. Every denomination was represented; Methodists, Baptists, Carmelites, &c., staying respectively for a week, some drove up in buggies and waggons, or rode, fully equipped for the month's or six weeks' encampment. The young people had a good time; match-making appearing to be combined with " conversions."

Cowboys, mustering in force, were often " moved " (by the girls) to confess their sins, such as horse-stealing, and led up to the platforms, where sobs, groans and wailings alternated with silent prayer. This is " finding salvation " or a " manifestation of the Spirit;" the Baptists " experiencing religion by baptism (immersion)."

The Church forbade its members to dance, and from August to December there were no festivities. But at Christmas the girls would admit that they had " danced themselves out." One sect always separated at sun-down for private prayer; the men taking one direction, the women another. Some of the preachers were eloquent; exciting their congregation to a condition bordering on madness. One hymn seemed to be a general favourite:

> " Ye must be a lover of the Lord,
>   Or ye won't go to Heaven when you die."

We heard it thousands of times from early morning until after midnight.

CHAPTER XXVI.

LETTING "THE FIELD"—FAREWELL PARTY—"FIX-
ING" THE WAGGON—SPANISH LESSONS—THE
"PRAIRIE SCHOONER" STARTS — VISITS EN
ROUTE — EAGLE PASS — BONDING WAGGON —
MEXICAN MONEY AND EXCHANGE—PREPARA-
TIONS FOR CROSSING THE BORDER.

ON being asked how long my absence in America would
last, I had answered "about a year." But nineteen
months had passed and I was still in Junction City, with a
furnished house and twenty-five acres of land on my hands.
However, about this time, when I was beginning seriously
to think of home, a tenant offered to take the orchard—
an eligible one; for in Texas it is easier to find a tenant
than to obtain your rent.

Eventually I came to terms with Mr. Royal, who,
greatly to my satisfaction, agreed to take the furniture
with the shanty.

There was some difficulty in disposing of the sugar-
cane so early in the year, although I could have sold
any quantity of Indian corn, which was scarce in consequence of the droughty spring and the bad harvest in
Kansas.

Now that we were free to return to England as soon as
we pleased, I began to think that it would be a pity to
leave America without seeing something of Mexico. This
idea gained strength, and we were poring over the map one

evening, when a friend, who had recently arrived from San Antonio, told us about a round-trip ticket by cars to the capital. Then Mr. Taylor made an important suggestion. Why not travel by our own waggon, thus seeing more of the country and enjoying a regular hunting trip at the same time.

The matter was discussed until at last it began to appear practicable, Mr. Taylor offering to accompany us provided that Tony's services could be secured for the occasion. On riding the following morning to Bear Creek, I found that Tony was willing, and would be ready to start on his return journey from freighting a load of wool to Kerville. The project met with a good deal of opposition, but, this only increasing the zest, I began to make the necessary arrangements for the journey in the waggon, creating quite a sensation throughout Kimble County. At first the Texans would not believe that we really intended to start ; but, convinced at last on observing our preparations, declared that they would never see us again.

We were thrusting our heads into the lion's mouth ; we were going to certain and utter destruction ! What, a journey through Mexico in a waggon ; sleeping upon the ground ! Your horses and mules will be stolen the first night, and you may think yourselves lucky if you escape without having your throats cut. This fate was said to be in store only for the men ; however, the ladies were to be taken prisoners and become Mexican señoras ! There was no need to pack our "tricks" for England, we were assured, since we should never return to Texas ; to say nothing about sailing to the Old Country !

Besides, the mountains were impassable ; there was a wide, unfordable river ; there were eighty miles of desert, which neither man nor beast could traverse without water, whereas we could not carry sufficient water in our waggon ! And the duties were enormous, even supposing we obtained a bond for the vehicle and passports for ourselves. Moreover, small-pox was raging so violently that the authorities would allow no one to pass, even the cars being fumigated at Porfirio Diaz. We were reminded that we did not understand the Mexican language, that even if we succeeded in reaching the interior we should not be able to get our money changed. Surely we should never be mad enough to carry sufficient money to tempt the Implacadores !

To all of which remonstrances and objections my reply was ever the same :

" I intend to go."

So our preparations advanced, and our start was fixed for September 25, on which day I was to give up possession of the house. A few weeks previous we issued numerous invitations, chiefly to our English friends, the party being intended partly as a farewell, partly to celebrate Didymusa's birthday. For the dinner we killed a young steer of our own rearing, which proved very different from the ordinary run of Texan beef ; nor did we omit to send some of the meat, with candies for the children, to our friends at Stewart's Camp.

Cards and music were the order of the evening, Mr. H. bringing his violin, whilst after the supper and ice-creams (a great success) Mr B. rendered the " Star-spangled Banner " with so much spirit that his wife, carried away by enthusiasm, caught me by the waist, and, calling for " Yankee Doodle," began to pirouette round the drawing-room, I trying to imitate her rapid movements, which were stiff and jerky as those of a marionette. This was the signal for more dancing, with " Sir Roger de Coverley " to wind up.

Our pets were to be left in charge of various friends; the cows had been sold. Dandy was to be sent out to grass until his time arrived to accompany me to England. Having letters of introduction to Mr. Riddle, of Porfirio Diaz, I wrote, asking him to purchase mules on his side of the Rio Grande, thus avoiding the duty, and saving my horses (which were then to be turned out with Dandy) such a hazardous and trying journey.

Then we packed our " tricks " (not forgetting the little collections) intending to leave the bulk of them ready for shipping to England. It proved a matter of difficulty to decide what should accompany us in the waggon. One thing was certain; the less we carried to Mexico the better, although there must be a straw mattress for Didymusa, blankets, &c., provisions and cooking apparatus, for which Tony fitted up a kind of cupboard with shelves and a padlock at the tail of the waggon. The door of this cupboard let down and, supported by one leg, formed a table on which to make our bread while in camp.

He fixed also an extra seat for me and Didymusa across the middle of the waggon, destined to be our perch during many long days, whilst on either side of the vehicle hung two small water kegs.

All this increased the weight, and, as we should often be compelled to carry corn and fodder besides, we were obliged rigidly to limit our stock of clothing.

Mr. Taylor and Tony certainly did not add much to our encumbrances in this regard, bringing only a small bag between them, and, as everybody declared we should be burned up, our own apparel was of the very lightest description. Some ladies advised us to wear masks— Americans are dreadfully afraid of becoming sunburnt— and cautioned us on no account to wash our faces in the morning. I could fill a volume with the advice we received concerning the preservation of our complexion alone.

Our farewells were made with regret at the first break in this delightful life of freedom, untrammelled by the conventionalities of modern society, both men and women speaking and acting as their hearts dictate, without regard for appearances or effect.

Not by any means is Texas peopled, as I had been led to suppose, only by fugitives from other States, such as the notorious refugees from justice of the Sam Vass and Kingfisher type in Edwards County.

Indeed, I enjoyed a delightful intercourse with many cultivated families, including Frenchmen and Germans and people from the more Northern States, to say nothing of my own countrymen, whose presence was due to reasons perhaps best known to themselves, some having suffered a reverse of fortune, others in sheer weariness of the vapid life spent at home with lawn-tennis or the many nineteenth century time-killers !

If, as was remarked by Goethe's mother, the object of life is to get to the end of it, surely there must be some satisfaction in feeling that the time has not been entirely frittered away, and that one has helped others, however little, to bear the burden and heat of the day ? I could but admire those ladies who, in order to further the comfort of their husbands and children, did not scruple to undertake work which, though it might be considered " menial," was surely more desirable than those feeble and futile attempts at art to which we are so accustomed.

There is a fine field for wives and sisters as colonists if only they go out with the fixed intention to be useful, while all " accomplishments " may be turned to account, lessons from Englishwomen being much sought after.

To Ernest I was indebted for lessons in Spanish, given during the last few weeks, on the gallery ; a post-prandial hour daily. When Didymusa joined us, I was in my first verb—" hablar ;" but this being far too slow a method in her opinion, she made Ernest teach her a few useful phrases, such as " No me mate " (Don't kill me).

I had never tried so hard to learn any language before, and my slight knowledge of Latin proved helpful. Having been nearly ten years in Texas, Ernest had seen a good deal of the Mexicans. He particularly cautioned me, when buying eggs, to use the word " blanchillos," instead of the Spanish " huevos," which would be considered as great a solecism as speaking of a cock to a Texan, instead of a " rooster."

September 25 arrived, and also our tenant, who was quite a girl and very pleased with the house, furniture, silver spoons, &c. Then, amidst the good wishes, fare-wells, and misgivings of our many friends, the waggon, which was to be our home for at least the next three months, our " Prairie Schooner," in full sail, took its course along the shore of the North Llano, *en route* to Eagle Pass, 200 miles distant. About two miles out, we remembered that Tige, the cat, had been left in the lot securely tied in a sack. His future home being at Viejo, our first halting place, Tony unhitched one of the horses and rode home to fetch him. At Bear Creek we were joined by Mr. Graham, who was to take charge of the horses from Eagle Pass back to Viejo, where they were to pasture until our return.

We spent a day with some friends at Roca Springs, and the next reached Fort Territt rather late, Button having been attacked by colic on the way. Tony adopted the Texan remedy, inserting a penknife in the roof of the animal's mouth, the warm blood being reputed a remedy when swallowed. All Texan remedies are more or less severe; for instance, the application of turpentine to cuts and wounds, bleeding, cutting off the tails of cows, &c. During this halt Mr. Taylor shot some wild turkeys and quail. After a two hours' rest, the animal still seeming to be in pain, contrary to the old custom of keeping a horse on his legs and moving when in this condition, I let Button roll. Tony then cantered him about, and so passed off an attack, which had, no doubt, been brought on by eating maize whilst he was rather warm.

We found our friends at Fort Territt in deep distress, Mrs. Trainer's second son having shot off two of his fingers while pursuing the same ' bunch ' of turkeys upon which Mr. Taylor had bestowed his attention. Having brought down several birds, Joe Trainer was running after the flock with his gun at full-cock, when the trigger caught in some thick brush. Mr W. and Mr. Van Buren were preparing an ambulance to convey him to surgical assistance. The following morning we set forth early, camping the first night at Lake Mackenzie, afterwards at Rock Springs and Hackburg. Then, passing William Prong, we spent a night on the west side of the Eastern Oasis, within a few miles of Barkswell.

The country here was magnificent and often mountainous, the roads always terribly rough. Before reaching Barkswell, Didymusa disturbed a rattlesnake whilst gathering wood for the fire, whereupon seizing his Winchester, Tony sent a bullet clean through the snake's head from a distance of over one hundred feet. It possessed a fine rattle, which I retained as a souvenir, but after stretching the skin on the pole of the waggon to dry, it became so offensive that we were obliged to throw it away. Near the oasis a panther crossed the road in front of us ; too quickly to afford the chance of a shot. At Barkswell we bought corn, bacon and lard at the little stores, and passing Martell, camped at noon on the Western Oasis, having now crossed the Divide. Having been able to find little broken wood the previous night, Mr. Graham skilfully " roped " the highest branch of a dead cedar, and uniting his immense strength with that of Tony and Mr. Taylor, pulled it down with a heavy crash, thus providing excellent fuel which burned all night. After Didymusa and I had played our usual game of whist, and betaken ourselves to our blankets, our three squires turned their attention to nap and poker. We could hear them bluffing, and I believe they kept it up all night, for on joining their camp next morning, we found breakfast, consisting of roast turkey, fried bacon, &c., all ready and waiting.

Having passed Bracketsville, Fort Clark, and Las Moras Creek, we entered Spofford Junction seven days after leaving Fort Territt, and at once perceived a great improvement in the roads. Spofford Junction is a station on the South Pacific line, where it joins the Mexican International railway, which was opened for traffic on March 1, 1888. About fifteen miles from Eagle Pass we came across a large cow outfit, and travelled with it some distance, Mr. Langford, the boss, furnishing us with information concerning our route.

This being Sunday and grass and water plentiful we determined to halt for the night where we were and enter Eagle Pass the following morning. Our little tent was pitched, we wrote letters, washed flannels, unpacked our zinc bath, made some water hot and indulged in a general setting in order, while the men bathed in the creek and shaved. The consequence was that on coming before the officials, we presented an appearance highly creditable to campers. Taking up our quarters at the Dolch Hotel, we were examined by Mr. Campbell, the health officer, and obtained a " clean bill." Mr. Addison escorted us over the fine iron bridge which crosses the Rio Grande, with a span of 930 feet, to the little town on the other side, formerly known as Piedras Negras (Black Rock), but now named Ciudad de Porfirio Diaz, in honour of the President. This border town, which possesses little interest for those who have seen elsewhere the curious adobe houses, is situated a thousand feet above the sea level and contains 5000 inhabitants, chiefly Mexicans, amongst whom at the time of our arrival small-pox was raging. Mr. Riddle was absent on the score of ill-health, and his partner, Mr. Seggermann, had received the letter, which I wrote from Junction City about the purchase of mules, only that morning. However, he treated us with great courtesy, promised to supply our wants as early as possible, and also to do his utmost to keep down the amount of duty and furnish us with letters of introduction.

The duty upon the transfer of cattle from Mexico to Texas was to be largely increased the following day, and having returned over the bridge to the American side, for more than two hours we watched a herd of 3000 or 4000 head being driven across the river, an animated scene ; the cattle " milling " round with the stream, whilst the Mexicans, anxious to push them over and to escape the increased tax, waded into the water and struggled with the animals, about half of which were over when we departed at supper time. We saw also a body of the White Horse cavalry come down to water their steeds, which were all in splendid condition.

When Mr. Graham started back to Viejo with our horses the next day, I fancied that Mr. Taylor and Tony followed them with lingering glances towards home. Although Tony had readily agreed to accompany the waggon, when the subject was first mooted, I really believe that he thought it was mere talk on my part, doubting whether we should ever get beyond the border at Eagle Pass. For now that we were actually in the despised Mexicans' country, his courage like that of Bob Acres, oozed out of his finger tips. But he was in for it, and none of the horrible tales related by himself and Mr. Taylor altered our determination to go forward.

A recent raid on the part of the Yaqui Indians had evidently had its effect upon them both, but as we were leaving Chihuahua hundreds of miles in the rear, I did not feel in the least alarmed, whilst Didymusa courageously looked forward to any excitement which might be in store for us. Having prophesied that the courage of our squires would fail when the time arrived, in spite of all their boasting, she felt a kind of satisfaction at their fears.

The morning after Mr. Graham's departure with the horses, the mules arrived to supply their place, and drew the waggon across the bridge, their pulling capacities having been already tested with a heavy load of bricks by Mr. Seggerman, who telephoned for me to return with the Custom House Clerk. This official made an inventory of the contents of the waggon, which Mr. Seggerman bonded at $20 a wheel; the money to be paid in default of its return. The mules were valued at $100 Mexican, or $85 American. The rate of exchange fluctuates, but there is usually a premium of from 30 per cent to 40 per cent on American money.

Little gold is seen, silver being the principal currency with paper notes of from $1 to $100 and upwards. Some of the paper money does not circulate outside the state which issues it, but notes of the Bancos Nacional, the Bank of London, Mexico, and South America, are received everywhere, as also bills on New York, though drafts on San Francisco are more easily negotiable at Vera Cruz and along the coast. The coinage is based on the metric system, the centavo or one-cent piece being the smallest copper coin, the tlaco (pronounced klaco) or $1\frac{1}{2}$ cents, the next, a cuartilla, equalling 3 cents. Prices are generally expressed in reales : 1 real $= 12\frac{1}{2}$ cents (called in San Antonio a " bit ") ; a medio real $= 6\frac{1}{4}$ cents ; dos reales $=$ 25 cents; cuatro reales $= 50$ cents ; a peso $= \$1$. There used to be some nickel coins, but after the nickel riots in 1883 these were withdrawn.

We had attached our coffee mill to the back of the waggon, together with the necessary apparatus for cooking and bread-making, two Winchester rifles, a shot-gun, my small English revolver, a deck chair, and a box of crackers (biscuits) in case we should run short of bread or the wood for fuel to bake it. In addition to these articles, we laid in a stock of various provisions from Messrs Riddle and Seggermann's store at Porfirio Diaz : 34lb. of bacon, 16lb. of ham, 50lb. of flour, 10lb. of lard, a dozen tins of condensed milk, 8lb. of coffee, 5lb. of onions, 1 bottle of vinegar, a dozen of tins of sardines, 2 bushels of corn, salt, baking powder, fresh meat, tobacco, &c., &c. The whole of which cost about $36, and made me think I was victualling a ship for a voyage.

While the goods were being packed, I accompanied Mr. Seggermann to the bank, and was introduced to Mr. Simpson, who wrote concerning me to his branches at Saltillo, San Luis Potosi, the city of Mexico, and elsewhere, provided letters of introduction and a certificate of signature. Mr. Simpson was a little more hopeful than some of our counsellors; believing that " God's Sun " would continue to shine upon us even in Mexico, and expressing the wish that he were able to participate in our travels. To this he added a long lecture for Tony's benefit, concerning his responsibilities, and insisted on my buying a Colt's revolver, which I accordingly did, at Holbrook's, for the sum of $14 (American) with a good supply of cartridges. I was introduced to Mr. Cloete, of the famous ranch which counts its acres in millions, and includes the San Marcus valley and something like 600 antelopes.

Mr Cloete offered his buggy to drive back to the hotel, and a pressing invitation to visit him, our route lying near his ranch. Having signed the necessary papers and passed the bridge with frontier and state customs, everything seemed now ready for starting. But we had still to get our papers signed on the Mexican side, and consequently were compelled to pass the night at the Internacional Hotel at Porfirio Diaz. On the following morning, however, we hoped to be under way.

CHAPTER XXVII.

FRONTIER CUSTOM HOUSE — BUYING MATCHES —
PEYOTES AND PELLOTES — CLOETE RANCH —
CROSSING THE SABINAS — MONCLOVA — MON-
TEREY—TOPO CHICO SPRINGS—SALTILLO—DIS-
PUTED BOUNDARY—COURTSHIP IN MEXICO.

THE following morning Mr. Alberto accompanied us to the
frontier Custom House, thus somewhat delaying our start,
and about three miles further on we endured another
inspection at the small village of San Antonio. But by
10.20 a.m. we were fairly on the road to the Halls of the
Montezumas, camping that night near Nava.

With trembling fingers Tony padlocked the mules to
the waggon, as we had been advised, little expecting to see
them there in the morning, or, indeed, to find much left of
himself or his friend Mr. Taylor. The mules stood only
about fourteen hands, a kind of chestnut and a grey,
named respectively Kate and Molly by Mr. Taylor.
Though I was wakeful that first night camping out in
Mexican territory, nothing molested us in any way.

Molly gave some trouble on being "hitched up" the
next morning ; breaking away from the pole and pitching
herself out of the harness, her exuberant spirits outlasted
1200 miles, increasing rather than diminishing as time
went on. Twice a day she went through her performance
with the most admirable regularity, the matutinal display

being the more vigorous, Didymusa usually walking the first mile or two, until Molly settled down by degrees and the course of the waggon became less perilous. It was just as well that Tony had come provided with nails, tools, and leather to repair the harness—freighters are seldom at a loss in this regard. But we had forgotten to bring any matches!

Now when you are dependent upon camp fires to bake your daily bread, matches are a desideratum, to say nothing about the men's pipes, and so forth. Consequently, it became necessary to supply the omission at Nava, but, unfortunately, I did not know the Spanish name for what we lacked, and, although Tony had picked up a little of the language from Mexican herders, he was equally at a loss.

On arriving at Nava we discovered another idiosyncracy of Molly's; she had the greatest objection to stand! Tony had only to give the usual salutation and inquire the way to any place (" Buenas dias, Señor! Este camino por— "), when the mule inevitably began to plunge. Nava is a pretty village, with about 1000 inhabitants and a plaza; standing 200 feet higher than Porfirio Diaz. Didymusa and I left Tony and Mr. Taylor struggling with the fractious Molly, while we went to a store to buy the matches. The black-eyed storekeeper would *not* understand; but she evidently regarded her customers as curiosities, and tried to detain us until she could summon her family to enjoy the novel sight. I used the words for fire and light, struck imaginary matches on my hands, and then, when I was beginning to despair of ever making my meaning plain, Didymusa espied the very things we wanted on a shelf.

" Como se llama eso ? " (What do you call that?) she exclaimed, pointing excitedly.

" Cerillos, señorita," answered the storekeeper, with a placid smile, which displayed her brilliant white teeth.

We had worked the oracle at last, and next enjoyed the satisfaction of paying four times as much as the matches were worth. It is said that Jews are never seen in Mexico; even they cannot live amongst a people who drive such hard bargains! At the best City shops you must begin by offering half the price demanded, and gradually ascend to that which the storekeeper will accept.

We had been particularly advised to travel as *pobres* (poor), and accordingly wore plain skirts of coarse linsey, dark blouses, and Texan sun-bonnets, thus saving also some of the trouble of washing. The sun-bonnets, although very comfortable, were perhaps a mistake, being calculated to attract attention, most of the women wearing the *reboso*, or shawl, which takes the place of the more costly Spanish lace mantilla. On nearing a large town we unpacked our smarter hats and dresses in order to make a more effective entrance.

The village of Peyotes lay in our route, but we had the misfortune to be directed to Pellotes, the names sounding very much alike. At Pellotes, therefore, we found it necessary to retrace our steps, and, the road to Peyotes lying across country, paid a Mexican a dollar to guide us. This delay was the more regrettable as it would make us later at Sabinas, and we might miss Mr. Cloete, who intended only a flying visit to his ranch.

On October 12 we came across one of his herders, Florencio, and camped on a pasture near Guadaloupe Creek, in sight of the magnificent Sierra de Santa Rosa, about forty miles distant, the coyotes keeping up an incessant barking all night. On reaching the ranch next day, we found that Mr. Cloete had departed, after awaiting our arrival till the latest possible moment. However, he had left instructions that the cattle raft, boat, and all available means were to be placed at our service for crossing the Sabinas, which was still swollen after the recent rains. We were very hospitably entertained at the ranch, besides being presented with a dog, for a guard, on our departure. He was tied behind the waggon, but took fright at Molly's erratic performances, broke away, and returned home ; the second dog presented to us and lost—our own having been prevented from accompanying us by a wound on one of his feet, received the day before we left Junction City.

Mr. Barrett and a Mexican led the way on horseback to the Sabinas crossing. The waggon was emptied near the depôt and railway bridge, and all our " tricks " put across with me and Didymusa in a boat, the Mexican conducting Tony and Mr. Taylor to a ford which it was hoped might be passable. I often wonder to what the Rio Grande owes its name. It may be large in the rainy season, but at El Paso and Eagle Pass we saw as much mud and sand as water, and although the current was rapid in mid-stream, there appeared nothing in the least *grand* about the river.

Mr. Barrett had told Tony and Mr. Taylor that it was not safe to leave us alone for a minute, which was not very reassuring ; and on bidding Didymusa and me good-bye, after ferrying us across the river, informed us that he and his friend would remain within hail until the men joined us from the ford.

We sat with our packages spread out on the banks and as time went on and the shadows lengthened, we grew anxious. It became darker and darker, so that we could distinguish little either across the river or up its steep well-wooded bank. What could have happened to the waggon?

Perhaps it had been carried away and lost in the deep waters !

As we sat wondering what to do, we distinctly heard approaching footsteps, and in an instant Didymusa seized one of the Winchesters, I the other; but the next moment, to our intense relief, we heard Tony's voice exhorting us not to fire.

Being uncertain as to the precise locality in the dark, and afraid of upsetting the waggon, he had left it higher up, so we quickly lighted the lantern and pitched our camp.

It had been a difficult business to get the waggon across, the water flowing over its floor and threatening each moment to bear it away down stream.

On reaching the opposite shore in safety, they had to exert all their strength to enable the mules to draw it up the steep, rough bank. If we had attempted to cross the ford without unloading, all our provisions would have been spoiled, even if the waggon could possibly have reached the opposite bank at all ; so that we felt extremely grateful for the timely help from the hospitable Cloete Ranch.

This being a delightful camping place, with ample supplies of water and wood, we rested till the next afternoon ; writing letters, washing clothes, roasting coffee, and making bread, or more properly, a kind of biscuit, made in round cakes, dropped into the skillet, above and around which we packed the fuel, thus forming a kind of oven in the open air. A joint of fine mutton that had been given to us at the ranch, was roasted on cross-sticks over the camp fire. There is bituminous coal in this district, and ironworks were shortly to be established on an extensive scale at Sabinas, a rich ore being found near Monclova.

For about seventy-five miles we followed the ascending

T

track in a westerly direction, posting our letters at Baroteran, and two nights afterwards choosing a picturesque camping ground near the Santa Rosa range, with Hermanos on our left. The water in the creek was quite hot, and we noticed a smell of sulphur in the air, though the water did not taste of it. At supper we entertained a Mexican, as I was desirous to increase my acquaintance with the language. He gave us a black dog, which I named Mungo, and actually succeeded in keeping !

Some geese flew above our heads, several falling to Tony's gun ; he said they were a sign of bad weather. We seemed to be followed by coyotes as we pursued our way parallel with the Santa Rosa range, passing some fine fields of cotton just bursting into soft, downy, white blossom, before reaching Monclova. We had letters of introduction to Señores Degetau and Garza, owners of large cotton mills, who did the honours of the place.

Didymusa and I always formed the advance guard on entering any town of importance, Molly being unhitched so that she should not break the harness.

This was the first time we had put up the waggon, and as livery stables are never attached to the hotels, I was once more at a loss for a word. Perhaps " campo-corral " (camp-yard) might serve, but at last someone suggested that I wanted a " meson," a yard with locked-up rooms round its sides, in which Mexicans often board, and we could secure some of our provisions.

Monclova was founded in 1686 by the twenty-ninth Viceroy, after whom the town took its name—Melchor Portacarrero Lazo de la Vega, Conde de la Monclova. It has about 5000 inhabitants, and attains an altitude of 2000 feet. Texas and Coahuila were formerly one State, with Monclova for the capital ; but the seat of government has since been removed to Saltillo. It is a great mining centre, sending vast quantities of ore and bullion to the United States and Europe.

From Monclova we travelled by Castaño and Bajan, buying corn for the mules at each of these little places, helping to shell it, and chattering to the people, who invariably afforded us a pleasant reception, and showed great readiness to serve us. Sometimes we bought sugar-cane as well as corn for the mules, and at San Barnabe some cart-grease, camping that night near Estancia, where Tony attended to the wheels. The journey from Monclova to Monterey occupied a week.

We were often astonished at the slowness of our pace, and began to think we had taken the wrong road (which, no doubt, was the case occasionally), until it appeared that the *legua* or Mexican mile is a little over two miles and a half; being, in fact, more nearly, though not quite, equal to our league.

The third day out from Monclova we camped in a gap of the majestic mountains of the Santa Rosa. The night was somewhat boisterous, with a fresh northerly breeze, grand lightning, and tropical rain. Our tent would have been flooded if Tony had not entrenched it, he and Mr. Taylor passing the night in the waggon, taking advantage of the shelter of its sheet with some misgiving, however, lest we should be surprised, and the mules stolen, during their sleep. I undertook to watch, Didymusa relieving me with the utmost cheerfulness. So boisterous was the earlier part of the night that we could hear nothing above the flapping of the tent, and, consequently, took our stand in the opening of the canvas. But the storm passing, and little rain falling after 11 p.m., we were able to peep out and even stroll round the tent. The high sugar-loaf cone, with its fire-burnt hematite sides glowing almost ruby-red in the rays of the morning sun, was surpassingly beautiful. A haze rose from the baked *mesa,* and the distant ranges loomed blue in front of it.

Two or three days before arriving at Monterey, grass and water became scarce. Forests of giant cacti and prickly-pear surrounded us ; sometimes twenty feet in height, with dense masses of thorny undergrowth, but the cactus branches supplied but little heat, besides being extremely difficult to handle (even our blankets and clothing picking up the sharp needles), so that by common consent we left it alone ; and, being at a loss to bake our bread, fell back on the cracker box. Some of the bushes were bright with purple and crimson flowers, and the scenery continued wild and beautiful to Monterey, the capital of the state of Nuevo Leon, and containing 30,000 inhabitants. It played a prominent part in the war with the United States ; the curious structure, Obispado Viejo, on the crest of the Mitras, a spur just outside the town, marking the spot which General Worth carried by storm.

Having found the " meson," we took cars to the Topo Chico Hot springs, about three miles, and enjoyed a bath in the famous waters ; temperature 100° Fahrenheit, curative in rheumatic and kindred diseases. On this account the place is gaining popularity as a winter resort ; but, although becoming rapidly Americanised, there still remain many features of interest ; notably the old church, forts, and convents. In the ancient convent of San Francisco we noticed a very stately palm.

The town is charmingly situated upon broken ground with a pretty plaza and a quaint fountain – the Ojo de Aqua—rising in the very heart of the city, providing a magnificent supply of clear water, the shores of the

CACTUS.

emptying stream in the distance being lined with bathers and washers of clothes.

In connection with the Topo Chico and the mountains —the Cerro de la Silla, rising over 4000 feet, to the east, to the west the Cerro de las Mitras, 3618 feet — is a legend. A lovely princess, daughter of the ancient house of Moctezuma. was stricken nigh unto death, and all remedies proved unavailing. In his palace by Texcoco, the emperor despaired at the loss of his inamorita, till one of a band of warriors who had recently returned from a raid, bethought him of a certain spring, whose waters were hot and reputed to be healing. He promptly enlightened his feathered and painted lord, who thereupon decided that the princess should be conveyed to the spring ; by what means, the legend saith not, but probably on the back of a *burro* (donkey). At all events, she arrived safely at Topo Chico, and was duly restored to health and the arms of her imperial lover, who, to commemorate the event, ordered one side of the mountain to be carved in the shape of a warrior's saddle. The other side is carved to represent a bishop's mitre, as a monument of the miraculous cure of some other noted personage.

The fact that horses, to say nothing of saddles, were unknown in Mexico at the time, is not taken into consideration ; but there are many surviving witnesses to the marvellous restorative powers of these hot springs, which rival those of Arkansas.

A three days' journey through unsurpassed mountain scenery brought us to Saltillo. Leaving the waggon near the bull-ring, with Mr. Taylor and Tony uniting their efforts to restrain the volatile Molly, Didymusa and I set forth to find Mr. Purcell, the banker, who had been requested by Mr. Simpson to afford us every help and information concerning hotels, &c., and on whom we counted to replenish our exchequer.

Saltillo is a typical Mexican city, unsullied by contact with foreign nationalities, and our first impressions were exceedingly enjoyable. There was ample opportunity to air my indifferent Spanish before we reached our destination, but after many " Donde vives ? " at last we found the Banco and Señor Parethale, as Mr. Purcell was persistently named. He expected our visit and showed us the greatest courtesy while it lasted, as also did Mr. Lynch, at once sending a messenger to escort us to the Hotel de San Esteban, attached to which was an ample *meson*, where we housed the waggon and mules.

Mr. Barrow, our American host, was extremely kind, introducing us to the few resident English, who were very sociable, and, together with some American and Spanish families, joined us in three or four interesting excursions.

November 1 was a gala day, all business being suspended and ourselves invited to a *tamalada* (picnic) in the beautiful grounds, beyond the town, of Señor Don Francisco Arispe. As the entertainment did not begin until afternoon, Mr. Barrow first drove us, with Mrs. Sharman, in his buggy, to the cemetery, which was crowded by the inhabitants, every grave being decorated, some very elaborately, with pictures of the dead, artistic drapery, exquisite flowers and illuminations ; others almost concealed by floral emblems. A combined odour of incense and guttering wax-candles pervaded the air. Earlier in the day Mass had been celebrated, the organ and choir being supplemented by brass and stringed instruments, as the priests passed solemnly from grave to grave. The very humblest grave was not forgotten, and since early morning the streets had been thronged with men, women, and children dressed in their best, and bearing wreaths and garlands. Gifts are exchanged, named *calaveras* (skulls) resembling in some degree our Christmas presents.

Before joining the picnic-party, we drove by a circuitous route and steep ascent to the American fort, and winding to the right, over the smooth table-lands to La Angostura (The Narrows) where we stood on the famous battle-field of Buena Vista, which I have already referred to in connection with the siege of the Alamo.

According to Mr. Barrow, the immediate cause of war was the disputed boundary between Mexico and Texas, when the latter country ceased to be a republic and sought admission to the Union. The debateable land lay between the Nueces river and the Rio Grande, being about 300 miles long and 75 miles in average width, with an area of 22,500 square miles. Mexico claimed the Nueces as a boundary, the States the Rio Grande, and to the present day trifling disputes arise with the alterations in the course of this river.

Bancroft in his History of Mexico writes as follows :—

If the injustice of all war was never before established it was made clear by the contest between the two republics of North America. The saddest lesson to learn by citizens of the United States is, that the war they waged against their neighbour is a signal example of might against right, or force, to compel the surrender by Mexico of a portion of her territory, and, therefore, a blot on her national honour. The United States had an opportunity of displaying magnanimity to a weaker neighbour, aiding her in the experiment of developing republican institutions instead of playing the part of bully. They could have secured peace by ceasing to assail the Mexicans, who were fighting only in self-defence ; but the much desired peace they resolved so to secure by war that a bargain, which was nothing better than a bare-faced robbery, should be secured. It was not magnanimity but policy which prompted Polk and his fellows to pay Mexico about twenty million dollars when she was at the conqueror's mercy. It gave among the nations, howsoever Almighty God regarded it, some shadow of right to stolen property. The total strength of the army employed by the United States in

Mexico from April, 1846, to 1848, consisted of 54,243 infantry, 15,781 cavalry, 1,789 artillery, and 25,189 recruits, making a total of 96,995 men.

The total number called out by the Government exceeded 100,000 men. The number that actually served in Mexico exceeded 80,000, not all called out at the same time, but in successive periods. At the close of the war, according to the Adjutant-General's report, there were actually 40,000 in the field. The gain in territory to the United States was immense, comprising a surface of 650,000 square miles. From the mines alone it is computed that precious metals have been extracted to the extent of 3,500,000,000 dollars. Besides this we must remember the vast wealth of Texas, California, New Mexico, &c.

The loss in money to Mexico will never be ascertained, and yet, unhappy as the results were for it, one must acknowledge that its honour was maintained. The treaty represents, indeed, its great misfortune, but does not involve perpetually ignominious stipulations such as many another nation has submitted to at the will of the conqueror.

Mr. Bancroft's severe criticism may possibly be due in some measure to the wide difference in political opinion between himself and President Polk.

Señor Arispe's large cotton and flour mills were closed in honour of the festival. His grounds were charmingly laid out in terraces, with artificial water, roses, lilies, and many semi-tropical flowers in full bloom. The refreshments consisted of *tamales* (which gave their name to the entertainment) and *pilon-cillas*, a kind of sandwich of sliced bread and the native syrup made from brown sugar, and grated cheese. Dancing was kept up throughout the afternoon. Several engaged couples were present, and it is not remarkable or conspicuous for them to dance together throughout the entire programme; in fact, the *danza* affords their principal opportunity of meeting. It somewhat resembles the old waltz-quadrille, the set consisting of two couples, who, after a "ladies' change" and more than one "balancez," and forming a circle, waltz away to repeat the performance at will; the dancers pausing at any time to go through the same figures with any other couple that may be so disposed, but not usually with the same pair twice during one " danza." This is distinctly the national dance, somewhat resembling the " Habanero " of Cuba.

Courtship appears to be a tedious affair in Mexico ; the lover being content to " play the bear " (*haciendo el oso*), that is, to walk slowly back and forth before the house of his " ladye faire," for hours at a time, days and nights indifferently. This term of probation may extend from five to ten years, or even longer. It is a serious matter for another man to come between the lover and the window ! Sometimes he " plays the bear " on horseback, content to obtain a glimpse of the head of his señorita, or of her finger tips as she salutes him in passing.

When she goes to church, or the plaza, or the baths, he is sure to be found not far away, a glance or a smile each day making the happiness of his life.

But there are means to exchange *billets doux*, and sometimes the " portero " is bribed to betray the movements of the señorita. When the wooer at last musters courage to call upon her " parent or guardian," she is asked whether she is willing to marry the young man, and quite reasonably replies that she cannot tell until she has met him.

On the occasion of this visit all the members of the household, even to the servants, are present, and the couple are never left alone together for a moment. Then he becomes the *novio oficial* (accepted lover) and marriage usually follows in six months.

The unlettered poorer class sometimes avail themselves of the services of an *Evangelista* (letter-writer), who, with a board on his knees, or a little table before him, a pen behind his ear, and a big mug of ink, is prepared, for the sum of a medio or a reale, to carry on the lover's correspondence, giving expression to his grief, love, fear, or jealousy, and always concluding with "à sus pies besa" (I kiss your feet).

Saltillo can boast of a nice little theatre, but on our first visit, after sitting in expectation for nearly an hour, our money was returned with the cool information that no performance would take place that evening. A few days later we met with more success, and I managed to follow the play fairly well.

———oo⟩o⟨oc———

CHAPTER XXVIII.

PONCIANO DIAZ—BULL FIGHT—THE VARA—FRUIT
— HOTEL PATIOS — TIPICHIL — THE FIESTA —
LEAVING SALTILLO — ENCANTADA — MEXICAN
GUEST — THE CURANDERA — HACIENDA DEL
SALADO — EMPLOYÉS ON HACIENDA.

HAVING been assured that we ought on no account to leave
Mexico without witnessing a bull-fight, on the following
Sunday, with some reluctance and a rather sickening dread,
we took tickets.

Mexico has had her own " stars " on the roll of tauro-
machy—Corona, Hernandez, Gonzales, and the great
Gaviño; and when Mazzantini, the famous Spaniard,
visited the Citadel, he was coldly received. The great and
only Ponciano Diaz was the idol of those days, and when
he went to the first bull-fight by Mazzantini at Puebla the
mules were unharnessed from the hero's carriage, which
was drawn through the streets by the mob. His father,
being an *aficionada*, used him in place of the *muleta* or
cloak at the weekly bull-fights at the Haciendo de Atenco
at a very early age.

Ponciano Diaz Gonzalez is an educated man; he was
born in 1858, and loves and reverences his mother almost
to idolatry, and this is supposed to be the reason why he
has never married.

As we walked round the large Amphitheatre (in small
towns the amphitheatre will seat the entire population) we

saw the five bulls, to be killed that afternoon, in a pen. Just as we were on the point of changing our minds and making our escape, the band ceased playing, and, with a flourish of trumpets, in dashed a horseman, galloping to the box occupied by the municipal officer, who threw him the key of the door leading to the pens. If he fails to catch this he is hissed. Then the procession entered ; matadores, banderilleros on foot, picadores mounted, all clad in gay colours, with gold lace and embroidery. Two men bore a long pole, suspending the gaudy banderillas. When the whole company had saluted the President's box, the fight began, the bull bounding into the ring with his breeder's colours attached to a steel barb through his shoulder. But the " charro " (sport) is so familiar in Spain, and has been so often written about, that a description here would be merely tedious.

The activity and grace of the banderilleros, the agility of the red-cloaked espada, struck me as being worthy a better occasion. The poor blindfolded horse of the picador is most to be pitied—nearly always wounded, frequently killed, old, and only fit for the knacker's yard, although fed up to friskiness for the ring.

At a signal from the president or official present, the matador despatched the bull with one thrust of his sword, the carcase being dragged away at full gallop behind four handsome mules, attached to his horns by a rope. The band played, men shouted, women waved their handkerchiefs and amidst it all we made our escape.

The bull was not a good fighter ; no one was injured, not even the horse. The performance once begun we sat spell-bound, and, however horrible and repulsive the " sport," our attention would have been held. The four succeeding bulls, as we heard, fought much better, and the general impression was that we had retired on account of illness. For that matter, we did feel ill when once the spell was broken. A group of idlers were waiting outside to see the carcase ; too impecunious to obtain admission to the Plaza de Toros. Seats in the shade command the highest price, which varies with the fame of the performers, boxes costing sometimes as much as $20.

This cruel sport is a blot upon the sunny land of pleasure, yet strange to relate, with Christianity and the planting of the Cross, came the introduction of bull-fighting. On reaching the City of Mexico we were thankful to learn that, in consequence of some popular turmoil, the President had seized the opportunity to interdict these repulsive exhibitions, though it has been recently stated that the cessation of their excitement tends to an increase of drunkenness, and bull-fights are even advocated to promote sobriety !

But such encounters cannot properly be described as fights ; in a fight surely the result is uncertain, whereas the fate of the bull is invariably sealed before he enters the ring. In towns possessing such arenas, we always avoided beef on Mondays and Tuesdays.

The letters we found at the bank were all satisfactory— both from England and from Texas ; a message being sent by Mr. W. "with kindest regards to those two crazy women in Mexico," hoping they " would not trust either a red-headed, a knock-kneed, or a cock-eyed man, as he would be sure to deceive them." Not meeting with any-one answering either description, we had no opportunity of putting his advice to the test.

We received much hospitality from Mr. and Mrs. Hayes, he an English resident in Mexico during nearly twenty years, his wife a Scot. They ran an extensive store, and

Mrs. Hayes was kind enough to do some work for us with her sewing machine, making Didymusa a new skirt in place of the old one which had caught fire from the embers while she was cooking one day. When we went to buy the material, Didymusa thought it looked too short for the number of yards, which fact, combined with the excessive price, was calculated to annoy. Her indignation waxed when the shopman explained that the "Vara" measured only 33½ inches, but her capacity for invective was limited by her knowledge of Mexican. Having lost her gloves from the waggon, she was unable to replace them for less than $3.25.

In this shop a card was exhibited: "English spoken here," and when I asked the linguist whether he did speak English, he replied "Just a few. But," he courteously added, "you speak Spanish," whereupon I also answered, "Just a few." Didymusa wished she could speak "a few more" in order to express her sentiments regarding the standard measure and the price of gloves!

The *portales* of the fruit market were very fine and we enjoyed the prickly pears—when they had been peeled for us. One evening in the dusk we bought some *chirimollas* and *aguacate*, mistaking the latter for figs. They were anything but pleasant, but after being dressed according to Mr. Barrow's orders, made a nice dish known as "huacamale." The figs and bananas at the hotel were delicious.

Men acted as chambermaids, and the absence of carpets gave a comfortless appearance to the rooms, which were all situated on the ground floor, round the *patios* (court-yards), where palms and bananas grew. The floors were hard, smooth and red. A kind of mortar is used for a foundation, which rapidly hardens; then a thin layer of gravelly sand is applied and polished with "tipichil" or "almagra;" an earthy deposit which is plentiful in dry streams. "Tipichil" is an Indian word, and for ages the substance has been used by those wild tribes to colour their bodies and faces.

Most of the windows in Mexico are fitted with iron bars, or wooden lattice work, affording barely space for a hand to pass between; "jealous husbands' windows" they are named in some places!

The best time to see the *fiesta* with the people all abroad, is at night. The scene is strangely picturesque; vendors of native pottery sitting on the ground surrounded by their wares; fruit sellers with large heaps of oranges, &c., smaller piles of *frijoles*, capsicums, red pepper, and pea-nuts. There are little fires intended merely for illumination; *tortilla* making goes on, the cooking brazier is in use, while groups of men sit beneath small pieces of canvas supported on three sticks.

This is the principal plaza, with gambling booths, roulette, picture-monte, and other games of hazard, surrounded by an excited pushing crowd. Many of these people are homeless and destitute; to be found by day crouching in corners of *portales* and *patios*, or on the cathedral steps, huddled up to their eyes in their *serapes*, which form a cloak by day and a blanket by night, their bright colours increasing the novelty of the scene. In the evening these gamblers wake to new life, even children bringing their centavos to place on their favourite monte: a picture game with cards representing figures and all kinds of animals.

Didymusa played at it with great success, eagerly putting her money on a white horse and a gaily plumaged bird— evidently popular favourites. At last, however, they

failed her, and having lost her centavos she foreswore monte
for ever and a day. But we still enjoyed looking on. On
the ground a man was performing the three-card trick with
shouts of " A donde color" (where is the colour); he had
the usual confederates, who were so importunate, that when
we pushed them away with " No dinero" (no money) they
still crowded round offering to lend us some.

In the city of Mexico this kind of thing is not allowed;
at least, in the open streets and plazas, and in all the towns
we visited, I never saw so much public gaming as at
Saltillo. It is lawful to carry firearms in Mexico, and these
are sometimes conspicuously displayed. In fact, though
the practice is illegal in Texas, even there everyone is
provided with " shooting irons" when occasion requires,
and at San Antonio a night seldom passes without some
casualty, fatal or otherwise.

Although our nomadic life was not without its dis-
advantages, and perhaps tended to monotony at times, it
enabled us to visit many out-of-the-way villages not
touched at by the cars, and to observe peculiar local
customs, whereas, in travelling by the cars, you cannot
obtain "stop-overs" at such places. And then, again, with
the more civilised mode of travelling, you are whisked past
the most beautiful scenery asleep in your luxuriously
upholstered berth. For my own part I preferred the less
conventional conveyance; what could be grander than the
view of these mountains flooded in moonlight, with the lofty
blue vault above?

Our delightful week at Saltillo came to an end all too
soon. Provided with a letter of introduction from Mr.
Purcell to the bank at San Luis Potosi, having reinforced
our larder, and procured new traces and chains for the re-
fractory Molly, the " prairie schooner" was once more ready

to sail, its harbour at present the third *patio*, or *meson*, of the hotel, to which was attached a laundry (unusual in Mexico), so that our *ropa* (clothes) had been nicely washed.

The mules looked all the better for their rest, but rather than trust herself in the waggon during Molly's preliminary performances, Didymusa set forth on foot, accompanied by myself. Mr. Barrow had added some presents for the commissariat department—none more highly appreciated than a jar of delicious honey. We had all been feeling somewhat giddy and bilious—not an uncommon thing at this altitude of 5300 feet. The air was very exhilarating, and a fine spring, " El ojo de agua," burst in countless sparkling cascades from the apex of the mountains, whence it descended in a crystal sheet to the valleys below. This capital of the Coahuila, indeed, takes its name from a word in the language of the Chichimecas which signifies " high land of many waters."

A stiff climb out of Saltillo brought us to our first camp at Encantada. Encantada, being interpreted, is "enchanted place," and, whether the evil eye was upon us or not, unfortunately, towards evening Mr. Taylor grew really ill and feverish. After administering a seidlitz powder and some Liebig, we covered him with all the blankets we could muster and placed him in the tent. A Mexican shared our supper of roasted meat, fish, hotel bread and salad, and after mixing the several comestibles together, insisted upon draughts from the vinegar and salad-oil bottles, washing down the whole with *mescal*, a spirit distilled from a small kind of maquey, the agave (species *Oyamec*). We had bought a bottle at Monclova, and, finding it far too fiery for our own tastes, now presented it to the guest. He was greatly concerned at Mr. Taylor's condition, and very courteously placed " mi pobre casa "

U

(my humble house) at our disposal; but the invalid preferred the tent.

The Mexican also helped us to roast some coffee and made neat little cigarettes in strips of corn shucks (which of course we accepted), talking volubly the while about the *curandera*. None of us understood in the least what he meant until he returned later on accompanied by a wrinkled señora—an old nurse or kind of medicine woman, not entirely free from suspicion of witchcraft, and held in considerable awe by the common people of these rural districts. The usual remedies are ground glass, crushed shells, white lead, and innumerable herbs. According to the *curandera*, every ailment under the sun is due either to excessive or insufficient heat; and some of their prescriptions are curious—for indigestion, frequent portions of white lead and mercury; for paralysis, ground glass beads, blue and red, in equal proportions, dose one tablespoonful! For children's ailments their treatment is supposed to be infallible: for backwardness of speech, a diet of boiled swallows; for incapacity to walk, an application of dirt to the legs, which accounts for the fact that poor children learn to walk earlier than the sons and daughters of the rich! But in this lady we reposed little faith.

Having finished his *mescal* the señor made his *adios*, promising to return in the morning with the bottle full of milk, which he did, though it was curdled. We were scarcely astonished when he complained of " Mal de estomago." " You bet he has, after all that stuff!" said Tony.

Mr. Taylor being no better, we decided to retrace the twelve miles to Saltillo, where Mrs. Hayes directed us to Dr. Bibb.

Dr. Bibb was a character in his way. Having shot

some too fervent admirer of his wife, he had been compelled to make himself scarce for a time, and only lately reappeared on the surface. He was an American, and decidedly clever; in a couple of days Mr. Taylor was on his feet again.

On the third day we once more set forth and reached the camping ground at Encantada, this time in more auspicious circumstances.

Wood being scarce, Tony had made a nice little collection and hidden it in some bushes, but not a trace of our fuel remained.

To name all the small ranchos and villages we passed would be tedious, although each had its little church, traditions old as the hills, and quaint pictures roughly painted on wood or tin, representing the life and temptations of its patron saint.

After leaving Gomez Farias, we came again to rich level lands hemmed in by lofty mountains; fertile valleys and broad plains with thousands of cattle, sheep, and horses, until we reached the Hacienda del Salado of General Juan Bustamente.

An *hacienda* is a large plantation (not a ranch for cattle) usually about 22,000 acres in extent, but this was an exceptionally large one. When one proprietor owns both an hacienda and a ranch, the farming is kept quite separate from cattle raising.

At half-past four in the morning we were awakened by the singing of the peons, whose voices sounded mellow and pathetic. The peon is invariably polite, always removing his clumsy straw hat: "Ave Maria Santissima," with "En gracia concebida," from the superior.

Although the rainy season lasts from June to October, agriculture depends almost entirely upon irrigation, and if a river runs by several haciendas the proprietors co-operate to construct the necessary dam and trenches, a man being at hand day and night to regulate the flow of water.

The rent of land is from half to a third of the crop, the average yield of corn about thirty-eight bushels an acre; and a church and store are indispensable adjuncts to a well-kept hacienda.

Being nearly always indebted to the stores, the peons cannot quit their employment, unless the proprietor of some other hacienda come to their aid. There are two classes of peons : those who are in debt and those who are not; the former (*calpaneros* or *gañanes*) being by far the more numerous.

The names and salaries of the principal *employés* are as follows :

		Dollars per month.		
Administrador	... ...	from 70	to	100
Mayordomo ...	... ...	,, 30	,,	60
Ayudante	... ...	,, 15	,,	30
Sobre Saliente	... ...	,, 8	,,	25
Capitan	... ...	,, 8	,,	20
Trojero (keeper of keys and accounts)		,, 15	,,	30

Besides these there is the priest, paid for his services as they are rendered, and sometimes a doctor, who receives so much a month. The founder, wheelwright, and carpenters work by the piece. In addition to their wages, the *mayordomo* and the *capitan* are allowed horses and certain perquisites. Although the *capitan* may be unable to read, he can count and carry as many figures in his head as any expert bookkeeper. He knows the antecedents and history of everything and everybody in the place, and while he is actually one of the peons, possesses great power over the rest, which he does not fail to exert. The *mayordomo* and the *capitan* come every night to the office of the *hacienda* to render an account of the day to the *administrador*.

There is a roll-call, and, the names of the peons being

MEXICANS BEARING THEIR CRATES.

read out, the *capitan* replies, " Cetonale " (he has worked), or " Homo cleno " (he has not), and at each answer a bean is pushed aside from a boxful, which the *mayordomo* keeps for the purpose. The roll-call finished, the separate piles of beans are counted and the result entered in the day-book. Then the *capitan* retires and the *mayordomo* receives orders for to-morrow—everything being conducted systematically and in order. The books of the *hacienda* are under the Government seal, so that anyone wishing to purchase the estate may satisfy himself by inspecting them.

The peons are by no means in such a state of servitude as to adopt any conditions which their employers may see fit to impose. They detest innovations and cling to their own rude methods of agriculture. One cause of want is the continual recurrence of feast-days, these consuming at least a third of every year. But their observance is prompted less by piety than an innate love of ease and indolence.

It is astonishing to observe how little suffices for the existence of these people, whole families sometimes living on twelve, or even six, cents a day. No wonder those who dwell near the border drift into Texas, where the pay is higher.

Enterprise is hampered by the difficulty of transport, so that an over-abundant crop is almost as bad as a poor one. The surplus is often wasted, and in times of scarcity the natives go on foot to carry " corn from Egypt." Of course, it is the " pobres " who suffer, and the need, not only for more railways, but even for waggons and roads, is a very real one. Nothing in Mexico is more pleasing than to see an *hacendado* " at home." His very apparel is picturesque : a suit of cloth or buckskin profusely trimmed with silver, a red sash about the waist, and loose neck-cloth, with the sombrero to crown the whole. He presents a striking picture on his gorgeously-caparisoned horse, whose equipments often cost 1000 dollars. When visiting the city the *hacendado* always appears in European cos-tume.

CHAPTER XXIX.

MATEHUALA—CATORCE—VANEGAS — SALT WORKS
—SAN LUIS POTOSÍ—THE MINT — LA PILA —
SAN DIEGO — LA CAMAL — TRONCAS — DOLORES
HIDALGO — HIDALGO RAISES THE "GRITO" —
MORELOS SUCCEEDS HIDALGO—AUGUSTIN DE
YTURBIDE — "THE THREE GUARANTEES" —
INDEPENDENCE OF MEXICO.

OUR intended visit to the silver mines at Cedral had to be
postponed owing to the absence of Dr. Mills. On leaving
Matehuala our troubles concerning wood and water began.
We had now reached the desert, foretold by our friends in
Texas, a broad, dreary expanse, unrelieved by vegetation,
save a few stunted *gobernadora* bushes, with towering
mountains on each side, their crests often lost in the mist.

On our left, between Cedral and Matehuala, Catorce could
be seen ; and perched on the heights to our right, a steep
path wound over the mountains, to a city in whose streets
no wheel has ever rolled.   It is a rich mining centre, first
discovered by brigands, who named it Catorce—fourteen,
the number of their own band.   Silver was found there in
1780, and the thirty years' output, dating from 1790,
amounted to $60,000,000.

Catorce is built on the side of a ravine near the top of
the range, and being only accessible on foot or horseback,
receives few but business visitors.   The population varies
from 8000 to 20,000, as the mines yield freely or scantily.
It is said that a wealthy mine-owner once sent a carriage

to Catorce, packed on donkeys, but, most of the streets sloping at an angle of 45°, the use of the vehicle was soon abandoned.

Didymusa and I had become so independent that we were half inclined to climb thither on foot, but relinquished the idea since it might have prevented us from reaching the City of Mexico before Christmas, to say nothing of the persuasion of Mr. Taylor and Tony.

Our waggon proved a great attraction in the various villages and small towns, the dogs came out to bark at us and to attack Mungo, while, to judge by the little crowd in our rear we might have been a travelling circus.

I generally went on in advance with Didymusa, to buy fruit, bread, eggs, &c., in the plaza (the butcher's shop was always indicated by a red flag), and to visit the church, which would be quickly filled by a curious, staring crowd. Whenever we turned to look at our spectators, they dropped upon their knees, crossed themselves and repeated paternosters.

During our journey of 1200 miles we met wheels only twice ; once the coach between Saltillo and Jaral, and once a rough cart drawn by several yoke of oxen near Estancia Grande. The oxen appeared at first to be without a driver, and to avoid a collision in the narrow pass we drove up a steep bank at the imminent risk of upsetting. But the driver was walking behind, and you may imagine his astonishment on seeing our " Camisa," or waggon-tilt. In some of the larger towns, there were, of course, " coches " and buggies, but few heavy carriages, owing to the prohibitive tax.

Trunks, packages of all kinds, even household furniture, is carried on the backs of *cargadores* (porters), who trudge wearily along with their heavy burdens.

Donkeys, in large numbers, form the freight trains in places where the locomotive is not yet, sometimes only the heads and tails of these poor little beasts being visible in consequence of their immense loads, carried in panniers, with occasionally a señorita perched between. Where the mountain paths are steep and narrow they walk in single file, and the raw condition of their backs must be seen to be believed. Sometimes men bearing heavy crates of fruit, pottery, wood, &c., from town to town, often travelling throughout the night.

These strings of donkeys often passed us at night, and the driver's cry of " Burro, burro ! " as he stimulated their exertions by vigorous blows, frequently intermingled with our dreams.

We spent several days passing the wide, level desert, taking the precaution to fill our two small kegs with water whenever opportunity offered, and sometimes purchasing six centavos-worth at little mud-holes. On one occasion the mules thirsted for twenty-four hours. There being no wood, we were compelled to use " buffalo chips " to heat the kettle and coffee-pot. During two days we spared no water to wash either ourselves or the crockery, and only a few drops to moisten the flour; but on the third day we met a man carrying on his back a load of the coveted *leña* (wood).

Two days before reaching San Luis Potosí we passed another region of the nopal-cactus, or prickly pear, growing in such dense thickets that we could not find sufficient space clear of needles to pitch our camp. Here and there was a tree-yucca, or *palmillo*, with splendid heads of large white blossoms, " clustering pyramids of flowers towering above their dark coronals of leaves." The natives make a marmalade of the prickly pear.

Between Vanegas and San Cristobal the people appeared to be almost in a state of starvation. Our camping ground was an improvement on that of the last night or two, but the occupants of some neighbouring huts besieged us at supper, and having finished our spread of bread, meat, &c., on the ground, turned their attention to the back of the waggon, so that we hastily replaced the supper utensils and prepared for the night. When they had all retired we arranged to be off at daybreak, without lighting a fire—not that we begrudged the poor creatures a little bread or money, but the difficulty in obtaining wood to bake more was immense, and it was possible we might be followed and molested.

Just as we finished hitching up, our tactics were perceived, and a crowd swarmed round the waggon.

For once in a way Molly's capers were an advantage ; after dashing right and left in a zig-zag course she rushed furiously ahead and soon left this hungry crew behind.

On leaving Venado, we diverged a little to the right, taking the town of Las Salinas, the largest salt works in Mexico, on our way. The salt is sent to all parts of the country ; being used to reduce silver as well as for dietetic purposes. The population is 5000, nearly all employed by this industry, but in 1842 when the Salt works were founded, the inhabitants numbered only 500.

A shallow fresh-water lake, which exists during the rainy season, disappears towards the end of the drought. The bottom of the lake is formed by a stratum of peculiar green clay, and beneath this, at the depth of a few feet, lies an enormous bed of brine, many hundred acres in extent. The pumping machinery is very primitive, no metal having been used in its construction.

Several leather buckets, each holding about two gallons,

are attached to a kind of water-wheel (*noria*) worked by mules. In these revolving buckets the brine is brought up and emptied into troughs which conduct it to large vats, when it is evaporated by the sun, though one extensive factory employs steam power for the purpose. Various parts of the valley have been bored, in the hope of discovering the deposits of rock salt which forms the source of this supply, quite in vain ; nor is brine found anywhere but in the centre of the valley. The works yield a large income, and belong to the Errasu family, whose palatial mansion, situated in beautiful grounds, is fortified, having

WATER CARRIER.—SAN LUIS POTOSÍ.

thick high walls with loop-holes, sentry tower, and a moat, crossed by a drawbridge. Such precautions were formerly necessary on account of the *mala gente* (banditti) who infested the country. The house, unvisited by its owners for many years, is occupied by the *administrador* (a Spaniard, who has had charge of the estate during the last 35 years), and wears a melancholy air of decay, strangely at variance with the prosperity of the works. Several miles of tracks connect the various storehouses, &c., and small railway tricycles are used for locomotion by the officials.

Following Mr. Barrett's advice, we stayed with Mrs.

Bennett, an American lady, who kept a boarding-house at San Luis Potosí, putting up the mules at the Meson Santa Clara. We arrived on November 25th, and remained until the 29th, spending our time in visiting some interesting churches. El Carmen contains some fine paintings by Vallejo, illustrative of the times of Santa Teresa and San Elias, with a Dolores by Tresguerras, who also designed the High Altar. The Cathedral is very handsome, with towers, a façade in the Churrigueresque style, and altars of hewn stone.

Mr. Pitman, of the Bank, sent one of his clerks to take us over the Museum, the State College, and the Library, containing 70,000 volumes. The Mint, which we visited also, much resembles that in London, save the size and the colour of the operatives ; the hair of some of the old Indians was white as the molten metal. The Mexicans possess a delicate sense of touch, and are very expert at detecting imperfect coins. Two young Indians, seated on stools, grasped a handful, without troubling to look—always twenty dollars ; never more, never less—and, transferring them from one hand to the other, at once detected the slightest scratch, all faulty coins being put through the mill again. Didymusa brought away a complete silver set. We were shown the gold coinage, though this is not often seen in everyday use—the onza de oro = $16 ; the media onza = $8 ; the pistola = $4 ; the escudo de oro = $2 ; and the escudito de oro = $1.

Two gentlemen who boarded at Mrs. Bennett's, officials on the Mexican Central Railway, wished us to see their pensioned mules, which had drawn all the steel for the line, and stood between sixteen and seventeen hands. Accompanied by Mrs. Bennett, we went to their large repairing works on a " push-car," or trolley ; obtaining a good view of the City of San Luis Potosí in the distance, with its handsome buildings, domes, and towers, fringed by trees and beautiful gardens. The Alameda is a charming spot, lying in the broad valley formed by the outspreading of the Cordilleras, a steep, lofty mountain range, which rises a few miles to the south. We sat in front while the gentlemen worked the trolley behind, Mrs. Bennett in the middle regulating the brake, which she put on during the ascent, causing our friends to puff a good deal.

The mules were splendid animals, and we spent some time in inspecting the well fitted houses, baths, &c., for the *employés*, the extensive works and immense storehouses containing bolts, nuts, bars—in fact, any article which could conceivably be needed for repairs. An engine had just been sent in for new wheels.

There are a fine market and a small native pottery, while the Indians exhibit gold and silver embroidery worked on slippers, cushions, and so forth, as well as leather and rope work.

We were told that some peculiar knives, with long, curved blades, were used for cock-fighting, the blades being attached to the birds' legs. The combat is usually brief, and of course affords an opportunity for gambling. This *sport* is common in the interior, the stakes sometimes being very high.

San Luis Rey was founded in 1583 by Fra Diego de la Magdelena, to whom came secretly an Indian chief with information concerning a rich mine (San Pedro) in the sierra hard by. Captain Calderon, commanding the military post at the time, was Spanish on his father's side, having for mother an Indian woman, highly esteemed by her own people. Calderon and the pious monk desired the treasure for their King, in order that it might enrich the mission and further the good work among the heathen. With the consent of the Indian they announced the discovery, and so secured the treasure of Cerro del Potosí. In 1666 the town was raised to the dignity of a city by royal order, and named San Luis Potosí, after the mines of Potosí in Peru, which its own rich mountain somewhat resembles.

A small green paroquet taking a great liking for Didymusa, and refusing to be kept out of her room, Mrs. Bennett gave her the bird, which was always in evidence during the remainder of our journey; often climbing to the top of the waggon-tilt, and settling there screaming, especially when it saw us buying bananas in the market.

Our difficulties regarding wood and water were now entirely at an end, the 362 miles to the City of Mexico being through a fertile and tropical country. But as we had to travel over a mountainous, and, in places, almost trackless region, Mr. Pitman advised me to procure a third mule. Several animals were brought up for inspection, all dear and none too good; amongst them a pony, which I bought for twenty-two dollars, Mr. Pitman requesting a bill of sale for him. Mr. Pitman did not seem to regard our journey as a particularly safe one, and cautioned me to set forth early, so as to place a few miles between the city and our first camping place.

The dog Mungo evidently preferred hotel life to our nomadic existence and generally tried to stay behind when the time came for starting.

Passing La Pila we camped near Santa Maria del Rio, and, the morning air being clear and crisp and the nights slightly frosty at this altitude, we pitched the tent for shelter. There seemed to be some kind of festival between La Pila and our camp; bells, drums, and the report of firearms could be heard in the distance, and later on a good deal of traffic went by, disturbing the pony (which we named Luis), and the mules.

Presently a mounted soldier appeared at the entrance of our tent. Starting up, I cried, "Cuidado!" and pointed my little revolver at the intruder, while Didymusa shouted "No me mate" and "Tony." The soldier proved quite harmless, however; and with bows and smiles and "Perdoname," retired apologising. Tony said he was tipsy, and perhaps the arrival of our stalwart teamster, armed with a "Colt," hastened the Mexican's retreat.

The following night we camped in the Hacienda of Jaral, which once mustered 20,000 peons, and in 1871 furnished a complete regiment of cavalry to resist the Royalists. Some one came to demand whether we had a *licencia* (leave to remain), but rode off apparently satisfied after I had done my best at an explanation. At San Felipe we saw a fine viaduct spanning a steep *barranca* of the railway, which must have required no little engineering skill to construct.

We left San Diego on December 1st—a sad anniversary! Years ago I had stood by my father's open grave on this day, and, while my thoughts dwelt upon the past, singularly enough, Mr. Taylor drew my attention to four Mexicans bearing a corpse on as many pieces of rough timber. It was merely wrapped in a sheet tied round the neck and feet. They kept alongside of us for some little distance, the form of their burden distinctly visible beneath its scanty covering, and at last stopped beside a wall, depositing the body (which must have been that of a man from its length) on the other side, where they made as if to dig a grave.

The next day we passed another funeral, the body being

carried in much the same manner. This was near the church of La Camal, where a child was being interred ; we saw the rude coffin and the officiating priest.

The weather having been somewhat colder of late, increased the mortality from small-pox. On another occasion, passing the village of Joya, near Bajan, there was a serious outbreak of this loathsome disease, due to a similar·fall of temperature. Not quite realising the danger at first, we frequently entered the *jacal*, talking to the women while we helped to shell corn for the team. The woman who brought the corn-cobs was still covered with sores, another lay scantily clothed in one corner of the mud floor. A little *cama* (cradle), roughly fashioned of maguey and palm, hung empty from the roof, and the mother sat beside it weeping as if her heart would break. The corn which the women were to shell lay untouched in the cob, and, making our *adios* as quickly as possible, we hastened from the hut. Vaccination is, of course, unknown.

At Troncas we camped near a large sheet of water covered with wild duck. The men shot half a dozen, and two falling into the water, Tony went to fetch them on Luis, the pony. He could never be induced to ride the mules.

The next day we reached Dolores Hidalgo, so named after the patriot, once the *cura* of the place. Hidalgo was an accomplished linguist, a man of science, philosopher, and political economist, occupying himself in the breeding of silkworms and the cultivation of grapes. He spared no effort to encourage industry amongst his people, and successfully started a porcelain factory in the neighbourhood.

His plans had long been maturing before he raised the "*grito*" (cry) in his fifty-eighth year. In the fine old cathedral we could picture him on that memorable night of September 16th, 1810; the central figure of the crowd; a priest transformed into a warrior, the voice which had blessed his flock now denouncing their oppressors, the hands which had been clasped in supplication now clenched to smite.

We could hear his clarion voice, see his thin hands waving with excited gestures, his slender body throbbing with emotion, until, carried away by enthusiasm, the eager cries of his hearers burst forth : " Viva nuestra Señora de Guadalupe ! "   " Viva la Independencia ! "

The banner of revolt is reared above their heads, Hidalgo makes the sign of the Cross, and having murmured a prayer, passes down the narrow street at the head of his dark-skinned followers ! They marched to San Miguel, where they were joined by the regiment commanded by Captain Allende. Then on to Guanajuato, capturing the town after a desperate struggle, and so to Valladolid, where Hidalgo's force was strengthened by the adhesion of another body of soldiers.

On the march to the City of Mexico, Hidalgo came into collision with Las Cruces and a number of Royalist troops, whom he defeated on October 30th, 1810. His cause might have been immediately triumphant had he marched at once on Mexico ; unfortunately, he decided to retreat into the interior, and being defeated at Aculco, concentrated upon Guadalajara, whither the Spanish forces were dispatched to meet him. The battle at the Bridge of Calderon, January 16th, 1811, resulted in the defeat of the Revolutionists. Intending to seek aid from the U.S.A., Hidalgo led his followers northwards, but they were betrayed by Elizondo (a compatriot and former friend) into the hands of the Spaniards, and taken prisoners to

Chihuahua (pronounced (che-wow-wa), where Allende, Aldama, and Jiminez were executed, Hidalgo sharing their fate a few days later, on July 31st, 1811.

The triumphs of his brief career were as marvellous as his defeat was signal. During the long trial which preceded his death, neither chains nor fetters could detract from his dignified fortitude. His life was valiant, nor did the "grito de Dolores" cease to reverberate over the mountains and plains of Mexico with his heroic death. The Washington of Mexico they name him, and with each succeeding generation his fame increases.

Morelos, his worthy successor, won many brilliant victories for the cause, until he was at last overwhelmed by Colonel Yturbide. From this time the sun of his success began to set. After several reverses, he was taken prisoner and suffered a traitor's death on November 16th, 1815, at San Cristobal.

During these five years' devotion to the service of his country, Morelos did not neglect the duties of religion.

He never struck a blow without previously confessing himself, although after his first battle the celebration of the Mass was delegated to his chaplain.

The military genius of Morelos won an encomium from so great a general as the Duke of Wellington. He was a native of Valladolid, now named Morelia in his honour. Far from being checked by the death of these heroes, the cause of Independence was stimulated: "The seed sown by Hidalgo was nurtured by Morelos, and in due time the whole grand scheme was harvested by the strong arm of Yturbide."

Mexico can boast of hundreds of noble, heroic sons, faithful alike in victory and defeat, not the least among them Michocan de Acampo and Señors Navarro and Escobar. After the death of Morelos the cause of the patriots seemed to languish for a time, although Vicento Guerrero offered a bold resistance in the mountains of the South. But in 1820 Viceroy Apodaca appointed to the command of this district Yturbide, who opened a correspondence with Guerrero, which resulted in a personal conference at Acatempa, on January 10th, 1821. At this meeting, Yturbide, who had hitherto fought against the popular cause, and had defeated Morelos, agreed to unite with Vicente Guerrero in proclaiming the independence of Mexico. Accordingly, on February 24th, Yturbide published the famous Plan of Iguala, the essential articles of which were : The conservation of the Roman Catholic Church to the exclusion of all other forms of religion ; the absolute independence of Mexico as a separate monarchy, with Ferdinand VII., or some other member of the reigning house, on the throne ; the amicable union of Spaniards and Mexicans.

The three clauses were styled " the Three Guarantees," and the colours of the National flag, to be adopted a little later on, were emblematic of these three articles of faith— white, of purity; green, of the union of Mexicans and Spaniards ; red, of independence.

Yturbide's army, converted by his efforts to the support of these principles, became known as the " Army of the Three Guarantees."

This action of Yturbide, which made him the supporter instead of the enemy of the cause, for which Hidalgo and many other brave men had died, together with his able direction of military affairs, secured independence for Mexico. Rapidly capturing the towns on his route, he triumphantly entered the City of Mexico on September 27, 1821. Cut off from the Capital, the sixty-second and last Viceroy, Juan O'Donojú, took the oath of office at Vera

Cruz, and sought a personal interview at Cordoba with Yturbide, whose only concession of any importance was that O'Donojú should become a member of the Provisional Committee of Regency, which was to govern the country until a king could be found to accept the Mexican crown.

On September 27, 1821, the Spanish power over Mexico formally ceased, and Yturbide made a triumphant entry into the Capital. Augustin de Yturbide was born in Valladolid (now Morelia) September 27, 1783, entered the Colonial Army at the age of sixteen, and, as a loyal soldier, fought against the insurgents. His change of sides is fully dwelt upon in the very remarkable " Historia de la Revolucion of Anáhuac," of Bustamento, translated by Dr. Mier, and published in London in 1810. Yturbide was elected Emperor, May 19, 1822, under the title of Augustin I., and, with his wife, anointed and crowned with great solemnity in the Cathedral of Mexico, upon which occasion the golden keys were handed to him on a silver salver.

Alas! for the instability of human felicity! Nine months after his coronation, Yturbide was forced to abdicate, flying an exile to Italy three months later with his wife and family. Weary of inactivity, solicitous for the welfare of his country, he subsequently returned to Mexico, was arrested and thrown into prison, and executed as a traitor on July 19, 1824.

Thirty years after his death, in 1853, his memory was honoured by the title of " Liberator of Mexico," an inscription was graven upon the house in which he had lived at Morelia, the anniversary of his execution was declared a public holiday, and a grand Mass was celebrated for the repose of his soul!

Those who are executed as " traitors " receive the fire in

their backs kneeling ; if priests they are stripped of their sacerdotal robes. Hidalgo, however, continued to wear his during his trial. We visited his house and the gardens he loved so well, but could not see the relics, these having been removed to the city museum. They consisted of his stole, gun, cane, chair, &c., and the banner of the Virgin of Guadalupe, taken from the sanctuary of Atotonilco, and emblazoned with the image of the Patroness of Mexico. This was the standard of the Cause of Independence, "Guadalupe" remaining always the war-cry of the Indians, all of whom are well-informed concerning its significance.

On the other side her figure is rivalled by that of " Nuestra Señora de los Remedios " (Our Lady of Succours), whose image was brought into the city by the royalists after the defeat of Las Cruces by Hidalgo. Amidst solemn ceremonies her aid was invoked against the victorious rebels, and she was formally made Generala of the king's army. Having thus become the symbol of the Spanish faction, Mexican feeling ran so strongly against her that on the attainment of independence an order was actually issued for her banishment. This order was never carried out, but, though the antipathy towards her may have become less, La Gachupina, as she was derisively named, has never recovered her lost ground, whereas thousands of children are christened in the name of the Guadalupe every year, When Hidalgo first placed the image of this virgin on his banner, the royalists cruelly persecuted those who worshipped at her shrine, and at once stamped upon their own banners the representation of the " Lady of Succours," whose shrine is magnificent, the value of her jewels and vestments exceeding $1,000,000.

CHAPTER XXX.

SAN MIGUEL DE ALLENDE—ZERAPE MAKERS—
GIANT CACTI, &c. — CELAYA — TRASGUERRAS —
INDIAN PROCESSION — FRAY SEBASTIAN —
ARRIVING AT QUÉRETARO — OPALS — MAXIMI-
LIAN—HERCULES MILL—SAN JUAN DEL RIO—
WAYSIDE CROSSES—ACCIDENT TO WAGGON—
TULA—THE TAJO DE NOCHISTONGO.

IT was with extreme reluctance that we quitted this historic town of Dolores Hidalgo, the next day reaching San Miguel de Allende, which takes its name from another patriot, and numbers 30,000 inhabitants.

The town is beautifully situated above the valley of the Laja, at the foot of the Cerro of Moctezuma, built on a declivity, and having an altitude of 6000 feet above the sealevel.

The baths, in the southern suburb, stand in grounds laid out in terraces with stone paved paths through which the water flows from the great spring Chorro, the plaza, also terraced, fronts the imposing cathedral. This edifice is unique in Mexico on account of its Gothic Architecture, and was designed by an Indian. The chapel of the Casa de Loreto, attached to the oratories of San Filipe Neri is a perfect gem in the way of decorations, with its carved wood, frescoes, gilding, delicate metal work and glazed tiles, the gift of Señor Canal and his wife.

What was once the palace is now the Hotel Allende, a

stone figure of the Virgin of Loreto over the main entrance being a relic of the former occupants. At San Miguel de Allende, *zerapes* and *rebozos* are still made by hand. These *zerapes* are wonderfully durable, their threads being tightly drawn in to render them almost waterproof. Some are really artistic, with figures interwoven as in old tapestry, requiring months to manufacture, and costing sometimes as much as $400 each. We watched one of the *zerape* makers at his primitive loom, using wool of many different colours, and harmonising the tints to perfection. The wool is received just as it is shorn, and the weavers' families wash, card, dye, and prepare it for the loom. The *rebozos*, nearly always black and quite inferior, are worn over the women's heads and used to wrap the babies in.

Several churches were interesting. In that of San Rafael we saw a curious figure of San Antonio Abad. In the parish church there is an interesting Camarin with a crucifix, known as the " Señor de la Conquista," and a crypt under the principal altar in which some distinguished ecclesiastics lie buried. The music at San Rafael was very good.

We left the town by a remarkably steep zig-zag track, and followed the fine Cañon de la Laja. Our whole journey would have been amply repaid by the walk through San Juan de las Vegas, alone ; the streets hedged by giant cacti, from 15 feet to 20 feet in height ; behind these the adobe houses, almost hidden by the luxuriant foliage of vines and banana, orange and lemon trees, with roses, camellias, magnificent poppies, flaming tulipan, the (*Hibiscus rosa sinensis*) scarlet, yellow, and almost chocolate coloured varieties. Crossing a bridge, we saw some women washing their clothes and themselves in the stream, especially their hair, which is generally full, long, and by no means coarse in texture, albeit swarming with vermin in spite of these ablutions. A favourite occupation of the women is to sit in a circle, each nursed in the lap of another, hunting for these creatures, like so many monkeys.

We concluded that Tito, the paroquet, had been brought up in the way he should go by a Mexican woman, as, whenever we said, ' Piojo, Tito ' he immediately began to examine our heads, and, on seeing the señoritas at their favourite occupation, flapped his wings and screamed with delight. Near this place Didymusa discovered the *Nopalea cochinellifera*, which stained her hands, while searching for fuel. There were the night blooming *cereus* species, also a few wonderful specimens of the *giganteus*, having a columnar trunk, one quite 50 feet high, and some of the *Pilocereus senilis* (old man's head), covered towards the top with long white hairs. After passing through a rich agricultural region, we came to Celaya, a city of 80,000 inhabitants, possessing several factories (cotton, wool, sweetmeats, soap, &c.), a good-sized market, and a theatre, though its chief claim to interest is as the birthplace of Eduardo Tresguerras, architect, sculptor, painter; indeed, one might say, the Michael-Angelo of Mexico.

He was born at Celaya, on May 13, 1765, and, dying in the same place in 1833, was buried in the chapel designed by and for himself, and dedicated to Nuestra Señora de los Dolores, to which Virgin he was especially devoted.

The noble church of Our Lady of Carmen is his most famous work. Standing in the form of a Latin cross, surmounted by a tower and dome of great beauty, it is remarkable for its size and grandeur, combined with lightness and grace, besides containing some frescoes by the same hand. In addition to these striking frescoes is the oil painting of Our Lady of Carmen, in the Chapel of the Last Judgment, while the work of Tresguerras also adorns several other churches and chapels.

Within a few miles of Santa Rosa, our attention was arrested by the sound of voices and music ; a kind of salute or *feu-de-joie*, and some objects advancing in a cloud of dust, threatened to meet us at a certain point ahead, where their road joined ours. Fearing that the commotion would upset Molly's temper, Tony suggested a right about face ; though I think he considered his own feelings as much as the mule's. I asked him to pull up and steady Molly whilst I alighted, when he might do as he pleased, for whatever it was I intended to be there. And sure (as the Americans say) sure it was the strangest procession you can imagine ! A large oil-painting, representing a venerable-looking person, supposed to be San Sebastian, was borne aloft on the shoulders of two men, surrounded by a mixed crowd of Indians and Mexicans with palms and canes in their hands. Some wore curious masks of a coarse kind of gauze, others wreaths of feathers, and tinselled, tawdry garments. Some were bare-footed, some wore ornamental mocassins, some played guitars or mandolins, headed by an Indian, vigorously beating a *jarana*— pronounced " harana "—a kind of drum covered with the skin of an armadillo. A crowd of wild-looking, fantastic creatures danced grotesquely on each side of the main procession, exploding fire-crackers and squibs the while. Sometimes the dancers formed a circle, always to the discordant jang-jang and tum-tum of their instruments and the din of Babel.

A qualm seized me when I found myself amidst this uproarious crew, but my salute being received with a unanimous " Ya ! " and one of the more respectable looking of the women addressing me in Spanish with a cordial " Vamos," I began to feel more comfortable.

Rosaries were being sold made of poppies and cempezuchitl, and, buying one of these for a few centavos, I passed it over my head, winning a nod of approval and a " Bien hecho " from the old señora. On through the dust I tramped, mingling with the motley throng. Now and then there was a halt, when the picture was changed to other shoulders, surrounded, and kissed, and always saluted by everyone who met it. During one of these halts I heard Tito screaming, and, turning, beheld Didymusa trying to overtake me with the bird perched on her shoulder, while the waggon followed at a more discreet distance. Both Didymusa and the bird came in for a good deal of attention, and as we went on our way one of the sky-rocketters cast furtive glances under our sun-bonnets, turning up his eyes and exclaiming " Bella " with great gusto.

I gathered from the old señora that this was the method of offering prayers for rain, and that the people were going to deposit the picture in the church of Santa Maria at Santa Rosa, where it would remain over Sunday— the following day. The pace being rapid and the dust intolerable, I was not sorry to reach the church, where the picture was placed before the altar with much solemnity, all who could manage to crowd their way inside falling on their knees and murmuring Ave Marias, while outside the weird dancing and singing went on without intermission. I was told that, in default of a satisfactory answer to the petition, the picture would be torn to atoms ; but, although no rain fell, I did not learn Sebastian's fate.

Fray Sebastian is not, strictly speaking, a saint. He

was merely a lay Franciscan brother, but having encountered numerous perils during his long life, and being loved by the Blessed Virgin, a great many miracles were wrought on his behalf, and he was made a "beato" by Pope Pius VI. in 1790. At no very distant day he will probably be canonised. It was he who first introduced wheeled carts (drawn by oxen) in Mexico, and for many years drove an ox-cart post through the dangerous Chichimec country, between the City of Mexico and Zacatecas.

We never travelled far on Sundays, making a "day-off" whenever it was possible, but not liking our camping-place near Santa Rosa, we decided to move on a little way, and after a short distance found ourselves near Querétaro ; too near in fact to camp. The road being full of people, we partook of a hasty luncheon in the waggon *en route*.

We had now left the State of Guanajuato and entered that of Querétaro, where a frontier Custom House had to be passed. Although I showed my protection papers, explained our business of pleasure, declared that the kegs contained nothing more contraband than water, and that the contents of the waggon were merely clothing and pro- visions for our journey, the official appeared incredulous. The kegs contained aguardiente or whiskey, the goods were a load of boots ! Mr Taylor began to air his Spanish and no doubt helped further to confuse the man, who accompanied us to the Customs Office in the town. There we were compelled to wait, as no one was on duty, and the Bank being, of course, closed, unfortunately I could not make use of my letter of introduction. But Monsieur Marin, owner of an opal mine, happening to pass, perceived the ridiculous situation at a glance, and, coming to the succour of the prairie-schooner in distress, succeeded in per- suading this obstinate official to permit her to "lie to" until

morning.   Mr. Marin kindly conducted us to the Meson
de la Luz and the Ferro Carril Hotel; the host an intelligent Frenchman, formerly *chef* to the Emperor Maximilian.

There were baths at this hotel, which, though barely
furnished with naked brick floors, was clean.   The coffee
was a great treat, though Tony did not like it so well as
the burnt concoction to which he was used in Texas.

We paid a visit to M. Marin's mine, and saw some red
opals, which were quite new to me, buying a few specimens and collecting some pretty pieces full of fire in the
quartz that had been discarded as worthless.   Some of
their veins were almost emerald colour.   The pure opal is
all, more or less, a deposit of lead, and where there are any
scratches, becomes opaque at a low temperature.   You
have to be cautious about opals; they are of all sizes and
all colours; you see them everywhere.   Indians hawk
them at street corners.   However a conversation may begin,
it is sure to touch on opals before it ends.   These stones are
said to bring bad luck; nevertheless, Quéretaro prospers!

After leaving the mine, we drove to the hill and the
redoubt where Maximilian with his two generals, Miramon
and Mejia, was shot, the spot being marked by three flint
shafts inclosed by an iron railing.   At the State Legisla-
ture we saw subsequently Maximilian's coffin and the table
used at his court-martial, and upon which his death
warrant was signed.   He requested that he might be shot
in the body, so that his mother might be able to recognise
his face.   This request was granted, and in the rough coffin
which temporarily contained his corpse, a stain of blood
marks the spot where his injured hand rested.   Having
been embalmed by order of Juarez, his body was placed in
a handsomely carved rosewood coffin, inclosed in a metal
shell, and sent to Austria.

This unfortunate man, cruelly brought to his death through the treachery of Napoleon III., lies buried at Miramir. It may be remembered that Maximilian accepted the crown under two conditions—the first, that he should be elected by a popular vote in Mexico ; the second, that Napoleon should give him armed support as long as this might be necessary. The Clericals were dissatisfied with his government ; he continued to enforce the Laws of the Reform, which he had been expected to abrogate. The summary execution of the Mexican generals brought to a climax the popular discontent at being governed by a foreign prince supported by a foreign army. It is believed that Maximilian was induced to publish the decree by Bazaine. His character was weak ; the extravagant expenses of his court and its pageants became a burden to the country, and when he was threatened by the U.S.A., Napoleon failed him.

To strengthen his position and conciliate the people, he adopted a grandson of the unfortunate Yturbide. The parents of the pretty, golden-haired, blue-eyed boy gave their consent, and agreed to leave Mexico immediately.

The child was three years old, and soon became the idol of Maximilian and his wife Carlotta. But, unable to endure the separation, Madame Yturbide returned to the capital, and, in a heart-rending letter to the Emperor, prayed for the restoration of her son. She was decoyed and forced to return to Pueblo, and going to Paris, held a memorable interview with Carlotta, who was striving to procure aid for the tottering empire, and already betraying signs of mental infirmity. When Maximilian found that his fate was imminent, he sent the young Augustin to Havana, where the mother and son were reunited. The

Princess Salm-Salm rode 120 miles across country to implore Juarez on her knees to spare Maximilian's life. But, though it appears that personally he would have been glad to remit the death penalty, his strong political convictions rendered clemency impossible.

Juarez (a "full-blooded" Indian) seems to have been born to right his country's wrongs, which served to develop his extraordinary strength of character. He was fully exonerated for refusing to annul Maximilian's death-warrant, and no stain dims the glory of his memory.

We drove past the great aqueduct which supplies the city on our way to the Hercules cotton factory, where, by permission of Senor Gabriel Ybambier-y-Villar, we inspected the combing and spinning rooms, and were each presented with a spool. About 500 Mexican operatives are employed, their wages averaging nearly three reales a day. The machinery (all of English manufacture) is driven by both steam and water power.

Beautiful gardens surround the house, containing ornamental water and statuary ; a figure of Hercules giving its name to the mills. On the terraced walks we were charmed by the lovely creeping vine Bougainvillea, in clusters of pink, crimson, and purple blossom ; while from the arches were suspended the long white bells of the *Datura arborea* or *floribunda* ; sometimes known as the *alcatras* (pelican).

The churches of Quéretaro are very handsome, and that of Santa Cruz possesses a curious history :

In 1531 an Otomite chief, a zealous convert, went forth to Christianize the members of his tribe, and accordingly recruited a little army at Tula ! Coming to Quéretaro he arranged that the heathen and Christian champions should fight only with their fists in order that no blood should be shed. During the fight the light of the sun grew fainter, and, floating in the air, so that it might be plainly seen by all, was the blessed Santiago with a ruddy cross ; which spectacle overawed the people of Quéretaro who forthwith withdrew their champions and begged to be baptised.

The saint's miraculous manifestation occurred on July 25, and the Christian town was called Santiago de Quéretaro ; a cross being raised on the spot where the church now stands.

Staying at the Ferro Carril Hotel was Mr. Rafle (who had fought and lost an arm at Gettysburg) with his wife : a pleasant couple.

On December 13th we set forth from Quéretaro, and camped that night at San Juan del Rio, hearing drums and bells in the distance. After visiting its three churches, fruit market, &c., we continued our journey through a lovely country of mountain and valley.

We had several times passed wayside crosses commemorating scenes of violence and murder. Near San Juan del Rio there is a little shrine, with quite a large pile of stones, each representing a petition offered up for the repose of a soul. Judging from the heap, the mute appeal must be seldom disregarded. On our return, near Zacatecas, our attention was drawn to other crosses, marking the graves of some men who met their death in a railway accident.

Just before arriving at Arroyo Zarco, while Didymusa and Tony were walking, by way of a change, Mr. Taylor and I applied ourselves to the study of the map, and not keeping a sufficiently sharp look out, found ourselves in a narrow gully with a fairly wide stream ahead.

There being no back view from the waggon, we were not aware that Tony was behind ; it was impossible to turn ; Molly objected to back, and, as we were on a slight decline, she showed an equally strong dislike to standing still.

Now, having seen artillery carriages cross the marsh ditches at Hayling Island on field days, I thought that our waggon would clear the stream if we approached it at a pretty quick run, especially as the take-off was good, and the bank on the opposite side lower. So we made for the obstacle at a rattling pace, the pony and mules gave a bound, but, alas ! the ditch was too wide, and our wheels dropped in the middle. A short struggle, and we were over ; but the next minute the bed of the waggon slipped bodily from the frame. If Tony had not hurried up and acted as a brake behind, matters would have been still worse, as it was, a good deal of trouble and our united strength were required to set the waggon right, and, of course, we had to unhitch the team while Tony repaired the harness. I managed to cling to the board during this scrimmage, and so avoided being thrown out.

The following day's journey lay through a wild, beautiful country, very mountainous, now thickly wooded, now so rocky that progress became extremely difficult. During the afternoon we seemed to lose the trail, and got into so thick a wood that it was difficult to turn back, and, indeed, it was necessary to remove a fallen tree before we could get round. Retracing our steps for a mile or two, we followed a track that we had noticed in passing, but this did not run in a south-westerly direction—about our proper course throughout the journey. Our camping ground that night was extremely picturesque, with a lake near at hand, where we shot some more wild duck.

On the morrow the road was remarkably rough and thickly wooded, and about three miles short of San

Francisco, in getting over some huge rocks our waggon once more gave way. It being nearly noon, we determined to camp, whereupon Tony made an examination and found that the main or "king" bolt (connecting the "bolster" pin, the sand-board, the axle, and coupling pole) had snapped. Taking the broken piece as a pattern, he rode Luis, the pony, on to San Francisco, where he was able to get a new pin made. But there was a good deal of trouble in removing the broken piece from the socket, and we had to hold the props, which Tony fixed as levers to raise the bed of the waggon, while he did the work.

The next day we lost one of the water kegs, but, fortunately, had not far to return before it was found—no doubt these several breakages were due to the jolt in crossing the ditch. Seeing a fine flock of turkeys in San Francisco, we bought a *pavo* from a handsome but uncanny-looking old señora, and roasted it for Sunday, in anticipation of Christmas, though where and how we should spend the festive season was more than we could imagine at present.

The people were very superstitious concerning the moon, and many of their failings are laid to the account of that luminary. Before lighting a fire they frequently make the sign of the cross, as also before killing fowls or preparing tortillas, or, if they possess ever so small a taper, they burn it all night, with a cross fixed close by.

The small town of Tula is very ancient, and believed to have been a Toltec foundation. At the time of the conquest it was an important Otomite town, and one of the first to embrace Christianity. It possesses some curious Toltec relics; the half of a colossal statue, some broken columns and an ancient font. The church (evidently intended also as a place of refuge from the Chichimecs) is more like a fortress, with its massive stone walls seven feet in thickness, and its battlemented roof. As we neared Huehuetoca on December 17th, we caught our first glimpse of the snow-clad summit of Popocatepetl, and passed the Tajo de Nochistongo—the great drainage cut, begun by Martinez in 1607, to draw away the waters of the lakes and of Zumpango and Texcolo, and save the city and valley from inundations.

In June, 1629, when the rainy season set in, Martinez caused the mouth of the tunnel to be closed, either from fear lest so large a volume of water should wreck his work, or to demonstrate to the people the necessity of the undertaking. The consequence was " the great inundation," which lasted nearly five years. In a single night nearly the whole of the city was three feet under water ; great misery naturally ensued and Martinez was imprisoned. But he was afterwards released in order that he might complete the work. Several earthquakes happening about this time, the cracks in the ground afforded natural means for the water to escape. As the tunnel showed a tendency to cave, it was eventually made an open cut (*tajo*), at the cost of 8,000,000 dollars. Fifteen thousand Indians were at one time employed on this work.

Never shall I forget the descent of that beautiful valley. One could imagine the feelings of Cortes and his little band when they first beheld it ! Stopping to look at the tiny chapel or shrine dedicated to Ermita San Antonio de Padua, and at the quaint pictures which depict his life and history, and passing Tlalnepantla (notable only for its enormous bull-ring), a journey of two hours through the suburbs brought us to the City of Mexico.

————◦◦⟩◦⟨◦◦————

CHAPTER XXXI.

ARRIVAL AT CITY OF MEXICO—NUESTRA SEÑORA
DE GUADALUPE—THE CAPILLA DEL POCITO
—HOTELS—THE VIGA CANAL—LAVANDERAS —
CATHEDRAL — PIÑATES — CHRIST CHURCH —
THEATRES.

YES, we had reached the Halls of the Montezumas at last! And our "prairie schooner" had escaped all the misfortunes which our friends in Texas had predicted.

Leaving the team at the Meson de Balvanera, we took up our quarters at the Hotel de Juarez, and shortly after our arrival were interviewed by the Editor of the *Two Republics*, who also presented Tony and Mr. Taylor with tickets for a supper to be given by the Christian Association.

Our first excursion was the holiest of the shrines in Mexico, the Guadaloupe. Taking cars from the " Plaza Mayor " we were borne swiftly along behind galloping mules about a *legua* from the city. The festival (*Posado*, signifying both an inn and a nine days' festivity) beginning on December 12th was not yet over, and in fact runs into that of Christmas. It reminded me of the procession at Santa Rosa, combined with the *fiesta* on the plaza of Saltillo, on a magnified scale. No fewer than 25,000 Indians had collected to celebrate the festival, frequently conducting their own ceremonies quite apart from those in the church. I fancy that the elaborate Roman Catholic ritual, with its processions and vestments, is calculated to appeal to the native mind.

The following is the legend of the church and chapel, very much condensed. In early times an Aztec divinity, known as Tonantzin (mother of gods) was worshipped where the chapel now stands. The chronicler (Vetancurt, 1672) goes on to describe "the miracle that occurred to change the worship of the pagan mother to that of the Christian God-mother. . . . . . Juan Diego went to hear Mass in the church of Santiago Tlaltebolco on December 9th, 1531.

" Near the hill called Tepeyácache heard the music of angels. Then beheld he, amid splendours, a lady who spoke to him, directing him to go to the Bishop and tell him that it was her will that in that place should be built to her a temple. Upon his knees he listened to her bidding, and then, happy and confused, betook himself to the Bishop with the message she had given him. The Bishop, Don Juan Zumárraga heard him with benignity, but could not give credence to the prodigy that he was told of. With this answer he returned, finding there again the lady, who heard what he had to tell and bade him come to her again. On the Sunday ensuing he was at the hill-side again, when she appeared to him for the third time and repeated her order that he should convey to the Bishop her command that the temple should be built. The Bishop heard the message still incredulously, and ordered that the Indian should bring some sure sign by which he might be shown that what he told was true ; and when the Indian departed, the Bishop sent two of his servants to watch him secretly ; yet as he neared the holy hill, he disappeared from the sight of these watchers. Unseen then of these he met the lady and told that he had been required to bring some sure sign of her appearance ; and she told him to come the next day and he should have a sign. But when he came to his

NUESTRA SEÑORA DE GUADALUPE.

house he found there his uncle, Juan Bernardino, lying
very ill (having the fever, which the Indians call *Cocolixtli*).
Through the next day he attended the sick man; the sickness increased, and early on the morning of December
12th he went to call from Tlaltelolco a confessor. That
he might not be delayed in his quest by that lady's impor-
tunities he went not by the usual path, but by another
skirting the eastern side of the hill. But as he passed the
hill he saw the lady coming down to him and heard her
calling to him. He told her of his errand, and of its
urgent need for quickness, whereupon she replied that he
need not feel further trouble, as already his uncle's illness
was cured. Then ordered she him to cut some flowers on
that barren hill, and to his amazement he perceived flowers
growing there. She charged him to take these miraculous
flowers to the Bishop as the sign that he had requested;
and she commanded that Juan Diego should show them to
no other until they were seen of the Bishop's eyes. Therefore he wrapped them in his *tilma* (blanket) and hastened
away. Then from the spot where most holy Mary stood,
there gushed forth a stream of brackish water, which now
is venerated and is an antidote to infirmities. Juan Diego
waited at the entrance of the Bishop's house until he
should come out, and when he appeared and the flowers
were shown him, there was seen the image of the Virgin
beautifully painted upon the Indian's *tilma*. The Bishop
placed the miraculous picture in his oratory, and Juan
Diego, returning to his house with two servants of the
Bishop, found that his uncle had been healed of his sickness the very hour that the Virgin declared he would be
well. As quickly as possible the Bishop caused the chapel
to be built upon the spot where the Virgin had appeared,
and, where the miraculous roses had sprung up from the

barren rock, there he placed the holy image on February
7th, 1532."

The papal sanction of the apparition followed in due
order. In a gold frame, and enclosed in plate glass, the
picture of the Virgin hangs above the altar of the Church
of Guadalupe, its colours still perfectly bright and fresh
after more than three hundred years. It is painted on
coarse cloth of *ixtli* fibre.

It was difficult to make our way through the throng of
Indians, whose wild gestures suggested that the old
divinity Tonantzin still held a place in their worship.
The altar rails are silver, and some millions of dollars
have been collected to provide a crown of gold, which still
awaits the pontifical sanction.

Several painters of high standing have examined the
picture; its glass covering having been removed for the
purpose. It does not seem to be either in distemper,
water-colour, or oils; though more like an oil-painting
than anything else.

The sacristy is extremely beautiful, with its wood
carving, its Mexican onyx and white marble. The value
of the jewels and gold and silver plate (nearly all of which
passed into the possession of the Government) is estimated
at $2,000,000. In 1836, the cost of the work, with reno-
vations, was $381,000, the original cost reached $800,000,
making, with alms-offerings, a total of $1,181,000.

The Capilla del Cerrito (chapel of the little hill) marks
the spot where Diego plucked the roses, and possesses an
endowment to provide for the performance of a solemn
service every 12th of December.

In order to reach the church, we climbed the long
stairway and path up the hill. On our right near the top,
stood the mast of a ship, with all sails set, carved in stone.

According to the legend, some tempest-tossed sailors in distress, appealed to the Virgin of Guadalupe, vowing to carry their mast to the shrine and erect it there as a memorial and thank offering, if she saved them from a watery grave. The ship reaching Vera Cruz in safety, they bore the mast and yards on their shoulders and set it up in its present position, encasing it in stone as a protection against the elements.

The Capilla del Pocito stands at the foot of the hill, a pretty little building with an iron grating surrounding a well (*pocito*), whence its name. Torres, the architect of this chapel, gave his services gratuitously. The handsome carved pulpit is supported by an image of Juan Diego, and opposite the door, at the beginning of the ascent of the hill, stands a pillar, crowned with a figure of the Virgin, which marks the place of her first miraculous appearance. We drank some of the clear bright water, but found its taste exceedingly disagreeable.

The Yturbide Hotel is the only one in the city with a restaurant attached. We often had our meals there, and found the cuisine excellent, as also at the Cántabro and Concordia Restaurants.

We had friends at the Comonfort and Ghigliazza Hotels, the rooms of which were very sunny—a great advantage in this climate. The Hotel del Jardin (pronounced "hardeen") also is sunny and picturesque, its gardens having once formed part of the grounds of the Convent of San Francisco.

This visit to the city of Mexico forms still a green spot in my memory. I often look back upon it as a pleasant dream. Such novel and marvellous scenes! Such kindness and hospitality!—thanks to letters of introduction from Mr. Seggermann and others. We were introduced to Mr. Kirkland, of Milwaukee, an attorney, whose visit was connected with some extensive mining operations, which had brought him into close contact with various Indian tribes. Singularly enough, we had mutual friends in England, Sir Charles C——, who had met Mr. Kirkland in Saskatchewan, being one of these. Nor must I forget Mr. Hector Thomas, ex-secretary to the Chargé d'Affaires de Belgique au Chili—an accomplished linguist, from whom I received much valuable information.

On the 23rd December we formed a party to visit Santa Anita and the shores of Texcoco, Xochimilco, and Chalco, by the Viga canal, probably so called from its wooden bridges : Viga=beam.

This was the work of the Aztecs, and is not really a canal, being, in fact, a navigable sluice to convey the waters of Lakes Xochimilco and Chalco to the lower level of Texcoco.

On reaching the Paseo de la Viga by cars we were besieged by boatmen, and a tremendous clamouring and bargaining ensued. The boats are broad of beam and flat-bottomed like Venetian gondolas, with bright coloured canopies and dusky barefooted gondoliers, who, clad in their short, white *mantas* walk briskly up and down the prow as they punt the craft along. After he has spent your " pour-boire " at one of the *pulqueria* on the shore, your gondolier becomes more communicative. The " Chinampas," or floating gardens, are now merely patches of nursery garden, with little canals, instead of paths, surrounding the beds. But the beds did formerly float above these little patches, separated by narrow channels. They supply the city markets with fruit and vegetables.

We moored for a while by the *hacienda* of Don Juan Corona. The house, which is shaded by trees and covered with climbing vines and flowers, is full of curiosities. The rooms form a perfect museum, containing, amongst other things, the pistol and sword carried by Hidalgo, pieces of Maximilian's table service ; several idols found in the Pyramids of Teotihuacan ; weapons, feathers, and war-dresses used by the Aztecs ; a magnificent collection of *chicaras* (chocolate cups), painted by the Michoacan Indians ; a very curious and ancient bull-fighter's costume, used by the Spanish matador, Gaviño, when he was killed in the ring at Texcoco, &c., &c. Collecting curiosities was Don Juan's hobby ; but out of his savings he established a school for the poor children of La Viga ; nor did his philanthropy end there. He cared for the bodies as well as the minds of the children, clothed and fed them, and was known as the " Father of the destitute." The school still exists. The villages being *en fête*, the smell of cooked *tamales* was all pervading, while the merry, light-hearted people wove garlands of brightly-hued flowers to crown one another—of course, they indulged in their favourite games of hazard.

In the quaint, old church of Santa Anita, we saw a representation of Santiago on a white horse ; and at Ixta-calco, a small and curious chapel dedicated to the same saint. Although we had brought some provisions, we did not fail to taste several native dishes at various *fondas* (restaurants). As we were returning on the evening of December 24, the Viga was alive with Indian canoes crowded by garlanded merrymakers with lanterns and other Christmas Eve decorations. We heard songs, accompanied by guitars, and on the larger boats there was dancing.

The banks of the Viga were busy with *lavanderas* (washerwomen), working on their knees, whose brilliant costumes formed a bright fringe along the edge of the stream. The *planchadora* comes to count the clothes and take them away to be starched, ironed, and finished. She also acts as *apuntar*, and carefully mends every article before sending it home. A real a dozen, with soap provided, is the price in most towns, but in the city there are laundries.

A description of all the churches would be impossible; in fact, they number nearly two hundred. We visited the most notable, amongst these, of course, the cathedral, consecrated as the Church of the Ascension Maria Santissima, and built on the site of the Aztec temple (*teocalli*), where, in the time of Montezuma, human sacrifices took place, until the city was destroyed and conquered by the Spaniards in 1521. The first stone of this enormous edifice was laid in 1573, its complete cost amounting to $2,000,000. The great bell in the west tower, nineteen feet in height, alone cost $10,000. The architecture of the interior is chiefly Doric, with traces of Gothic, the aisles being divided from the nave by fluted columns. The choir is inclosed by a handsome railing of tumbago—an alloy of gold, silver, and copper, made in Macao.

Amongst all the numerous chapels and altars, the finest is the Altar of los Reyes, in the apsis rising from pavement to roof, and executed by the architect of the altar bearing the same name in the cathedral at Seville. Six large paintings cover the walls of the sacristy—" The Glory of Saint Michael," " The Immaculate Conception," " The Triumph of the Sacrament," " The Entry into Jerusalem," and two others.

The interior of the cathedral was seen to great advantage when fully lighted on Christmas Eve. We arrived at eleven o'clock at night, and remained until nearly two o'clock on Christmas morning. A truly wonderful scene!

The gorgeous vestments of the priests and acolytes; the array of wax-work figures, reinforced for the occasion; the vast congregation, including high-born Spanish ladies wearing their mantillas, Mexican women in their *rebosos*, and half-clad Indians with babies suspended to their backs. Some were doing penance; we noticed one man on his knees for hours, crouching with his hands outstretched in what must have been an exceedingly painful attitude. And then the music swelled through the immense interior; two organs, several auxiliary instruments, and many beautiful voices.

The pretty gardens of the Zócalo, which surrounded the edifice, were a gift from the Government to the people, who assemble (rich and poor alike) on Sundays and two or three times a week to hear the band. The view of the cathedral, however, is obstructed by trees.

The market was a mass of surging, struggling people, eager to buy decorations; Venetian lamps hung in the *patios*, fireworks exploded, *posados* sang.

Mexican children are ignorant of the existence of Santa Claus, and never wake to find their stockings full of presents on Christmas morning. Their chief pastime is the breaking of the *piñates*—earthen jars filled with sweet-meats, covered with bright ornaments and tinsel, and decorated to represent turkeys, horses, bull-fighters, brides with trains, veils and orange blossom, &c., &c. They are sold in the streets and market by men, who carry them suspended on long poles, and Didymusa was inclined to buy one, until she realised that our space was too limited to pack it. So she turned away from the stall with a sigh.

A *piñate* is hung in the *patio*, or to the ceiling of a room, whereupon each person in turn is blindfolded and strikes at the figure until it breaks, scattering its contents over the floor. Then the children scramble for them. *Posados* (festivities) are given by the wealthy on a grand scale, with balls, dinners, and various other entertainments. In rural districts and on the borders of Rio Grande the *pastorela* begins several days before Christmas. The infant Jesus, represented by a doll, is rocked in a cradle swinging from the ceiling and is baptized on Christmas Eve, sponsors being selected from amongst the company, with children dressed in white and bearing crooks for angels.

We attended several nicely conducted Anglican services at Christ Church ; which is in the north wing of the San Francisco Cathedral. On Christmas morning the British Chaplain preached an excellent sermon. In the evening, while listening to the band in the fine Alameda (so-called because it was first planted with *álamos*, or poplars), we enjoyed a good opportunity of watching the people *en fête*. The " Principal " and "Nacional " Theatres each seat about 3000 persons, but are poorly decorated. There are good Italian opera troupes, however, and at the " Principal " we saw " La Dame aux Camellias " acted by a Spanish company. I was greatly impressed by Madame Prodescini's treatment of the last scene, and, although I hesitate to say so, prefer her rendering of the character to the more sensational method of the famous Sarah Bernhardt : a rapt, silent gaze, a slight totter, and droop of the arms indicating that life was over ! As the curtain fell the lines of Milman's prize poem, " The Belvedere Apollo," came to my mind :

> " Slowly she wan'd, and, cold and senseless grown,
> Clos'd her dim eye, herself benumbed to stone ;
> Yet love in death a sickly strength supplied,
> Once more she gazed, then feebly smil'd and died."

————oo:o:o:oo————

CHAPTER XXXII.

OUR PARTY BREAKS UP—MULES, PONY, "PRAIRIE
SCHOONER," &c., SOLD — SANTA GERTRUDIS
MINE—"PATIO" PROCESS — APAM — PULQUE —
MUSEUM AT CITY OF MEXICO—AZTEC GODS—
NAHOAN INDIAN SUPERSTITIONS.

It now became necessary to think about returning to
Texas; Tony's mother was ill, Mr. Taylor's cattle required
their owner's attention, whilst my own letters suggested
duties at home in England. There remained, however,
several excursions yet to be made from the city of Mexico,
and for these the waggon would be unpracticable. Moreover, we were strongly advised not to think of returning to
Junction City with Mexicans for our only escort.

To take the waggon to England was out of the
question, consequently it must be sold; and, Mr. Thomas
having discovered someone who wished to buy the whole
turn-out, I finally agreed to sell it and the mules for 220
dollars—an excellent price.

The poor mules certainly owed me nothing. They had
pulled us over a long stretch of rough country, exhibited
marvellous powers of endurance, and now looked as fresh
as when they started. Luis, the pony, also fetched his
money again.

Finally, I said good-bye to our "prairie schooner"
with great reluctance; also to Tony and Mr. Taylor, who
started to Texas by the cars on December 29th. Previous

to their departure we held an auction : the guns, revolver, tent, &c., fetching ridiculously high prices.

In this benign climate, Didymusa had lost her rheumatism, and her mattress had been burned bit by bit in default of wood.

Mr. Carden dissuaded us from climbing Popocatepetl, an expensive and uncomfortable task, and the view at its end by no means a certainty. But he gave us a letter which enabled us to visit Captain Frank Rules's silver mine, Santa Gertrudis, at Pachuca, whither we started at 7 a.m. from Peravillo Station on the National line. An hour's drive from Pachuca brought us to the mine, which we descended by a shaft, although at many others there is only a bucket to go down in, worked by a horse and windlass.

The staves looked somewhat treacherous, but they bore us safely ; even at the pit mouth the air seemed sulphurous and suffocating. The ore is raised by a *malacate* (horse-whim) ; some specimens we received contained fifty per cent. of silver.

Ladies are not generally welcome, as the miners imagine they bring bad luck ; nevertheless, the Cornish manager showed us the greatest courtesy, and took infinite pains to explain the mysteries of the " patio " process while conducting us over the large concentration works. The ore is first crushed by the hammer, then more finely ground by the Chilian mill (mule power), afterwards being reduced to powder in *arastes*, or small stone tanks, where a little water is added. The mud which results is conveyed to the *patio* (floor), and mixed with ore pulp—sulphate of copper, occasionally cyanide of potassium, lime, salt, and quicksilver. Mules are then driven through this muddy compound in circles, until the quicksilver has amalgamated with the gold and silver, when the pulp goes to the washing room. Here more water is added and sticks are drawn through the now very wet mixture (worked by a wheel and mule-power) until the earthy matter is washed away, depositing the amalgam at the bottom of the agitator, After this it is placed in buckskin bags and thoroughly squeezed in a press until all the lighter particles of pure quicksilver have passed through, leaving only the amalgam—heavy and solid. This is carried to the retort-room and condensed by a slow fire at a heat of 600°, leaving the gold and silver combined in a spongy mass, which is melted down at the bullion furnace into solid blocks of alloy, these being subsequently shipped to the various mints or refining works for separation.

The " patio process " is employed only for ores which are free from sulphur, antimony, zinc, and lead ; otherwise the roasting process has to be resorted to. Insufficient capital brings many mines to grief, as also inferior machinery, which allows water to gain the upper hand. But at Santa Gertrudis the machinery was all of English manufacture ; the house and engine costing 60,000 dollars. Each stroke raised thirty and a-half gallons, and the rate was six strokes a minute. Some of the coal came from Pennsylvania, but more from England by sea to Vera Cruz, the price being twenty-two dollars a ton. From 500 to 600 men were employed, about sixty from Cornwall. At this period the mine yielded 60,000 dollars a month clear profit, and had been equally lucrative ever since it came into full " bonanza " (boom) some time ago.

The silver workings were discovered by a shepherd at Pachuca shortly after the conquest of Mexico, and a mining camp sprang into existence in 1534. The so-called "patio process " of amalgamating silver ore was invented by Bartolome de Medina in the time of Luis de Velasco, second viceroy (1557), who emancipated 150,000 Indians enslaved by the Spanish. When it was pointed out that their liberation would ruin the mining industry of the province, the Viceroy made answer : "The liberty of the Indians is of more importance than the mines of the whole world." A noble sentiment destined to be soon forgotten, the enslavement of the Indians in one form or another having continued almost to the present day. The same Viceroy founded a university and a hospital, built the dyke of San Lázaro, cleared the roads of robbers, and died greatly lamented and beloved in 1564.

On our way back to the city we passed through Apam, the great pulque district. Far as the eyes can reach over these plains one sees the maguey or century plants (*Agave Americana*), from which the national beverage is obtained and conveyed to the city by special trains every morning.

Sometimes the plants are laid out irregularly, some-times in parallel rows. When about to flower (which occurs oftener than once in a hundred years) the plant throws out a shoot from fifteen to twenty feet in height. The heart being extracted, the sap which would otherwise go to nourish the stalk and blossom, rises in the cavity thus formed. This is crude pulque. The *tlachiquero*, or Indian whose business it is, collects the sap in his skin bags every day until the plant dies. He carries a gourd with a small hole at each end; placing one in the centre of the plant, he puts his lips to the other and sucks until the gourd is full, when he empties it into a skin bag, which in its turn gives up its contents to one of the casks waiting in a cart at the end of the row. A single plant yields about a gallon of sap a day, or about twenty-five gallons in all before it dies. Pulque does not keep, and unless it is drunk after a short process of fermentation, becomes extremely intoxicating. As the bags are made of hog or sheep skin, the smell of the pulque is even worse than the taste, and this is certainly an acquired one. It is desirable, however, to make an effort, for it is not only very wholesome, but tends to counteract the biliousness induced by the altitude of this district. We found pulque very

TLACHIQUERO WITH BURRO.

efficacious at Saltillo. It is also a specific for Bright's disease and diabetes, being bottled for exportation. In colour it resembles cocoa-nut milk or butter-milk, and in taste is something between bad cider and sweet-wort. Hot pulque is used by inhalation in lung weakness and drunk for coughs. For indigestion it is mixed with starch or "tequis quiti," a mineral containing soda and ammonia.

z

Mescal and *tequila* are distilled from the root of the maguey, and somewhat resemble whisky.   Brandy is known as *aguardiente* (tooth-water), that imported from France fetching a high price.   Toluca beer is both good and cheap.

From the cars near San Juan Sebastian we saw the pyramids of the Sun and Moon.   They do not look imposing in the distance, although one measures 216 feet and the other 150 feet.   The latter had been entered (but not the former) from its southern face, whence there is a narrow declined gallery 65 feet from the ground.   Beyond this both pyramids remain unexplored.   They are connected by a causeway, flanked by a notable group of tumuli, and named Calle de los Muertos—the City of the Dead.   Some of the tumuli on being opened revealed only empty chambers, but in others were found boxes of wrought stone, enclosing skulls and ornaments of obsidian pottery.   These tombs are supposed to be older than either Toltec or Acolhuas, and it continues doubtful whether the civilisation of Mexico does not date back further than that of Egypt.   The museum contains a rich collection of antiquities and pre-historic remains : the Chac-Mool, or god of Fire, about the origin of which have raged bitter controversies not yet entirely extinguished ; the Aztec calendar stone (the stone of the sun) ; the Indian Triste (sad Indian) ; Huitzilopochtli, a huge idol of porphyritic basalt, the war god or Mexican Mars ; and the famous stone upon which from 20,000 to 50,000 victims were annually sacrificed.   This is a circular stone with a cup-shaped cavity in the centre and a radiating channel extending down one side to carry away the blood.   The sight of this horrible relic caused a shudder, and recalled the description in Prescott's History of the five priests binding their victim, while a sixth, clad in a " scarlet mantle, emblematical of his bloody office, dexterously opened the breast of the wretched victim with a sharp razor made of *itztli*, a volcanic substance, hard as flint, and, inserting his hand, pulled out the palpitating heart."

In the carving of these curious stones, the forms of

AZTEC CALENDAR STONE, 12FT. IN DIAMETER; WEIGHT, 53,790LB.
THE AZTEC YEAR CONTAINS EIGHTEEN MONTHS.

animals, lizards, and other reptiles are seen. Two colossal heads of snakes (from Tenochtitlan) in the south gallery, were discovered by Señor Cubas, and shown by him to be part of the ancient Cohuatepantli, or Snake Wall.

Quetzalcoatl is also an interesting specimen of the serpent symbol : pyramidal in form, the body covered with feathers, it is carved in basaltic porphyry. As pointed out by Cubas, this fantastic effigy is repeated in many ancient Mexican monuments, often of colossal proportions. It is accepted as one of the most ancient and famous deities of the American Pantheon, since it is found, but slightly modified, in all parts of the continent. In this myth is preserved, in Mexico, the memory of a mysterious, white, and bearded personage, who expounded a strict and pure system of morals, bestowed a knowledge of the Arts and Sciences, and was at once the priest and civilizer of the people. In a semi-barbarous and superstitious country, as time effaced all recollection of his personality, his apotheosis was only natural. By the Peruvians he is known as Manco-Capac ; by the Muiscas as Bohicá ; by the Yucatanos as Kukulcan ; and by the Mexicans as Quetzalcoatl.

Astonished to find traces of so pure a system of morality amongst a semi-barbarous and heathen people, the Christian missionaries fancied that this mysterious personage must have been one of Christ's Disciples, or at least one who had heard Him or His Apostles, and come to preach the true faith in the New World. Dr. Mier, a celebrated Mexican writer, demonstrates that he was no other than St. Thomas, arguing from the fact that in Spanish Quetzalcoatl is rendered Tomás. Señor Orozco-y-Berra was the first to draw attention to the circumstance that the quasi St. Thomas figured in Mexican history about the tenth century, A.D., while nobody could dispute the fact that the genuine St. Thomas belonged to the first ! But Señor Orozco-y-Berra not unreasonably suggests that Quetzalcoatl may have been a Christian missionary from Iceland. Cubas shows that the meaning of Quetzal-coatl is " serpent of Quetzalli." " Quetzalli " had anciently a variety of significations, albeit all akin. Its root, Quetzal,

THE AZTEC IDOL, HUITZILOPOCHTLI (TEOYAOMIQUI SIDE).

signifies a species of bird-of-paradise, and especially the two long, brilliant, tail-feathers of that bird : one of the principal articles paid to the Mexican chiefs by way of tribute. Its metaphorical use to describe anything very precious, naturally followed, and thus the term was applied to the man-god Quetzalcoatl.

There is a close similarity between the Aztec and the Mosaic records. The account of the Creation in the Book of Quinches of Guatemala, named also the Popul Vuh, bears a remarkable coincidence both in style and incident to the early chapters of Genesis.

The Aztecs taught that eternity was not of unbroken continuity, but divided by mighty events which occurred in cycles of several thousand years : one a cataclysm that swept everything from the face of the earth, another the blotting out of the sun from the heavens to be rekindled only after all things had perished.

These Mexican antiquities furnish food for a world of research and reflection. It is said that, even recently, garlands have been placed upon the idols in the museum, and that descendants of the ancient races, who inhabit caves in remote mountain regions, whither the light of Christianity has never yet shone, still worship their ancient deities, and that the old men and women still keep the young in awe of the grim gods worshipped by their ancestors. Some of their superstitions are singular ; according to " Mexico á Través de los Siglos," it was believed that Mictlan (hell) was reached by the dead only after a long and painful journey. Their hieroglyphics indicate that the dead must first cross the Apanohuaya River, and to accomplish this the aid was necessary of a little yellow dog (*techichi*) with a cotton string round his neck, placed in the dead person's hands. Neither white nor black dogs could cross the river—the former said, " I have been washed ;" the latter, " I have been stained." The dogs must needs be yellow, and were specially reared by the natives. The *techichi* is that well-known favourite amongst *perros*—the present Chihuahua dog. After crossing the river the dog led his naked master between two constantly colliding mountains, next over one covered with jagged rocks, then over eight hills on which snow was ever falling, to eight deserts where the winds were sharp as knives. After this a path was reached where arrows were continuously flying, and, worst of all, where the dead traveller encountered a tiger, who ate out his heart. After falling then into a deep, dark foaming river full of lizards, he at last appeared before the King of Mictlan, whereupon his journey ended with his own identity.

Before beginning this arduous voyage the body must have lain in the earth for a period of four years ; yet it was not the soul, but the actual body which performed the journey. The name of the last stopping place was Izmictlanapochcalocca, on which the alligator Xochitonal is encountered. The alligator is the earth's symbol, and Xochitonal the last day of the year. Here the body reached the final stage of existence, and became dust of the earth again.

" El Arbol de Leche de los Niños muertos " (" the milk tree for dead children ") embodies another tradition of the Nahoan Indians—the existence of a mansion to receive children after death. This was named Chihuacuauhco, after a tree which is supposed to grow there. From its branches milk dropped to nourish the children who cling to them. It was believed that these children would return to populate the world after the present race had passed away.

CHAPTER XXXIII.

THE AGUADOR — MEXICAN SERVANTS — MEXICAN
RACES — ORIGIN OF NATIONAL EMBLEM —
"NOCHE TRISTE" TREE—CHAPULTEPEC—RARE
FLOWERS — NATIONAL LIBRARY, &c. — THE
ARMY—POPOCATEPETL AND IZTACCIHUATL —
CHOLULA—TLAXCOLA—FRANCISCAN FRIARS—
ESPERANZA TO CORDOBA.

As the houses in Mexico are not provided with pipes, the *aguador* or water-carrier is in most towns an important functionary. At San Luis Potosí the water was carried in a low cart with a pole and one ox; at Queretaro in a kind of hand-barrow, but at Quanajuato and the city of Mexico it was borne on the head of the *aguador*—a picturesque figure in his jacket and trousers (turned up to the knees) of blue cloth or tanned buckskin.

The *chochocol* (water vessel) are attached to straps which cross on the forehead over a palm-leaf cap with a leather visor. The *aguador* wears a leather apron with a flap to guard his back, upon which the *chochocol* rests, another flap from waist to knees, and another (*rosadera*) to protect one thigh; all these pieces being fastened to his leather waistcoat by thongs which support and balance the jars. It is necessary that these should be of the same size and weight; if they do not exactly balance, or if one be suddenly broken or emptied the *aguador* loses his balance and falls. On the side opposite the *rosadera* he carries a deer-skin pouch (*barrega*) adorned with figures and containing coins and *pitoles*—small red beans, one of which he leaves at every house he visits. These are counted when he is paid, once a week or once a fortnight, as the case may be ; their number being checked by his own tally-sheet.

The *aguador* usually knows everything connected with the household he supplies, and is frequently employed as a

AGUADOR (WATER CARRIER.)

go-between by lovers. He scarcely ever dines at home ; his wife meeting him with his dinner, which is perhaps shared by his children or companions at the entrance to a house ; then he goes to the fountain where he obtains his water, and, freeing himself from his jars, takes a siesta in the shade, or spends the rest of the day at a pulque shop, or playing at *monte* and *rayeula* with his companions.

On Saturday in Passion Week (Sabado de Gloria) the *aguadórs* strew flowers on the water of the fountain and burn an image symbolical of their trade.

Mexican servants seldom quarrel, each having his or her separate duties, which never clash. An average city house employs from ten to twenty servants, some of the larger from thirty to thirty-five.

The chief servants are:

El portero ...... the doorkeeper.
El cochero ...... the coachman.
El lacayo .... the footman.
El caballerango the groom.
El mozo .... a kind of odd man for errands, &c.
El camarista ... the valet (in hotels this man acts also as chambermaid).
La recamerera ... the chambermaid in private houses.
Ama de llaves ... the housekeeper (literally mistress of the keys).
Cocinera .... the cook.
Galopina .... the scullion.
Pilmama .... the woman who takes out the children.
Chichi .... the wet nurse.
Molendera ...... the woman who grinds the corn.
Costurera .... the sewing woman.
Planchadora ... the ironing woman.

The *portero* is responsible for the safety of the house, both day and night, and usually sleeps under a staircase or in some dark nook of the *patio*.

The *tortilleras* are a separate and distinct class: making tortillas for sale, or sometimes going at stated hours each day to prepare them for private families.

On the frontier the mistress of the house is "Señora,"

but in cities of the interior " niña " (child), although her
years be a hundred.

Servants often serve one family for a lifetime, and
become strongly attached to it ; especially the *pilmama*,
whose pet name is " nana." A cook's wages vary from
$2 to $5 a month, a coachman's from $10 to $30, a serving
woman's from $3 to $8—beyond which sums they receive
a *medio* and *quartillo* a day (or sixty-two cents every eight
days) for coffee, bread, and pulque ; whilst soap, to the
value of a *medio*, is allowed each week for washing
clothes.

Servants are summoned by a motion of the hand—
turning the palm outward ; to attract their attention the
hands are generally clapped. Signs and gesticulations with
hands or fingers are frequently employed by the Mexicans ;
the graceful señorita at the window moves only her middle
and third fingers rapidly back and forth by way of a
salutation — not the whole hand. With " No es
costumbre " (a negative), the forefinger goes outward and
upward.

One cannot but be struck by the curious mingling of
races ; some Mexicans are extremely handsome, others
remarkably repulsive, the children of the upper classes
being generally very pretty.

According to " Mexico á Través de los Siglos," in the
sixteenth century the various types were classified as
follows, and they remain about the same to-day :

Children of Spaniards—
    Born in the country .... are Creoles.
Children of a Spaniard—
    And an Indian .... ,, Mestizos.
Children of a Spaniard—
    And a Mestizo .... ,, Castigos.

Children of a Castigos—
    And a Spaniard..................... are Españoles.
Children of a Spaniard—
    And a Negro....................... ,, Mulattos.
Children of a Mulatto—
    And a Spaniard.................... ,, Moriscos.
Children of a Negro—
    And an Indian .... ,, Zambos.

The Mestizos are the handsomest, the Zambos the ugliest and least attractive. Sometimes, nothing of the kind having happened for several generations, a black child crops out unexpectedly in a family : " Salta atrás " (a leap over several generations).

The various types seem almost unlimited : the dark, olive-tinted type is one ; the pale, though dark, swarthy, bloodless face, with melancholy, expressionless eyes, and dejected bearing, is characteristic of another ; but the type which interested and pleased me the most possesses a rich brown skin, carmine cheeks and lips, glistening white teeth, and eyes wondrously bright, yet soft and shy as a gazelle's. Figures and gaits differ as widely as faces : one thin and shambling, another plump and lithesome. The politeness of even the most ragged and degraded is conspicuous, not only to superiors but to each other.

The City of Mexico was founded in the twelfth century by one of the Northern tribes which invaded the lovely valley of Anahuac, and named it Tenochtitlan (cactus on a stone).

After leading a nomadic life for more than a century they rested on the borders of Lake Tezcuco, where an eagle with wings outspread, and holding a serpent in his talons, standing upon a *tunal* that grew from a fissure in a rock on the water's edge, impressed the tribe as an omen of future sovereignty—hence the emblem on the American escutcheon. They at once made preparations to build the city, and the slender huts of reeds and rushes erected by the Aztecs in the marshes of Tezcuco were in due course replaced by the more solid structures of the Spaniards.

Wherever you turn there is something of historical interest. The Calle de Tacuba is the ancient causeway of Tlacopan, where the Spaniards suffered their terrible defeat at the hands of the Aztecs, and Pedro Alvarado made his famous leap on the memorable night of July 1st, 1520, the " noche triste " (sad night). The " Arbol de la Noche triste," the tree against which Cortes is said to have leaned and wept, stands at Popotla, two miles from the capital : a giant Ahuehuete or cypress—at present guarded by an iron railing against the vandalism of tourists !

Near here the great Aztec slave market was situated, at Atzcapotzalco (ant-hill). On the church tower facing the plaza the figure of an ant is graven, symbolical of the town and its once swarming population.

Behind the monastery, by a pond of sweet water, is a ruined aqueduct haunted by Malinche. At Chapultepec, where she spends half her day, she is a benign spirit, but here malignant, of extraordinary beauty, and with a voice so sweet that it is dangerous to pass at early morn or eve, when none can resist her syren-song. One's only hope is to stop one's ears and fly. Otherwise, overcome by a delightful languor, he is drawn unresisting to the pond and the haunts of men know him no more. An old Indian will tell you of an enchanted grove of giant Ahuehuetes hard by, and whisper confidentially concerning hidden treasure concealed in the depths of the pond by Guatimotzin, who refused to reveal its locality, even under the cruel torture inflicted by Cortes.

A permit is required before you can visit Chapultepec, a fine fortress, built by Montezuma, now the residence of the President. It also accommodates 300 cadets, who receive their education gratis. Here lived Maximilian ; we climbed the drive, which he constructed, round a mountain of solid porphyry, and were rewarded by a magnificent view ; the dazzling snow-clad heights of Popocatepetl and Ixtaccihuatl, lakes, plains, towns and villages, the fields of Cherubusco and Malino del Rey on one side ; on the other in the foreground grand cypresses, Montezuma's bath and old aqueduct, with mountains stretching away far beyond.

The interior decorations of the castle are extremely handsome ; it is quite a royal residence. At the foot of the hill, a monument marks tho site of the conflict between the U.S.A. troops and Mexicans in 1847.

The National Library contains over 200,000 volumes, some new, some very old ; amongst others, an English atlas, printed in Amsterdam in 1659, with steel plates, and colours still bright. There are numerous original MSS. and a roll of deer-skin with despatches (painted pictures) sent by Montezuma to his allies and intercepted by Cortes.

The Monte de Piedad, founded by Count Regla, is under Government control. At the flower market at any season of the year, a profusion of the choicest kinds may be bought for a few centavos—roses, camellias, heliotropes, sweet peas, pansies, calla-lilies, and gorgeous poppies. Some of these are rare, such as the Plumeria, with rose-coloured, white, and yellow flowers and a sweet scent. Its Aztec name, *Cacolox ochitt*, means " flower of the raven." The " flor de noche buena" (*Poinsettia pulcherrima*) puts forth its brilliant scarlet flowers at Christmas, and the remarkable " arbol de las manitas " (tree of the little hands) (*Cheirostemon platonides*). It grows in the valley

of Toluca, and attains great age.   We saw it in the garden
of San Francisco—the flowers a bright red, with well defined
miniature hands.

At the *portales* near the Zócalo on Sundays, all kinds
of second-hand articles are on sale.   Hundreds of vendors
spread their goods on the pavement or hawk them in
baskets—jewels, pictures, string, furniture, books, &c.

On the occasion of the President's re-election there was
a grand march past, the troops covering the Plaza Major
and its outlets.   The evolutions were rapid and precise, the
horses in splendid condition ; each man carries a light
lariat at his pommel, and a crimson blanket strapped to the
cantle, whilst the silver mountings of saddles and bridles,
and frequently stirrups of the same metal, glistened
brightly in the sunlight.

The army is composed of three divisions—the permanent army, the reserve, and the general reserve ; about
130,000 infantry, 26,000 cavalry, and 4000 artillery.   The
permanent force consists of 40,000 men, 14,000 being
cavalry.   Mules are used in the batteries, as they are
supposed to work in this climate better than horses.   The
artillery and cavalry carry the Remington 50-calibre rifle,
the infantry the 43-calibre ; but both are to be replaced
by breech-loaders of a different pattern.   The nominal pay
of an enlisted man is four reales a day, but of this one and
a half reales are deferred until his time expires.   The pay
of an enlisted man in the cavalry and artillery is five reales
a day, of which two and a half reales are deferred.

All payments are made in silver, and the paymaster's
cart, drawn by a string of mules, is often as heavy as an
ammunition waggon.   An important sub-division of the
army is the gendarmeries, a section specially detailed to
clear the highways of robbers, being known as the *rurales*.

The *rurales* number about 4000 ; each man provides his own horse, equipment (arms excepted), rations, and forage, and receives ten reales a day.

Some of our friends were bound for Vera Cruz, but as we intended to return to Texas before leaving America, we could not sail for home from that port. However, I decided to accompany them to Cordoba, and visit other places of interest by the way ; the first being Puebla de los Angeles (City of the Angels) with its innumerable churches and pictures.

It is said that during the building of the magnificent cathedral, when the artisans ceased their work at close of day, the angels continued it by night. Here, too, is obtained a better view of the volcano Popocatepetl, his rugged peak towering 17,000 feet above his neighbours, and seeming to keep majestic watch over his snowcapped, sleeping companion, Iztaccihuatl—called familiarly La Mujer Blanca (woman in white). On the brow of the rugged mountain which forms her bier she lies with her face upturned to heaven ; white, cold, beautiful, her arms folded over her ice-clad breast, her knees drawn slightly upwards ! The figure is completely outlined ; her tresses seem to hang over the mountain sides ; a sheet shrouding the dead frozen woman in graceful folds !

Concerning this gigantic couple the Indians weave a romantic story, Popocatepetl's convulsions and eruptions are lamentations for the beautiful Iztaccihuatl, who sleeps on ever regardless of his thunderous notes. Of course we did not pass Cholula and its great pyramid without a visit. It may be seen for miles before it is reached. According to Prescott, its base covers about forty-four acres, but other authorities say sixty. The adobe walls were sun-dried— not burnt, and all the material was obtained near at hand.

The bricks vary in size ; a fact which seems to show that the pyramid was not constructed entirely at one period. Mr. Bandelier concludes that it was certainly not built by Indians at the time of the Conquest, and that its beginning may be ascribed to Olmecs or Toltecs. Upon its top, where the church now stands, the idol Quetzalcoatl was found and thrown down by the Spaniards. This temple is supposed to have been erected in his honour.

There is a pyramid at Xochicalco (Hill of flowers) and another at Papantla, built in six storeys with a great stairway of fifty-seven steps leading to the flat top. On the sides of this pyramid serpents and alligators are carved in relief. It is believed that the 366 niches in the walls have some connection with the ancient Toltec calendar.

The district of Huactunango contains gold, silver, and iron mines. Emeralds are found in Tefiji, but the natives of the Zapotecos have succeeded in concealing them' from explorers. In a small town near Cholula, an emerald, threequarters of a Spanish yard in length, formed the *ara*, or consecrated altar stone. Maximilian had it actually in his hands, but the Indians refused his offer of 1,000,000 dollars. The stone was worth double this sum, and later on an armed force attacked the town in the hope of obtaining possession of it, but met with a repulse. Eventually it fell into the hands of the Jesuits, who promised the natives eternal salvation in return. The emerald was cut into many pieces and sold abroad.

The town of Tlaxcola wears an air of picturesque decay. Its archives contain some curious documents of the sixteenth century, an illuminated volume with the signature of Philip II., and there is an interesting collection of idols. In the church of San Francisco is preserved the pulpit from which Christianity was first preached in the New

World. It bears the inscription : " Aqui tubo principio el Santo Evangelio en este nuevo mundo."

The Tlaxcolans were very faithful to Cortes, their conqueror, who consequently emancipated them. The twelve Franciscan friars who arrived after the conquest, were men of profound learning : pioneers of Mexican literature. One of them, Toribio Benavento, being at first ignorant of the language, instead of preaching, pointed to the heavens, to show whence he derived his authority. Observing his humble dress, the Indians spoke of him pityingly as " Motilinia." Learning that the word signified a poor person, the friar declared that Motilinia should be his name henceforth. Father Bernardino de Sahagún laboured here for more than thirty years, dying amongst the Indians, whom he had striven to educate, in 1590, aged ninety-one. His best-known book is the "General History of the Affairs of New Spain."

The writings of Father Las Casas, Bishop of Chiapas were at first condemned to oblivion, but only for a time. Father Olmos, who arrived in 1524 was the first to write a grammar of the Mexican language. The MS. lay long in the Paris library and was published in 1875. After a period of decadence, there was a revival of letters in the 17th century. Clavigero, Veytia, and Guma were celebrated historians, Boturini was a collector of hieroglyphics and modern MSS. Next came the famous Quintana Roo, Ortega, Galvin, and Fernandez, amidst the storm of civic dissension.

The separation of the Church and State was brought about by the action of the Church itself, which, as its power and influence increased, burst its own bonds. The wealth of the Church has been estimated at $300,000,000, the whole of this vast sum being applied to the use of the Government under Juarez.

The wearing of clerical dress in the streets was forbidden under penalty of fine and inprisonment, religious parades were suppressed, as also the ringing of church bells; whilst Sisters of Charity and Jesuits were expelled from the country. Although religious marriages, &c., are permitted, they are not legally necessary; but notwithstanding the limitation of clerical power, the dignity and influence of the Church has distinctly increased. It has been purified by fire.

Esperanza ships large quantities of cereals, ores, &c., conveyed thither to the cars by donkeys. At this station a monster Fairlie engine is attached to the train, in reality two complete engines on one set of wheels, heading both ways, two smoke-stacks and head lights with one long boiler. It draws the train up the steep gradients, and holds it back when descending. The cars would run over an ordinary engine going down hill, and instead of trusting to air or steam brakes on these gradients, a man is stationed at each brake wheel on every car.

In a few minutes we reached Boca del Monte, the down grade beginning at an altitude of 7849 feet above sea level, and descending 2305 feet. It takes sixteen miles of track to reach the lower point, which is always in sight.

The scenery of this grand, wild cañon surpasses description. Sometimes we crawled round horse-shoe curves or passed along the edges of frightful abysses hundreds of feet below, This line took thirty years to make, at a cost of $30,000,000; it has been under about forty different managements, and there has never been an accident. Following the Rio Blanco through the valley of La Joya (jewel) on leaving Orizaba, there were more sharp curves, tunnels, bridges, and deep cañons ; then we crossed the Metlac gorge by a curved bridge, with far below a foaming torrent rushing down the *barranca* under the arches of the old stone bridge. Cordoba was the end of our journey ; Cordoba, with its tropical fruits and flowers (including orchids), its coffee and sugar plantations, orange and lemon groves, its pineapples, bananas, mangoes, wild cherries, and guava.

———oo✦oo———

CHAPTER XXXIV.

CLIMATE—WANT OF ENGLISH IMPORTING HOUSES
—THE PASEO—LEAVING THE CITY—GUADALA-
JARA POTTERY—AGUAS CALIENTES—RETURN
TO TEXAS — A MEXICAN OFFENDER — DEER
HUNTING WITH "BUFFALO DICK"—STARTING
FOR ENGLAND—LANDING AT HULL.

ON returning to the City of Mexico our time was short.
We had a pleasant entertainment at the Castañeda, and at
the Panteone saw the fine monument to Juarez, but were
compelled to leave the Sacro Monte shrine, and several
other places of interest, unvisited. We had seen many
wonderful sights, yet many still remained to be seen in this
sunny land of a sunny people. There is uninterrupted
sunshine during twelve months of the year; the crisp, clear
mornings reminded one of a pleasant English October.
As the sun gets higher the temperature rises quickly, but
we never found the heat oppressive. Joaquin Miller, on
being asked his opinion, replied enthusiastically, "Mexico
is Italy, France, and the best part of Spain, tied up
together in one bunch of rapturous fragrance."

The shops are chiefly in the hands of Frenchmen and
other foreigners, and Mr. Carden has directed attention to
the want of English importing houses:

"The trade of Mexico is undoubtedly worth looking
after, and several branches, in which our manufacturers
and exporters might compete successfully with other

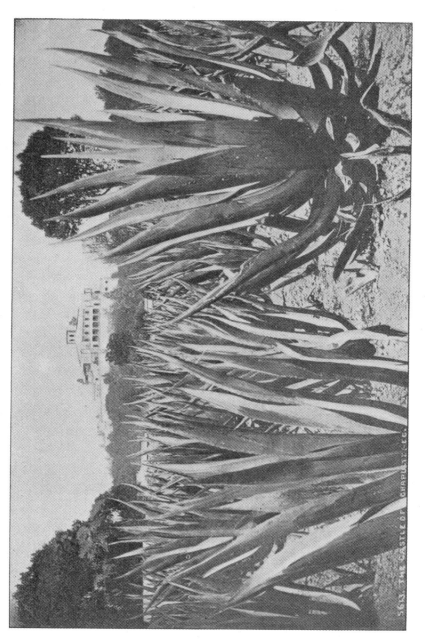

PULQUE PLANTS IN FOREGROUND AND CHAPULTEPEC IN DISTANCE.

nations, have been quite neglected hitherto. Earthenware, glass, china (for the better kinds of which there is an increasing demand), scarcely appear amongst the English importations. The carriages and carts in use are almost exclusively of American and French make, though there is no reason why English carriages should not be imported for town use. Again, English leather goods—saddlery and harness, boots and shoes—are rarely to be found in Mexico, though their superior quality is so well recognised as to insure their acceptance among certain classes, if properly pushed. Besides these, there seems to be no reason why English lamps, furnishing hardwares, cutlery, tools, arms and ammunition, should not find a market there as much as American or German goods of a similar kind."

I would add that silks, hats, ribbons, woollens, and ready-made clothing would find a profitable market if properly introduced, whereas the natural resources of Mexico are immense in its fine woods, ores, cereals, &c.

With regret we took our last drive on the beautiful *Paseo,* where, from 4 p.m. to dark, the people of fashion most do congregate. It is about two and a half miles long, and widens at intervals into a *glorieta* (circle) 400 feet in diameter, with statuary and seats in the middle. At its end is the hill on which stands the castle of Chapultepec, surrounded by magnificent cypresses. The sunset cast a roseate glow over the snow-capped mountains as we took our last lingering look.

We left the city of Mexico by the Central line at 8.10 p.m., accompanied by Mr. Kirkland, who was bound for Milwaukee, a few of our kind, new friends assembling at the station for the last *adios.*

"Vamonos!" cried the conductor; the train started,

and we were borne away, but not without a hope of returning some day to see our friends again, and inspect more of
the wonders of this fascinating country.

At Encarnacion we bought some Guadalajara pottery,
and at Irapuato, very early in the morning, Mr. Kirkland
brought us some fine strawberries. At Lagos he suggested
that we should see the scenery better from the engine,

MARKET AT AGUAS CALIENTES.

whither we eventually transferred ourselves. Having been
introduced to Mr. Harding, the engine driver, an extremely
well-educated and agreeable companion, we sat one on each
side of the locomotive, listening to wayside anecdotes, and
thoroughly enjoying the novel situation. In the evening
Mr. Harding very politely escorted us to supper at Aguas
Calientes (hot waters); a delightful place, its waters useful
in rheumatic and skin diseases. The old bath house is in

the town, the water being supplied by conduits. The new one is half a mile distant at the springs. The waste water extends along an *acequia* (ditch) with an avenue of cotton-wood trees, where the people freely indulge in the luxury of a bath, men, women, and children lining the banks, and even the dogs participating. At the head of the ditch are more pools of hot, clear water, where one can bathe in the open in January.

There are some interesting pictures in the churches of San Marcos, the Encino, and San Diego ; a beautiful *plaza*, with a good band ; and an excellent market, inclosed on four sides by heavily columned *portales*. We bought some beautiful specimens of maguey work in coloured baskets, &c.

Between Guadalupe and Zacatecas we were invited to ride again upon the engine. Mr. Kirkland bade us good-bye at Torreone, where we changed cars, finally reaching Porfirio Diaz about 11.30 p.m.

Here we remained one day to arrange the payment for bonding the waggon and to pass the Customs (a very informal proceeding). We boarded the train at midnight, but were not fairly off until 2 a.m. Just as we were comfortably settling ourselves to finish the night's repose, Dr. Crook arrived to interview me about our journey, for the Eagle Pass newspaper. At 3 a.m. we changed cars again at Spofford Junction, reaching San Antonio at 8.35 a.m. The journey from Kerville to Junction City was accomplished through a " Norther," and we found considerable trouble in keeping ourselves from freezing. At Junction City we took up our quarters at the hotel, intending to devote a few weeks to farewell visits before leaving Texas.

Early one morning there was an unusual bustle and excitement in the quiet little *plaza*, and a clerk from the store ran over to the hotel. A reserve party of sixteen men with the Sheriff and Under-Sheriff had been called out in pursuit of a runaway : Would I lend them one of my horses, " Monte ? "

Of course I assented, and off started the pursuers at full gallop in all directions. The crime was rape and the perpetrator a Mexican. "Give him Lynch law ! " "Hang him like a dog ! " were the cries ; but happily Mr. Corder, the new sheriff, was imbued with a sense of justice, and issued orders that the criminal was to be taken alive.

Towards the close of the day he was caught in a small cañon sixteen miles east of the town. His captor, a well-known Mexican ranger and a dead shot, who could bring down flies with a six-shooter, covered the wretched man with his gun, and would no doubt have blown out his brains there and then, in spite of the Sheriff's orders, but for a witness in the person of a sheep-herder.

The daily stage brought up the culprit, who was put in the town prison. That night was pretty lively for the inhabitants of Junction City. Two or three hundred cowboys surrounded the gaol, but the Sheriff courageously elbowed his way through the crowd, planted his back against the prison door, and refused to surrender the criminal to their mercy. A guard was told off to help him keep the door during the night, but the " boys " hung about, " fooling " with their Winchesters, and it was said there were only three sober men " on the streets," including both guard and mob. The ladies of the city were afraid to stay in their beds, and felt anxious for the safety of husbands, brothers, or lovers. However, they wisely kept within doors, for random shooting went on everywhere, across the *plaza* and all round the town ; the sole object being to draw the Sheriff and guard from the gaol and to get at the prisoner. Failing in this, they began to fire at him through the windows of his cell, one bullet making a hole in his *zerape* (blanket), another grazing his cheek.

The enterprising owner of the best saloon, with an eye to business, kept it open all night. Its walls were riddled with bullets, and in another house the stove-pipe was shot clean in halves—a short time previously the occupants had been cooking their supper at it.

As the Court would not sit for nearly a month, and there was no military force nearer than San Antonio, while the civil guard could be called out only so many nights a week on account of the business occupations of its members, the Sheriff determined to remove the Mexican to Mason, a larger town seventy miles off, where the Court sat earlier. Owing to lack of ammunition and to some wedding festivities which engaged public attention, the following night was quieter, and just before daybreak the prisoner was placed in a hack and driven away. His ultimate fate I never heard, as I quitted the country before the case was settled. Had he been a Texan, it would probably have fared very differently with him from the first ; but it is difficult to convince these people that a Mexican is a human being. He seems to be the Texan's natural enemy ; he is treated like a dog, or, perhaps, not so well. It seems scarcely credible that even a fairly educated Englishman, holding a good position in Junction City, an influential member of the Episcopalian Church, should have become so imbued with these ideas that he actually looked forward with delight to the hanging of this man without trial or time for repentance, and gleefully boasted that he had the promise of the rope on which the "beast" swung, and also of his scalp as a trophy. " I have one Mexican scalp already," he exclaimed.

I was acquainted with the unfortunate victim of the crime and her husband, and naturally all one's sympathy went with them ; nevertheless I could but rejoice that the Mexican had the prospect of a fair trial before being condemned to death.

A fair trial ! Money, influence, a good array of daring, well-armed witnesses, go far towards winning a case in an American frontier town.

We enjoyed a successful deer-hunting expedition from Fort Territ under the clever guidance of " Buffalo Dick," and brought our trophies to England. Monte was sold, but poor Button mysteriously disappeared, together with some other horses, and was never found. When the day of our departure arrived, Gerino jumped into the stage, and Dandy, tied behind, trotted his fifty-five miles in the day to Kerville. Thence Mr. Taylor took charge of him in a freight train from San Antonio to New York, we travelling to Galveston, thence by the s.s. *Nueces*, of the Mallory Line.

Captain Risk did a great deal to render the week's voyage agreeable, and made a pet of Gerino, who was the first to recognise land on nearing Key West, Florida. Here we went over a cigar factory, and saw some Cuban boys dive after coins. I had already secured berths for England on the *Egyptian Monarch*, but on arriving at New York, finding she was not to sail for a fortnight, transferred them to the ss. *Martello*, of the Wilson Line. The faster lines do not carry horses or cattle, and, as I wished to sail with Dandy, there was not much choice. When I first saw him again at New York he looked like a skeleton ; the journey had frightened him, and for several days he refused

"BUFFALO DICK" IN CAMP.

food and water. However, he greatly improved on the *Martello*, which took sixteen days to reach Hull ; not a fast boat certainly, but a very steady one.

We had a remarkably calm voyage, and there was only one passenger besides ourselves, a Danish lady, who proved a very agreeable companion. Capt. Rea was kind enough to have Dandy twice unboxed and exercised on deck, but it was a year before he fully recovered his condition. The first English winter tried him, but he has now become acclimatised, and has even learnt to roll over like our own horses. Texan horses never turn in rolling ; they prefer to get up and lie down again to finish the other side. Dandy's former owner writes that he is pleased the horse is "spreading himself in England." Gerino thrives, and has taken two prizes at the Crystal Palace and Agricultural Hall.

At Portland Bay the pilot came on board. How we shivered on entering the Channel, though it was the 2nd of May, 1891, when we landed at Hull !

And so our absence from home came to an end. During the interval we had seen innumerable objects of beauty— works of art, works of nature. We had lived amongst peoples whose civilisations were both more ancient and younger than ours. We had made many friends, and laid up a rich store of pleasant memories little likely to fade. I have written them here in the hope that they may afford at least a passing interest to others.

THE END.